THE ENGLISH DEPARTMENT BOOK

A GUIDE TO ORGANIZATION AND RESOURCES

ILEA English Centre

The English Centre is a teachers' centre in the Inner London
Education Authority.
This book had as its starting point an earlier English Centre
publication called ' The English Department: Organisation and
Resources'. Many of the ideas here have been developed as a result
of suggestions made by ILEA teachers who have attended English
Centre courses on the organisation of the English Department.

English Centre Sutherland Street London SW1
ISBN   0907016030

Printed and bound by A.Wheaton, Exeter and London

The English Department Book :
A Guide to Organisation and Resources

Written by: David Marigold, Mike Raleigh, Michael Simons
Edited by: Mike Raleigh

Additional material for a number of sections was contributed by:

Andrew Bethell: for 'Time', 'English and Media Studies', and
'English and Drama' (with Claire Widgery)
Paul Ashton: for 'The Composition of the Team', and 'Non-
Specialist English Teachers'
Don Shiach: for 'Money'
Gwenlian Evans: for 'Covering for Absence'
Daphne Denaro: for 'Outings and Visits'

Thanks to the following for their help and advice:

Richard Exton, Terry Furlong, Philippa Hunt, Jacqui Nunn
(on 'The Team') Bronwyn Mellor (on 'Special Help:Reading
and Writing') Jane Leggett (on 'Examinations').

Thanks also to Battersea County, Walworth, Haverstock and
Woodberry Down Schools for the use of illustrative material.

Typeset by: Kate Haggart
Designed by: Steve Morley, assisted by John Hookway
Photographs: Keith Hawkins, Andrew Bethell, Michael Simons,
                Andrew Wiard (Report)
Cartoons: Neil Dishington, John Moreland, Colin Wheeler,
                Garry Kennard

Foreword

'The English Department Book' is a valuable addition to the English Centre's list of publications. It draws on the wide range of experience of the community of ILEA English teachers, pondered, discussed and represented here by three of its members.

The Centre has previously published materials for the English classroom developed by teachers to meet their expressed needs. It has also explored in 'The English Magazine' many of the seminal concerns of English teaching.

This book addresses itself to the vital issues of good organization and communication in the English department, without which effective and imaginative teaching cannot for long flourish. It affirms the importance of good relationships between the department and the wider school community and asserts with splendid conviction that English teaching is at its most successful when organized by people who work together as a team.

I welcome this book. It was written for ILEA teachers of English and I hope it will be read by all of them: specialists and non specialists; full-timers and part-timers; probationers and heads of department. I think it will also be read by teachers across the whole country. My colleagues and I owe the authors of 'The English Department Book' a heavy debt of gratitude.

John Welch
Staff Inspector for English, ILEA.

This Book...

▪ is not for heads of English only

It is predicated on the idea that an effective English department needs to work as a co-operative team and that this can best be achieved if knowledge is available to all members of the department. Obviously, we hope this book will be useful to heads of English but we wrote it for all members of the department.

▪ is not the blueprint for every department

Needless to say, we know of no department which embodies all the policies advocated in this book; it is an amalgam of our own experiences and our knowledge of the achievements of many ILEA English departments. Readers will need to decide which aspects of the book are relevant to the particular circumstances in which they work. They should certainly be aware that the text assumes a department that is properly staffed and reasonably well funded. We hope that readers in departments without adequate resources may at least find this book useful in presenting arguments for better provision.

▪ is not to be read at one go

This advice does not arise from false modesty. Reading straight through this book could seriously damage your health. We suggest an occasional trawl; use it as a reference book.

We have crammed a great deal of information into this book and anyone who reads it in one go may not only suffer from indigestion but may also begin to feel that running a good department is an impossible job. In fact, it is far more explicit than it needs to be; we have drawn out and unpacked what is inside most teachers' heads. We decided to be overcomprehensive rather than risk leaving anything out.

▪ is not about English teaching

Because this book concentrates on organizational matters the living quality of ideas in action and descriptions of children learning don't appear. It deals with what goes on behind the scenes, not with what happens on the stage.

David Marigold   Mike Raleigh   Michael Simons

Contents

The Team

Helping Ourselves

The Syllabus

Assessment, Exams and Grouping

Time, Space and Money

Teaching Materials

The Department and the School

Bibliography

The Team

9

The Team

Working as a Team

We start from the assumption that an English department ought to function as a team, that its members ought to be actively engaged together in developing and sharing common approaches to the teaching of the subject. There are schools in which the English department is seen simply as a collection of individuals who are supplied with timetables and exercise books and then expected to devise programmes of work entirely on their own. On the other hand there are schools in which the English department is seen as something like a set of production-line operatives who are supplied with all necessary materials and then expected to follow programmes of work devised solely by the head of department.

In either case the prospects for both teachers and pupils shrink. English teaching is a complex business covering a wide spectrum of concerns; it can be a particularly difficult and frustrating business for for teachers who are required either to draw entirely on their own resources or to act merely as agents for someone else's ideas. Being involved in a common enterprise, identifying and solving problems, sharing ideas and resources with others, is not only a more relaxed and stimulating mode in which to work, but one more likely to produce good English teaching — by experienced as well as inexperienced teachers.

Everyone who reads this book will drink to the idea of a working environment in which English teachers think, plan and share as a team. Most will be working in a department which is not a perfect co-operative unit. It probably won't be a monument to laissez-faire individualism or to the feudal spirit, but a well-intentioned community marked by eneven harmony and incomplete efficiency. Differences in philosophy and strategy will not have been resolved; there will be bad practices as well as good ideas, half-formed schemes as well as established policies, unfinished organization as well as clear patterns of responsibility.

The nature of the subject and the conditions of school life mean that unevenness and imbalance are inevitable in the way most departments work; but for most teachers there is personal and professional satisfaction in the effort towards greater departmental coherence and efficiency.

A PARTICIPATING DEMOCRACY?

We think that a department is at its happiest and most efficient when decisions about the way it should work are made together and not by the head of department alone. Nothing is worse than major decisions being taken without reference to those colleagues who are affected by them: it can lead to bitterness, conflict, a loss of morale and energy. Clearly not every decision is a major one needing full consultation and debate; and some quite important decisions may in some circumstances need to be made quickly by the head of department (or whoever is responsible) simply to enable the department to function until such time as consultation can take place. Nevertheless, the general rule stands: decide together.

The ability of a department to reach agreement on matters of policy and procedure depends on three things:
- a free flow of information;
- well-organized meetings;
- a sharing of responsibilities.

These three areas are considered in what follows.

Information

There are very broad lines of communication which are necessary in order for everyone to function efficiently. Information needs to be shared so that colleagues can plan ahead, can help make informed decisions when consulted, and can feel that they know what lies behind many of the problems and patterns in a departmental or whole school context.

General administrative matters may be dull, but for colleagues simply to know in good time may help to avoid a kind of nagging frustration which can accumulate over weeks and months. Broadly, administrative information might cover all matters related to:
- meetings, including dates, agendas, reports of discussions, deadlines;
- staffing, money, timetabling;
- events which might affect the daily routine, like exams, medicals, school trips, visitors etc;
- comments, reports or actions taken about pupils by pastoral staff, parents or other departments.

Curriculum information should also be available. This might include information which comes to a head of department from sources external to the school — like exam boards, publishers, inspectors/advisers, teachers' centres — so that colleagues can keep in touch with new developments in English or can apply for courses; it might even avoid people embarking on a set book which is no longer on the syllabus. Some of this information might flow from within the department itself — such as minutes from the last department meeting, or occasional articles which are relevant to aspects of the syllabus which might feature in future discussions. Perhaps the most vital information of all is simply being aware of what kind of work is being done and what materials and approaches are being used by colleagues in the team.

SPREADING IT

Much of this information can be spread by casual chats in the staff-room or English resources room; but the problem with this informal approach, even in small schools, is the danger of missing out colleagues and forgetting the bits and pieces. However, it is also clear that saving it all up for a department meeting can lead to stupor and to the agenda being sucked down the drain. As an alternative, information might be spread in some of the following ways:
   — a notice-board in the department's base (if there is one) to be used by everyone. Someone will need to keep it tidy, take down out of date information, and organize it into

sections;
- assigning the distribution of particular kinds of information to different colleagues;
- short, informal meetings (once a week, fifteen minutes before school starts? ten minutes in a lunch break?). Meetings as short as this have the virtue of cutting out unnecessary waffle. However, it is best to set a routine of the same place, same time, same regularity, otherwise it is difficult to ensure that everyone will be present;
- distributing a weekly or fortnightly bulletin. This is particularly useful in large or split-site schools. It is possible to rotate editors, and for everyone to make a contribution. If a bulletin is used, it is helpful to establish headings for the information e.g. 'Courses', 'Interruptions to Timetable', 'My Brilliant Lesson', etc.

Department Meetings

Spreading information is the easy part of the democratic process. But how can differences of philosophy and approach be cemented into agreements about what a syllabus should be, for instance, or about whether teaching groups should be set or mixed ability?

Although casual chats and ad hoc debate can contribute much to the forward movement of the department, it is the full department meeting which is the forum for major decisions. No department can do without some full meetings in the year; their timing and precise nature need to be the subject of discussion and negotiation. Some suggestions follow on how they can be arranged and made into productive occasions.

1.   DATES AND TIMES

How often full meetings take place will partly depend on the size and composition of the department and the nature of its current concerns. The regularity of full meetings may also be affected by whether the school as a whole has a policy about meetings. Some schools have established a sensible system of early closure one day a week: the available time is used in a 3 week rotation for staff, pastoral and department meetings — which go on for an hour after school if necessary. It is worth proposing such a system if it doesn't exist. As an alternative the department can request that meeting time be formally put on to the timetable. This is a reasonable request for a department to make and it should not be beyond the wit of the school timetabler to meet it (at least for the full-time teachers in the department). Last period in the day is the best time so that the meeting can run on after school. Once the meeting time is on the timetable it should be protected from encroachments like cover for absent teachers: make sure it is written into individual and master timetables and that deputy heads appreciate its importance.

Where no school time is available for full meetings (or where the time is too short for real discussion), a pattern of meetings after school (say fortnightly or monthly) needs to be established. Some departments favour lunchtime meetings, but these tend to be rushed and unrelaxed — though they can be useful for getting through administrative business which can't be dealt with any other way. Some departments favour the occasional use of evening meetings at someone's house as semi-business, semi-social events. Whatever the pattern, a series of dates for after-school meetings should be established at the beginning of the year and booked into the school calendar; the head of department needs to argue for the protection of these dates against rival claims made by staff or pastoral meetings. If conflicts emerge regularly, suggest a simple system in which all department meetings take place on the same day in the week.

2.   ATTENDANCE

Most people will come to a department meeting willingly if they've been given adequate notice, a reminder and an agenda relevant to their concerns. It also helps if there is a prompt start, a cup of coffee at the beginning and a time-limit for the end of the meeting. Where meetings are not in school time attendance is voluntary: a department can expect but not require people to come. Part-time members of the department (whether part-time in the school or teaching more than one subject) can find regular attendance difficult; there are also people whose domestic circumstances impose constraints on their after-school time. The head of department needs to make a point of passing on to absentees information on matters arising from meetings — and making sure they know when the next meeting is and what the agenda will be.

It is the practice in some departments to extend a standing invitation to attend meetings to other staff in the school who have an interest in the activities of the department (e.g. the school librarian, the media resources officer, senior staff responsible for the curriculum, and teachers of drama, remedial work, ESL, Humanities and so on). A standing invitation is very nice — but a specific invitation to attend a meeting in which there is a particularly relevant issue on the agenda is probably more likely to be of immediate mutual benefit. Students on teaching practice in the department should be invited to meetings as a matter of course.

3. THE AGENDA

Full department meetings should be concerned with the theory
and practice of English teaching and the provision and use of
resources; administrative items should be kept to a minimum. It
obviously makes good sense if the agenda is planned and circulated
in advance so that people can collect their thoughts on the issues
and so that part-time teachers can make a special effort to attend
where items are of particular relevance to them. There will always
be more items for possible inclusion on the agenda than there is
time. One suggestion is that the head of department circulates in
advance a list of possible items for people to choose from — and,
if necessary, add to. Alternatively, the head of department might
consult people with major responsibilities in the department about
items for inclusion.

Where a major issue has been nominated for the agenda of a full
meeting (say, for example, the development of a policy for encouraging independent reading) it may be worth thinking about ways of
preparing the ground and organizing the discussion, perhaps by:
- making a list of questions about the issue which need to
  be addressed;
- passing around copies of a relevant article or account of work
  done in the area;
- asking one or two members of the department to prepare
  a list of suggestions for action;
- inviting a teacher from another school to come and talk
  about the policy in their school.

4. RUNNING THE MEETING

Running a large meeting so that the business is properly aired *and*
moved along at a reasonable speed is not an easy matter. There is
no reason why the head of department should hog the role of
chairing meetings; the chairing can be revolved or alternatively
different people can be asked to open and direct discussion of
items about which they have particular knowledge. However, the
head of department has a particular responsibility to ensure that
everyone has a chance to contribute to discussion, that minority
points of view are fairly represented, and that proposals for action
resulting from discussion are clearly put. It is helpful also if someone makes brief notes of discussion at the meeting so that a record
of key points can be distributed afterwards to those present and to
absentees. The minuting might be done on a revolving basis.

5. THE FRANCHISE

We have outlined the importance of spreading information, the
importance of regular meetings, and the advantages of behaving in

a democratic manner, so that a context is prepared in which issues needing decision can be discussed. In other words, we have suggested ways in which colleagues can be *involved* in the process leading up to a decision. But what next? Is there a vote?

Taking an informal vote can be useful for cutting the cackle on less-than-crucial issues ('a drama festival this year or not?'), but a decision based on a simple majority vote can be counter-productive where it is likely to have a marked effect on all teachers' working conditions. Decisions which force a number of teachers to do things unwillingly, especially in the area of curriculum organization (for example, in the nature of remedial provision), can sour personal relations within the department as well as affecting classroom work.

Important decisions are clearly best reached through consensus. If full agreement on a curriculum innovation is not forthcoming after discussion it may be worth proposing a trial period or a reduced-scale experiment. However, the head of department will need to use his/her judgement and discretion here. If the considered views of the full-time specialist English teachers (on, for example, mixed ability teaching) are being resisted by one or two part-time members of the department who teach only a few classes of English, it may be advisable to vote and end the matter once and for all. Achieving consensus on important issues, in other words, is not always possible; although voting highlights disagreement, it can also end frustration.

A System of Responsibilities

Making democratic decisions is one thing; putting them into action is another. No head of department can do all the work a department needs. Nor should it be the case. When other people do their share, it's not only good for the department but good for the morale and professional development of individuals. But unless there is some kind of system of responsibilities negotiated and monitored it's very easy for jobs to get left undone, decisions to be left unenacted.

WHO DOES WHAT?

Clearly the way in which responsibilities are organized will vary in different schools, depending on the size of the department, the pattern of scale posts and on the strengths and interests of individual members of the department. But the following general points are worth bearing in mind.

1.   SPREADING THE JOBS

People with scale posts in the department will naturally be expected to do more than those without, but it is a healthy policy to try to give everyone in the department a specific responsibility, however small. This might be, for example, taking charge of a working party set up at a full department meeting to collect information, draft a policy or make materials and then to report back to the whole department. A short-term commitment of this kind, with a clear brief and a deadline, is likely to be acceptable to most teachers, including part-time members of the department.

2.   MIXING THE JOBS

Those people with more than one responsibility (including the second in department) should have a mix of different kinds of job to do. It is not uncommon for the second in department, for example, to end up doing most of the routine administration and none of the more interesting and demanding tasks; that's not a good idea. If the responsibility involves just one area, it shouldn't be just the dull clerical bit of it. Most jobs that need doing in the department (see example list below) have 'classroom' and 'liaison' dimensions as well; the responsibility should also include these.

3.   REVOLVING RESPONSIBILITIES

A scale post can't be switched around once it is handed out until the holder leaves. But there is no reason why responsibilities can't be re-defined and revolved on, say, a yearly basis. Some jobs (like ordering stock) become almost bearable if you know you won't have to do it next year. It is particularly valuable for teachers at an early stage in their career to be given experience in different aspects of department management; older hands may find a change almost as good as a rest.

4.   DEFINING RESPONSIBILITIES

It's not uncommon for a responsibility to be allocated with neither the giver nor the receiver being too sure of what exactly is to be done. In consequence, nobody is then sure whether or not the job is being done adequately. The device of a formal written job specification might seem over-elaborate (especially if the job is an apparently simple one like ordering and distributing consumable stock), but a properly negotiated description can make things clear and save strain. Specifying a job includes saying when and how things need to be done.

5.   MAKING TIME FOR IT

People who carry major responsibilities in a department may be given extra money, but they may not get the extra time needed to carry out their responsibilities efficiently. In the absence of a national policy on how much non-teaching time secondary teachers get in a week, schools make up their own. A common pattern in ILEA is for a head of English to be given around 25% non-teaching time, a second in department (scale 3) to be given up to 20%, and other post-holders (scale 2) to be given just the normal minimum allowance (or one period more). That's a common pattern, but by no means a universal one. There are serious problems and inequities in some schools, perhaps because of imbalances in departmental staffing or because of the way the time of senior staff is used — or perhaps simply because no-one has given much thought to what a post-holder in a department like English is expected to do.

A rational basis

If the whole business of non-teaching time is opened up to staff scrutiny and discussion so that the system is put on a rational basis, an English department is unlikely to suffer. A number of questions might be raised in such a discussion:

- what should be the minimum allowance of non-teaching time to a scale 1 teacher?
- should a differential be used to award more time to teachers in departments with exceptional preparation or marking loads?
- should all post holders on the same scale receive the same extra time allowance regardless of the size of the department or the nature of the post?
- what proportion of the work which a particular post involves needs to be done (a) on the premises and (b) when pupils and other staff are available?

Some schools may prefer, for one reason or another, not to have an open discussion of this sort. In that case special pleading, using the device of describing in exhaustive detail (and with approximate timings) the precise duties which the various responsibilities in English involve, may do the trick. It may, for example, substantiate a case for a teacher who runs a bookshop to be given some additional free time even if there's no scale post available; at the very least it can be used to argue for a 'cover-free' (or invigilation-free) period during the term for post-holders without extra time to get on with their job uninterrupted by other calls.

WHAT'S TO BE DONE?

It is a useful and illuminating exercise for a department to compile a list of all the jobs which have to be done in the course of a school year. Such a list will persuade even the hardened sceptic that a major department like English has a lot of work to do; it may provide powerful ammunition in a fight for a fair distribution of scale posts within the school. Within the department it can offer a basis for discussion of job allocation among those with scale posts for English and those without; it can also be used as an aide memoire for thinking about agendas for meetings and deadlines for action.

The jobs on a department's list will include:

- curriculum development work on classroom strategies and materials;
- the maintenance of departmental procedures and routines;
- liaison with people outside the department.

The example list below (taken from an ILEA school, 8 form entry, teaching in mixed ability classes) reflects these categories. Other departments might prefer to list the jobs in another way.

Curriculum co-ordination (by year group)

1st year: including liaison with feeder primary schools and Integrated Studies department
2nd year: including arrangements for Bookweek
3rd year: including drama festival, supervision of transfer to upper school exam classes
4th/5th year: including responsibility for work towards O/CSE exams, organizing set texts, mocks, oral and coursework standardizing
6th year: including responsibility for CEE/A Level, consortium arrangements

Curriculum development (through the school)

Reading (including independent reading, special help)
Writing (including special help, writing for audiences)
Talk (classroom strategies; communications element)
Drama (lower school programme; CSE option)
Media Studies (ordering films; video work; newspapers)
Language across the Curriculum (contacts with other departments; reports)

Department Procedures

Student teachers: liaison with tutor, timetabling, support, reports
Probationers: support, liaison with school induction supervisor
Assessment: new intake, maintaining pupil profiles and records
Disciplinary procedures: report books, liaison with year heads
Reading help: books/materials, timetabling arrangements for withdrawal groups, liaison with remedial staff
Bookshop: ordering books, duty rota, accounts, publicity
Teaching materials: 1) selection — catalogues/reviews, inspection copies, consultation with dept.
Teaching materials: 2) ordering, accessing, storage, distribution, stock control
Home-made materials: liaison with MRO and office typist, advice on design, indexing
Publications: magazines, anthologies, displays
Outside visits: information on theatres/museums/trips, liaising with senior staff and office
School Play: direction, scripting, co-ordination of other staff

Administration

Public exams: entries, correspondence with boards, arrangements for orals
Timetable: staffing, consultation with dept., planning, liaison with deputy head
Budget: estimates, accounts
Dept. meetings: convening, agenda, minutes
Dept. bulletin: compiling, printing, distribution
Dept. documents: syllabus, records of work, dept. library
A.V.A. equipment: purchase, storage, liaison with MRO
Consumable stock: ordering, controlling supply
Rooms: furniture and equipment, liaison with schoolkeeper

Liaison (i.e. not mentioned elsewhere)

HoD meetings: papers, resolutions, reporting back
Inspectorate: visits, appointments, divisional meetings etc

Librarian: 1st year library course, library use, book suggestions
Teachers Centres etc: information on courses
PTA: school play, parents' evenings

Head of Department: Special Responsibilities

TAKEN BY SURPRISE

If I'd taken over the department I'd worked in, I think it would have been relatively smooth. However, walking into a department in a new school took me completely by surprise. I had to spend time attempting to do a lightning 'read' of the personal politics which, of course, had become part of the air I breathed in my last school. The second in department (who didn't get the job) was being very pleasant but wouldn't actually do anything I asked — and I suspect he was quietly undermining me with the rest of the department. The Head was clearly unhappy with the department, which he felt was too traditional and staid; in the course of several interviews he suggested that I begin leaning on certain members of the department. I was too daunted by the consequences of risking a conflict and so I decided to leave it until the department had settled down. I'm still sorting out in my mind a way of approaching these teachers, some of whose work I think is really dreadful.

RELIEVED TO SEE ME

I knew from my visit and interview that I was taking over a good department. I'd had several hints that the previous head of department didn't cope very well and that they'd really worked together just to make sure they survived. So they were close knit. Also they were stable — I mean they'd been together for a few years and had worked out what their views of English were and had certainly done a lot of hard work on materials. I had a real shock when I learnt they had a fortnightly workshop which went on to six or six thirty; my last school was empty by ten past four. They seemed really relieved to see me after I got the job. I thought the best tack from my point of view was to say what good stuff they'd got together — and I was quite frank about my own limitations. I decided to leave the curriculum side to them until I'd caught up with their ideas, so to speak, but to see if there was anything I could begin to work on that they saw as problems. Fortunately it seemed to be exactly the right line to take — because there were a lot of admin problems which were getting in the way of a lot of good work, as well as a need to sort out relationships with other departments in the school.

Being the head of any subject department in a school is a difficult job; being head of an English department is especially difficult.

English — like Maths — is a particular focus of attention in any school; it is at the centre of every child's experience of secondary education and, with its responsibility for the development of the child in and through language, it occupies a crucial place in the curriculum. The nature and the range of concerns the English department encompasses make it a peculiarly complex department to organize and to lead. Good heads of department come in all shapes and sizes; there is no blueprint; there would be no point here in trying to define the qualities and skills which the job requires — beyond saying that it needs, among other things, a commitment to the subject and knowledge of the variety of topics covered in this book, and a desire to ensure that things *happen*. (A streak of masochism and a flexible home life are also helpful.)

THE IDEAL

This section is concerned with the special responsibilities a head of department has — in addition, that is, to those administrative and curricular jobs which s/he draws from the list of things to do in the department (see page 20). These are themselves in addition to a teaching load and to participation as an ordinary member of staff in the whole range of school business. Whatever the size of the school and the nature of the department this is a lot for any normal person to do — let alone do brilliantly. It is the sheer variety of roles — and the contradictions and tensions among them — which can make any head of department, however conscientious and hard-working, feel horribly deficient in face of the ideal.

But the ideal head of department (on top of everything else, a managerial wizard, a subtle director of operations) is not a real one. We want to emphasize in what follows that the real satisfaction for a head of department lies not in being Head of it but simply part of it: a useful and developing member of an effective and developing team.

WHAT ARE YOU DOING FOR US?

What does a head of department need to do — as an absolute minimum? Answer: get stuck in and make yourself useful. The basis of a head of department's ability to forge a team is the contribution that s/he makes to the department's life day to day by making things easier for colleagues to get on with the job of teaching and enjoy it. So:

1. S/he must take a full range of classes so as to share the same experiences and problems as other members of the department. Sticking as closely as possible to A Level and top band classes is not on.

2. S/he must arrange for the immediate needs of teachers in the department to be met. 'Immediate needs' means things like writing paper, 20 copies of *Of Mice and Men* at short notice, help in sorting out a troublesome child, and so on: that is, the day-to-day routine business without which nothing else can happen. There ought to be systems which deal with immediate needs; but if the system breaks down, the needs must be met on the spot.

3. The head of department must adhere to agreed departmental policies; if s/he does not, then no-one else will feel any obligation to. That goes for things like hogging the best materials, using 'comprehension books' on Thursday p.m. when you have agreed not to, sticking to policies on homework and so on.

4. The head of department needs to be aware of what other teachers in the department are doing with their classes. That does not mean ceaseless interrogation. It means taking five minutes at break-time and making a special effort to leave the stamping of books (or similar urgent business) at 4 p.m. — in order to chat with teachers about special projects they have got on or things they want discussed. The point is not just to be aware of what people are doing and how they feel about it, but to be able to make constructive suggestions: 'Why don't we combine the 3rd year classes to watch the film so that you can take the 12 from your class to finish off the play?'

WHERE ARE WE GOING?

The development of an English department often seems uncertain and piecemeal to the teachers who work in it. There are spurts in one area, pauses in another; ideas for improving the quality of the department's work get raised and get shelved. Most people would like to see the department making steady progress towards defined goals; it needs to matter more to the head of department than to anyone else. Let's look at the issue of the department's development from the point of view of a new head of department.

101 THINGS TO DO

When a new person takes over the running of a department there seem to be 101 things to do. That is true even if the department has been run well in the past; an outsider with a fresh view can always see plenty more things which need to be done.

Some of the 101 things which need doing may be suggested by the head, the governors, the inspector/adviser, the ex-head of department, teachers in the department, the deputy head(s), or other teachers in the school. The school-keeper may also offer some positive suggestions. Some of the 101 things may be obvious to you as an outsider but not to anyone else. Some of them may seem like enormous tasks, others may be trivial; some may be to do with processes (like what happens at department meetings); others may be to do with material resources (like getting a cupboard in Room 23).

It is vital that some sense is made out of all these things to do, so that some things, at least, become manageable. It is important:
- for the new head of department, so that s/he does not collapse under the strain of trying to do everything simultaneously;
- for the department, so that pointless turmoil is not set in motion;
- for the school hierarchy (etc) so that expectations are not established which are impossible to fulfil.

So what should the priorities be? How can plans be made to develop this particular department as an efficient and co-operative unit? Obviously:
- You can't do everything at once
  but some things can be done quickly which are of immediate practical value (e.g. setting up a system for recording and using ETV programmes). And some things *have* to be done quickly (e.g. getting the probationer's room timetable sorted out).
- There is a good order in which things can be done
  but it will not necessarily be the order which one individual may recommend (e.g. setting up a mode 3 A level may be the second in department's pet scheme, but that may not be the best place to start).
- The sense of momentum in a department is often intangible
  but there are things which can make it visible, even in the early stages (like agreeing to work together to produce some home-made materials or on an anthology of children's writing).

PLANNING

Bearing these principles in mind, it may be helpful to a new head of department to take the planning of the department's strategy in four steps.
1. Organize your list of 101 things into sections (e.g. 'timetable', 'materials', 'exam policies', 'physical arrangements' etc).
2. Further divide your list of things to do into those which can be tackled immediately (i.e. this term or next term), those which can be done within a year, and those which are going to take some winding up to (i.e. next year).
3. Discuss this list informally with key members of the depart-

ment and with sympathetic members of the school hierarchy, looking for their reactions and advice.

4. You should now have a rough set of plans outlining the sequence in which various issues might be tackled. Ideally these plans should now be presented to the department as a whole for discussion so that everyone has a sense of how the department is going to develop.

HOW ARE WE DOING?

Inevitably things won't be accomplished with anything like the neatness that plans promise: some jobs will take longer to do than you thought, unexpected problems will crop up, and particular intentions will need to be re-routed. But it's worthwhile looking back at your plan of action on a regular basis to check on how far you've got — and perhaps spending part of the first department meeting of each term assessing the progress you've made on particular issues and discussing priorities for the future. Evaluation of the department's development in this way shouldn't be abrasive or heavy-handed, but it should be reasonably open and honest — remembering of course that members of the department will have to work with one another tomorrow. Broad questions of the following kind may help to stimulate discussion about possibilities for future development:

— what are the good things about the department's organizational procedures? what things need tightening up or rethinking? (the ordering and distribution of stock? the nature and timing of pupil assessment?)
— which aspects of the English curriculum is the department as a whole now pretty confident about? which aspects need further consideration? (poetry in the upper school? a form of language study which recognizes and welcomes the diversity of languages and dialects in the school?)
— are there any more ways in which teachers in the department can help one another? (by sharing ideas for work on CSE books? by observing one another's lessons?).

Some LEAs or individual schools require departments to submit to the head and governors a formal written evaluation of their development over a period of time. That's a different matter from the department's own informal internal review and one which needs to be discussed fully with other heads of department in the school. If a new head of department comes into a school already operating such a scheme, it's a good idea to ask to see previous examples of written departmental evaluations before writing a word.

The question of the evaluation of exam results is considered in the section 'Assessment, Exams and Grouping'.

WHERE AM I GOING?

One of the key responsibilities for a head of department is the oversight of the professional development of individual members of the department. This doesn't just mean newly-qualified teachers; particularly in the context of falling rolls it applies to everyone. That may seem a heavy responsibility; but it is important and it is possible to take it on without behaving like a prescient vicar. It means thinking about where individual teachers are going — or could be going. The 'going' may be in terms of intellectual or organizational contribution to the department. It may mean promotion — either within the school or elsewhere (though encouraging a valuable member of the department to go elsewhere is clearly not something to do lightly!).

Part of the head of department's responsibility here is discharged within the normal work of an active department. Working in a department where people are continually meeting and sharing new ideas with one another is obviously conducive to individual professional growth as well as to the collective development of the department. Arranging responsibilities so that individual members of the department take charge of an area of concern (like books for class libraries or media study) will also add to the special expertise an individual teacher can claim.

The following suggestions grow out of the overall policy of sharing and developing practice and giving teachers in the department specific responsibilities.

IN-SERVICE COURSES

Keep an eye out for courses (either evening or day-time short-courses) which would be of particular interest to individuals. The first thing here is to make sure that the information about what courses are available gets through to you from whoever in the school gets it in the first instance. The second thing is to put the idea of going on a particular course directly to an individual or indirectly at a department meeting where people agree that a course sounds worthwhile and nominate someone to attend it. The third thing is to work out some way of feeding information or materials from the course back into the department. That may not always be easy or appropriate, but if it can happen (by making it the focus of a department meeting, for example) it is likely to be good for the department and for the teacher who attended the course. It is worth ensuring that the school hierarchy is aware that this feedback is taking place. Getting release for courses during the day can be a problem because of the disruption absence causes. Making the case that individuals going on courses is doing the department good is a powerful way of easing the problem.

PUBLIC RELATIONS

A regular bit of public relations (with the school hierarchy, governors, inspectors) on behalf of individual teachers is an excellent thing. When one person has done all the work to produce an anthology of pupils' writing or an informal drama show, make sure this gets known; don't put all the credit for it down to collective departmental energy. When one teacher is about to do a particularly interesting sequence of work with a class, you might want to invite the inspector/adviser in to see it in action. That helps to ensure that when a head or inspector/adviser comes to write a reference or report on the teacher they have got some additional knowledge of the teacher to call on.

MAKING A MOVE

Take the time (and choose the moment) to talk to individual teachers about what their plans might be for the future. It is a delicate matter but there may come a time when to say 'maybe it is a good idea to move on' would be a helpful thing to do for the person concerned — and maybe for the department. Where a member of department does apply for jobs elsewhere, the head of department will probably be asked to write a reference and/or to contribute information towards the head's reference. (The ILEA is one of the few education authorities which has an open rather than 'confidential' system of reporting. For an application for a Scale 3 post or below, within or outside the authority, the head or other referee is obliged to show the testimonial to the applicant before sending it. No other report is sent.) The writing of a reference (open or confidential) is a tricky business. It is a great help if you are writing or contributing to one to know the details of the post so that the reference can be geared in the right direction, using particular illustrations of the applicant's work and experience as well as making general statements. It is also helpful to show a draft to someone senior in the school to make sure that there are no possibilities for misinterpretation by the receiving school.

REPRESENTING THE DEPARTMENT

Another of the head of department's responsibilities in the department is to think beyond it. There's every good reason to do so and to avoid the danger of isolationism:
— because an English department's work is directly affected by the policies of the school as a whole, and its collective voice needs to be heard in discussion and planning of these policies;
— because governors, parents, senior staff and other teachers in the school all need information about and illustration of what the English department is up to (see the suggestions in the section 'The Syllabus');
— because what goes on in English lessons needs to be seen in relation to what goes on in other subject classrooms (see the section 'The Department and the School');
— because a positive case has to be made in the appropriate forums for the department to get its fair share of material resources (see the section 'Time, Space and Money').

The head of department will not be the only member of the team who wants and needs to look beyond the details of the department's work to the school as a whole. All teachers of English in a school are more than just that. But the head of department has a particular need to think big, to positively look for ways of relating the department to the school — and to encourage other people in the department to do the same.

MAKING FORMAL MEETINGS WORK
Most schools have regular meetings of heads of department and senior staff to discuss and plan curricular arrangements. It is important that the head of department collects the views of people in the department on issues which come up at these meetings and is pre-

pared to present a case on the basis of these views. Some of the issues will bear directly on English teaching, while others will be of a general nature or of particular concern to other departments in the school. Representing the views of the English department doesn't inevitably mean proposing a partisan and unanimous opinion.

The simplest way to ensure that the department's views are represented is to set up a department meeting prior to the curriculum committee date. Agenda items can then be discussed in advance. Subsequently the department can expect a report from its representative on key decisions taken, even if, as in many schools, such decisions are publicized through other channels too.

The same sort of procedure can apply to school policy working party meetings in which the department is represented (as it should be — though not necessarily by the head of department). It won't be possible for the whole department to be kept informed of the details of a working party's discussions, but the department's nominated representative can collect general views before a series of meetings and provide an opportunity for comment on recommendations at an appropriate stage in the working party's life. Some of this collecting of suggestions and comment can be done on paper to save time at department meetings.

OILING THE WHEELS

The transaction of school business doesn't take place exclusively at formal meetings. Much of it is conducted in the creases of a school day, person-to-person, with no explicit policy decisions or recommendations made. So: oil the school wheels. We don't wish to suggest that the head of department should carefully engineer significant interactions with other staff every break-time, but a certain amount of premeditation at this level of school life (as in the examples below) won't do any harm.

Bumping into the head
Heads of schools (and their deputies) can be isolated people. It's good sense to make informal contact when you've got nothing much in mind to say or to ask for, but just want to air some ideas for the future and find out what the head's current concerns are. This may sound daft (and implausible to people in some large schools), but it does work. It makes a change for a head to talk to someone outside the executive circle who doesn't have a bellyache or want an extra £200; and it gives you a chance to share the head's perspective and seed a few ideas of your own. The more you are at loggerheads on a particular issue, the more useful this kind of contact may be.

Informal contact with other departments
While it's a good general policy to circulate other departments with

" ASK THE HEAD OF ENGLISH... "

A head of department is hourly required to make lightning reactions to problems and requests. Test your own reflexes on the situations below. Consider each situation and check how your decisions compare with those recommended by the Experts. Keep track of your score. You begin with 10 points, representing the reservoir of respect and good-will with which you begin the week. Once you have worked through the situations soberly repeat the process when drunk. Compare your scores. Does this tell you anything about yourself?

1. The largest member of the P.E. department approaches you at break-time and says the Head thinks he may have to do a bit of English next year to fill up his timetable. Do you:

(A) smile and say that you are looking forward to his contribution to the department;
(B) go straight to the Head to offer your resignation;
(C) laugh out loud, spill coffee on his tracksuit and say not on your life?

2. The Head suddenly asks you to address a full staff meeting after school tomorrow on the issue of reading in school. Do you:

(A) accept with enthusiasm and mention Bullock;
(B) say you can't do it for tomorrow night because you need to consult the department?

3. A parent governor sends you 30 free tickets for an amateur production of *Macbeth* (set in downtown Los Angeles) which she is involved in. Do you:

(A) offer the tickets to your 5th year literature class;
(B) send the tickets back with a note saying thanks but the children have already seen the Polanski film?

4. Over lunch, your probationer (with whom you have recently had a long discussion about discipline and classroom management) asks to come and see you

teaching your difficult 3rd year after lunch. Do you:

(A) say you will just be carrying on with the class reader, which won't be very interesting so how about next week;
(B) say certainly, by all means, skip the pudding and quickly hunt out a guaranteed worksheet from the filing cabinet?

5. You are addressing a meeting for lower school parents about the teaching of English in the school. At the end of your talk about collaborative work in English and the importance of reading, a parent calls out from the back of the hall, 'And what about spelling?'. Do you:

(A) immediately give the assembled parents a spelling test in order to demonstrate that everyone has difficulties with spelling;
(B) ask the parent concerned to see you privately after the meeting;
(C) tell a funny story about a doctor who couldn't spell 'enema'?

6. You ask a junior member of the department to take over the requisitioning and distribution of consumable stock. He accepts gladly and asks for £400 to spend immediately. Do you:

(A) agree without hesitation;
(B) agree and then go to the school secretary and request her to check with you before forwarding any requisitions for consumable stock in the future;
(C) ask him to draw up and cost a list of possible items for discussion at the next department meeting?

HOW DID YOU SCORE ?

1. (A) Excellent on diplomacy. Score 2 points. But the next day you have to spend a whole double free period listening to the P.E. teacher's proposed schedule of English work for next year. It seems to almost exclusively centre on the split infinitive. Lose 2 points.
(B) A mistake. The Head seems quite interested in your offer of resignation and promises a testimonial by lunchtime. Lose 3 points.
(C) Crude but effective. The P.E. teacher goes back to the Head to express an interest in the teaching of Economic History. But your place in the staff badminton team is now at risk. Score 2 points and buy a squash racket.

2. (A) Full marks for enthusiasm. Score 3 points. But unfortunately you have forgotten you're supposed to go to the theatre tonight; you'll have to cancel and re-read the Bullock Report instead. Lose 1 point. (You can't find it. Lose another point.)
(B) In theory a good tactic. Unfortunately the Head calls instead on the probationary remedial teacher, who blinds the staff with phonemes and accuses the English department of waffling to non-readers about literature. Lose 2 points.

3. (A) Your courage is rewarded. The performance is a huge success; everyone is pleased. Score 3 points. But later, in an acid letter to the Head, the Chief Examiner wonders why all your candidates described how Macbeth met his tragic end, struck down by a hail of bullets in a drive-in movie. Lose 3 points.
(B) A foolish move. The parent governor is offended and points out that the Polanski film is an X certificate and shouldn't have been shown to pupils under 16. She will raise the issue at the next governors' meeting. Lose 2 points.

4. (A) Pity. This week's lesson on *A Kind of Loving* goes unusually well; now you'll have to worry about next week. The next chapter features Vic and Ingrid on the park bench. Those who have read on are very keen for you to read this bit aloud. Lose 2 points.
(B) You should have stuck to the class reader. Somehow the worksheet on writing haikus about city scenes in pairs on sugar paper just doesn't take off today — something to do with the pudding? Lose 2 points.

5. (A) Unwise. 14 parents immediately get up and go; the meeting ends in disarray when your mind goes blank on 'occasionally'. Lose 4 points.
(B) Not a particularly successful tactic; some parents wonder what you've got to hide and start to ask awkward questions about your attitude to the split infinitive. Lose 2 points.
(C) Brilliant; your joke brings the house down. Carried along by waves of laughter you make four punchy remarks about the department's spelling policy. Score 3 points. But the person in the front who left rather smartly at the end turned out to be the local G.P. the head was trying to woo on to the PTA committee. Lose 1 point.

6. (A) Your confidence in your colleague is appreciated by him. Score 2 points. But the three gross tins of copydex which subsequently arrive present a bit of a storage problem. Lose 1 point.
(B) Odd that you hadn't noticed that your colleague and the school secretary are having an affair. Your two-faced-ness creates a bad odour. Lose 2 points.
(C) Strong on democracy. Score 1 point. However, having spent an entire department meeting discussing the tensile strength of different kinds of rubber bands, your CSE entries will now be late. Lose 1 point.

regular, brief information sheets about what the English department is doing, experience shows that a high proportion of interesting cross-curricular developments grow out of casual chats about matters of shared interest (assessment, group work, projects, using reading for learning, the design of teaching materials . . .). Having a departmental base is an enormous advantage to an English department (see 'Time, Space and Money'), but if you've got one don't live in it: take tea in the Science prep room; have a bun with Home Economics; beard Maths in their staffroom corner. On that basis, you may not feel at all tentative about inviting yourself to a Humanities department meeting, or inviting French to one of yours.

Second in Department

THE UNCERTAINTY OF THE SITUATION

I've been second in department for three years, in a team of eight. My head of department has been quite reasonable towards me — I mean she sat down when I first came and discussed my responsibilities and I had some say in what I do. Basically I look after the CSE groups, the second year programme and a pile of bits and pieces like keeping class libraries stocked, ordering films etc. I've got a free hand to initiate new ideas and to order materials and to make decisions about exam entries and groupings of kids, things like that. But I find it a strange job because in the end you don't have complete responsibility for final decisions although you do all the groundwork which counts. Sometimes I get frustrated about the uncertainty of the situation. For instance, last year I put together a completely new package for our 2nd year, which involved a new kind of assessment programme. Although I talked about it with my head of department — and she agreed with it — when we had a department meeting to explain it to the team she treated it as an item for discussion and decision. The result was that most of the work I'd done was discarded because some people weren't happy with it. I felt really let down. Our relationship is a good one, personally, but I feel now that I'm treated differently from the way she'd treat her own initiatives. If the 2nd year exam ideas had been her own I think she would have handled the meeting differently — to make sure the team agreed with them.

CREATIVE TENSION

I really enjoy being a second in department. It gives me a chance to take real responsibility for things I'm good at and to share in work and decisions on other things I'm not too sure about. Not that there isn't some 'creative tension' in the job: I sometimes find myself

*thinking I'm doing far too much of the dogsbody stuff and that
people in the department use me as the clerical officer. But that's
partly my fault, because I've got an obsession with tidiness and
keeping things straight. My outbursts about disappearing books and
so on are a regular department joke; in return I make fun of the head
of department swanning about and playing at 'management'. But
most of the time the sharing of the jobs is pretty well-balanced — and
I particularly enjoy the fact that people in the department are genuinely grateful when things get done which they find helpful. I don't
really want to become a head of department — I don't think it's
worth the aggravation you get in the school as a whole. But I probably will.*

WHO AM I?

A second in department is a person for all seasons; the role is one
which it is impossible to define except in terms of its relationship
to that of the head of department. Some heads of department might
see the second in charge primarily as someone to come up with
bright new ideas and schemes; or as someone who can look after
complete year programmes; or as someone who can be expected to
absorb much of the admin. drudgery (exam entries, stock checking
and so on). The head of department's view may or may not coincide
with the conception the second in charge has of his/her most useful
role. Clearly open discussion is the only way of ensuring that a
proper relationship between the two views is established and maintained.

Discussion about the allocation of jobs between the head of department and second in charge ought to acknowledge the fact that a
second in department generally has it in mind to become, at some
point, a head of department. Having an opportunity to experience
the whole range of responsibilities within a department will obviously be useful from that point of view. It is also likely to benefit the
department as a whole if the second in charge is given an active and
wide-ranging role. As well as discussing the allocation of jobs, it's
also worth raising the question of whether the second in department
is to be consulted separately from the whole team on all major issues
of policy — and, on the other hand, whether s/he is free to take
initiatives or make decisions in particular areas without reference to
the head of department.

SUPPOSING . . .

For a second in department to negotiate and carry out a role in a
department overseen by an active head of department is one thing.

Doing so in a department which is not effectively led is quite another. All heads of department to some degree fail to meet the specifications for ideal head of department behaviour. That is not in the least surprising given the range of roles a head of department is required to adopt in addition to being an ordinary teacher and an ordinary member of a school staff. But there are heads of department who find themselves ill-equipped, for one reason or another, to provide enough leadership and direction even to keep things going on an administrative level. While we should point out that heads of department are no more prone to ineffectiveness than, say, headteachers or LEA inspectors, an ineffective head of department is in a position to affect directly the day-to-day working lives of colleagues in the department.

Where it's a matter of simple inefficiency or idleness on the part of the head of department, it may be possible for the second in department to gently take over the key administrative functions while leaving the head of department with the trappings of authority and with a warm feeling that things are humming under his/her sensitive supervision. One consequence of a badly run department is that the staff feel that they do not have access to teaching material appropriate for their classes. A sensitive second in department can, in these circumstances, negotiate a way of remedying this relatively straightforward deficiency.

However, there are heads of department who don't do the minimum of jobs required and won't delegate either — let alone exercise a positive role in the development of the department's work. Clearly there are awkward implications for a second in department where a department has become so run down and disorganised that children's education is at risk. Other members of department may well expect the second in department 'to do something' on the grounds that s/he is the next in line for decision-making. It is a highly problematic situation in which the possibilities for action can be severely limited, partly because of the particular personalities that may be involved, partly as a result of legitimate constraints arising from codes of professional conduct. The second in department and other members of the team will need to make a fine judgement about whether to let things ride, to discuss the issues openly at a department meeting or to find some way of taking the matter beyond the department in order to exert pressure from outside. Situations of this kind are far too complex and delicate to offer useful generalisations or reliable lines of action.

O.K. so where's the bit about the duff second in department ?

The Composition of the Team

The composition of an English team is largely determined by factors well outside the control of the department or the head of department or indeed of the school as a whole. One couldn't change the fact, for example, that in the mid 1970's a large number of fairly experienced teachers moved out of inner-city areas to find cheaper housing; nor is it possible now to ignore the impact on staffing of falling rolls and a shrinking job-market. Within the school, questions of personalities, hierarchies, efficiency and inefficiency, job security and insecurity, re-deployment from department to department and the status of English in the school — all may affect, in their different ways, the composition of a departmental team.

In some cases, then, there won't be much room for a department to manoeuvre on this question of staffing. But where there is some room for manoeuvre, the head of department, consulting the rest of the department and calling on the LEA inspector/advisor as appropriate, can — and should — exert influence in three ways:
- arguing for a reasonable balance in the department between experience and inexperience, between full-time and part-time commitment, with a spread of scale posts to reflect a healthy spread of responsibility;
- having a decisive voice in choosing who teaches English (where there is a choice);
- requiring of anyone teaching English (including non-specialist teachers) that they conform to at least a minimum of 'how this department operates' (see the suggestions on ways of supporting non-specialist teachers of English in the section 'Helping Ourselves').

A BALANCED DEPARTMENT

English departments come in all shapes and sizes, but a well-balanced department will probably comprise:
- mainly full-time specialist teachers;
- a mixture of experience and inexperience, pragmatism and idealism;
- a sufficient spread of scale posts to allow delegation and promotion.

The three examples which follow are real ones from ILEA schools. They illustrate quite different department composition, although the department is in each case responsible for 'English only'.

EXAMPLE 1: 1200 pupils
    10 people teach English:

8 full-time specialists, Scales 43222111
1 Year Head (20/40 English periods)
1 Drama teacher (6/40 English periods)
This is probably as good a situation as can currently be achieved. The department is a coherent administrative unit in which solid commitment can be expected from almost everyone. The spread of scale posts allows for expertise to be developed and rewarded.

EXAMPLE 2: 750 pupils
9 people teach English:
2 full-time specialists, Scales 42
1 Drama teacher (5/40 English periods)
1 Remedial teacher (5/40 English periods)
2 Year Heads (30/40 English periods)
2 Deputy Heads (14/40 and 6/40 English periods)
Head (18/40 English periods)
The difficulties of co-ordination, attendance at meetings and delegation of jobs in the department seem overwhelming here, as must the production of teacher-made materials. The presence of senior staff in force will make the head of department's leadership-role especially difficult, although their experience may be helpful.

EXAMPLE 3: 800 pupils
10 people teach English:
2 full-time specialists, Scales 42
1 Remedial teacher (5/40 English periods)
2 History teachers (23/40 and 17/40 English periods)
2 PE teachers (12/40 and 10/40 English periods)
1 Maths teacher (6/40 English periods)
1 Social Studies teacher (4/40 English periods)
This is hardly a department at all, and a suitable case for consultation with the head and the LEA inspector/advisor.

PICKING THE TEAM

Where new appointments involving external applicants are to be made to the department team it is essential that the head of department, acting on behalf of the whole department, should make strenuous efforts to ensure that s/he plays a real part in the appointing process. There are four phases in this process where the post is advertised nationally or within the LEA. (Where the LEA has a policy of offering available posts to teachers subject to re-deployment, the procedure will be different, although in most cases the school can still exercise some degree of choice over whom it accepts to fill a vacancy.) Different LEAs and individual schools vary in the extent to which heads of department are encouraged to be involved in some or all of these four phases; the head of department should ensure that s/he sticks out for the maximum involvement possible.

PHASE 1: THE ADVERT

It is unlikely that there will be a general shortage of applicants for English posts in the foreseeable future, but it's always worth giving thought to the wording of the advert for a post. There should be some attempt at job definition and some mention of interesting things going on in the department. The more teachers you can interest, the wider the choice. Compare the information offered in the two examples below of adverts for Scale 1 posts.

Alfred Bishop School
(roll 1400, 11-18, mixed)
Helmwirth Rd., London SE20.
This is a locally popular school in a pleasant part of London. The English Department is part of the large Humanities Faculty. Courses lead to GCE O and A Level and CSE. Required for September: Scale 1 teacher for English with an active concern for the subject and an interest in extra-curricular work in the school as a whole. Possibility of advanced work for suitably qualified candidate.

Application should be made by letter to the Headmaster giving full curriculum vitae and quoting two referees.

Freston Grove School
(roll 1000, 11-18, boys)
Pawn Rd., London E8.
Required for September: a teacher of English to share in the work of a vigorous department. There is an integrated studies programme in years 1 and 2, mode 3 CSE in years 4 and 5. Classes are mixed ability. Candidates would be expected to share in production of materials and the teaching of courses for all years. There are opportunities for specialist interests in remedial work, drama and media studies.

Short-listed candidates will be invited to visit the school.

Additional information.

Schools normally send out further information about the school's pastoral and curricular arrangements to those who request application forms. The department might put together a simple-and-honest description of itself on an A4 sheet to go out with this material; it might include reference to things the department would like to get under way as well as things which are established policy and practice. Where the advertised post involves specific responsibilities these can be spelled out on a separate sheet in more detail than space in an advertisement allows.

PHASE 2: SHORT-LISTING

The people who do the job of short-listing applicants will vary from school to school: the head will certainly be involved; other senior members of staff may be involved, along with a representative of the governing body; a member of the LEA subject Inspectorate is usually involved in the short-listing of head and deputy head of department. The head of department can make an invaluable professional contribution at this stage.

The only things you can go on here are the application forms and the references/testimonials (if available at this stage). Read the application form with two questions in mind:
- does this person have the kind of qualities and interests which will be of value to us?
- if there is no direct or substantial evidence of this being the case (as perhaps with new teachers), are there *any* indications that this applicant would be able to develop them?

A considerable weight may be placed on the 200 word personal statement on the application form by those doing the short-listing — especially where there are a number of candidates whose qualifications and experience are similar. Any teacher who has tried to do the 200 word essay knows that it is a real pain to do: there are problems of both content and tone to resolve. Some members of the short-listing group may be looking for a cogent educational stance, while others may be more interested in an ability to string sentences together.

References and testimonials

References/testimonials also take a bit of careful reading. There tends to be a set of codes operating in the writing of these things, but the codes aren't very explicit and so they're open to misinterpretation. Having open testimonials (where negativity tends to be muted) alongside confidential references (where negativity can be irrelevant or 'judicious') can complicate matters. Excessive praise may not be generous in intent; there may be significant omissions or ambiguities; there may be messages in the way descriptions of personal and professional qualities are phrased. On the other hand, there may be no great art in the writing at all; there's a danger in being too cunning a reader. What the head of department can do is to ensure that the professional strengths recorded in the reference/testimonial are actually registered in the short-listing procedure, rather than overwhelmed by general stuff about 'serious contribution to the school' and 'receptivity to the views of others'.

PHASE 3: PRELIMINARY VISITS

As the formal interview usually only lasts 20-30 minutes it's worth trying to ensure that prospective appointees visit the school beforehand. This obviously causes some disruption, but it can be of real value both to the department and to the applicants. Visits provide an opportunity for the applicants to see the department's resources and to visit some classrooms so as to get a glimpse of the children, the running of the school and the department's working style. Visits also give an opportunity for lunch-time or after-school informal chats with members of the department; paradoxically, the informality of the occasion can allow people to ask applicants more specific and probing questions than they may face at the formal interview.

The visits of applicants to the school are sometimes organized so that the four or six people turn up together for a day; it may be less strenuous if they are split into two groups to come on separate days, if this can be arranged. Alternatively some schools expect applicants to look around the school during the day of the interview itself. Whatever the arrangement, it will clearly be useful for the head of department to elicit the views of the department (whether individually or collectively) after the visit so that these can be presented to the interview board. Obviously, it's much easier to organize this in a small department.

PHASE 4: THE INTERVIEW

It seems to us inexcusable for a head of department not to be invited to participate in the interviewing of candidates for a job within his/her department. Heads and/or governors may have a number of reasons for excluding the head of department — possibly among them being the fear that the head of department's views on the characteristics of candidates as English teachers may not match with their views on the general characteristics of the candidates as potential members of a school's staff. If the head of department *is* excluded, s/he should at least ensure that the head and teacher-governor are given a list of points, comments and questions from the department.

Assuming that the head of department is able to be present at the interview (and is permitted to speak, if not to vote should the occasion arise), s/he can perform two valuable functions:
- offering an opportunity through his/her own question(s) for candidates to describe areas of special interest or concern in English teaching;
- interpreting or translating questions from governors about aspects of English teaching (which can sometimes be crude or vague) so as to make them easier to formulate a reply to.

Helping Ourselves

Covering for Absence
Discipline
First Year Teachers
Student Teachers
Non-Specialist English Teachers
Not So Brilliant

Helping Ourselves

The first part of this book considered how a framework for co-operation within the department can be based on the active participation of all teachers, whatever their particular responsibilities. This section looks at ways in which a department committed to a co-operative working style can organize itself to meet some of the demands of school life and offer support to members of the team with specific needs.

Covering for Absence

The business of covering lessons for absent teachers probably causes more bad feeling, dispute and organizational angst than any other in schools. Ideally all teachers ought to feel that none of their free periods (properly 'non-teaching periods') should be used for cover. Non-teaching periods should be for marking, preparation or just relaxing. For a teacher to be asked instead to take another class for another teacher is, at the very least, a nuisance.

From the department's point of view cover arrangements for English lessons (which include arranging the work the class is to do) can involve both time and strain, as well as affecting relationships with teachers in other departments. In what follows we look at the question of cover and at different systems which are used to manage the business. No system solves the problems. Only adequate staffing of schools based on their actual needs would provide a proper answer. But under present circumstances some systems (or, indeed, just having *a* system) may minimize the problems.

ABSENT AGAIN

The majority of teacher absence is due to illness or personal need. There is nothing to say about that — except for obvious things like illness being associated with tiredness and stress and tending to hit teachers towards the end of a term. But teachers are also absent from their normal lessons for a variety of reasons to do with school

or departmental work. These reasons may apply more to some teachers or some departments than to others. English teachers, like teachers of other subjects, may need to be out of school to:
— attend meetings to do with exam work;
— take pupils on trips and visits;
— attend an in-service course.

There are some teachers and some members of school hierarchies who suspect that these reasons to be out of school are fraudulent, and resent the disruption caused. If this suspicion and resentment is voiced it needs to be met head-on and necessary absence clearly argued for on the grounds of department policy and professional need. If arguing needs to be done it will probably be the head of department's job. Obviously it will help everyone if necessary absence of this kind is notified well in advance and the reason for it made plain. It will also help if the request itself is framed in terms of departmental rather than individual need, i.e. 'We need someone to go to the CSE exam meeting next month. Paulette has agreed to represent us.'

WHO COVERS?

If someone in one department is going to be out of school, for whatever reason, who is going to cover the class?

SUPPLY TEACHERS

LEAs, and individual schools within them, have different policies on the use of supply teachers. Some deny that such people exist; others make liberal use of them even when the absence is only going to be a day or two. Generally speaking, the shorter the absence and the shorter the notice you get of it, the less likely it is that a supply teacher will arrive. Even with a liberal policy and efficient communication supply teachers can't always be summoned out of a bottle. But there's nothing to stop a department pooling its knowledge of friends who might be available to do a few days work at short notice and passing these names and phone numbers on to the deputy head responsible. This obviously makes particular sense if you are looking for someone with experience of English teaching to cover an absence longer than a few days.

If supply teachers are used to cover English lessons it's worth remembering that they need some basic information about the department in order to operate effectively. It may even be worth doing an A4 sheet especially for supply teachers which answers questions like these:
— are classes banded, set or mixed ability?
— where are the main rooms that English is taught in?
— do pupils do their writing in exercise books or on loose

paper? where are supplies kept?
— what is the policy on homework?
— what discipline procedures operate in the department?

OVERTIME FOR PART-TIMERS

If the department has any part-time teachers one of them might be
interested in working extra sessions to cover absence if the LEA
policy allows this. It isn't possible to claim overtime on anything
like a permanent basis, but the scheme may help with absences of
something in the region of four weeks. If it's possible, there are
obvious advantages in using someone who knows the school and
knows what the department is doing.

A ROTA SYSTEM

Where a supply teacher or someone doing overtime is not available,
many schools work out cover arrangements within the school on a
rota basis for each period of the week. The advantage is that teachers know which free periods are safe and which are at risk. If records
of cover are kept by the deputy head responsible, the head of department can check that a member of his/her department is not
suffering too much. The disadvantage from the department's point
of view is that cover teachers come from every subject and are likely
to want to supervise work set rather than teach it.

SUBJECT PLUS POOL

Under this system English teachers with free periods are on first
call to cover English lessons. Where an English teacher is not available,
then other teachers are called on. The advantage is that English teachers will be prepared to cover the lesson actively and will be able to
devise work if none has been set. The disadvantage is that all your
free time is at risk. The system can only work fairly if there is an
agreement on a minimum protected free number of periods — otherwise you'll find yourself covering English and then having to do pool
cover for a small department as well.

FACULTY COVER

Under this system departments with common interests are grouped
together into faculties of roughly the same size. Some schools have
a faculty system anyway for reasons other than administering cover;
in this case English is usually with Humanities and Drama. Teachers
within each faculty only cover lessons in their group of subjects,
partly by re-distributing pupils from a class without a teacher and
partly by using their free period allocation. The advantage lies in the
limited range of work which cover teachers have to familiarize themselves with and in the possibilities for flexibility within the faculty
grouping. The disadvantage — if it is one — is that the administration
of cover needs to be done by teachers in the faculty. More import-

antly, the flexibility the scheme makes possible may in fac[...]
the spreading of dislocation if classes are regularly divided [...]

COVER WORK

It's demoralizing for both pupils and teacher in a cover lesson [...]
there is no work available. If it's an English teacher doing the [...]
ing, s/he may have a bottomless stock of wonderful one-off lessons
which go a treat with a strange class. But most people prefer to be
given something rather than try to produce a rabbit out of a hat. In
any case it's better for the class if the work they are asked to do
continues in some way from previous lessons, though that's not
always easy. It's a matter of developing a system which causes as
little strain as possible to all concerned. Some suggestions follow.

Someone in charge

Nominate one teacher (or two on split sites) in the department to
oversee the arrangements for cover work. This job is such a nuisance
that no-one should have to do it for more than a term at a time,
though senior members of the department should take on the major
share. Alternatively pair teachers together so that when teacher A is
away teacher B ensures that work is set and available and vice versa.

otes from the absent teacher

When absence is known about in advance the absent teacher should write out a reasonably detailed programme of cover work and give it, together with any materials and cupboard keys, to the person responsible. If the absence is unforeseen and the absentee has to phone in it's often easier for him/her to describe the cover work to a department colleague than to the school secretary or deputy head. Having a duplicate set of cupboard keys within the department is a real boon on these occasions.

The resource bank

When it's not possible to set up work which continues from previous lessons — and it's sometimes more trouble than it's worth — a resource bank of wonderful one-off lessons is invaluable. This might include sheets of suggestions for writing (not just single-word starters but fully outlined ideas), dictionary and word games, and special sets of short story and poetry anthologies with accompanying notes to the teacher. A resource bank of such items shouldn't take long to build up if the work is shared or if one person spends time on it. The material needs to be reasonably self-propelling (if not idiot-proof); it mustn't be raided for any other purpose; it must be readily access-ible (packaged in special boxes perhaps); and there needs to be some simple recording sheet with it so that the cover teacher can write down which class has done what. A simple alternative to the resource bank is a couple of spare book-boxes to be used for short-term cover purposes only.

Long-term pairing

Where long-term cover is being done by a supply teacher, there is obviously a need for something better than emergency arrangements for cover work. In this case the supply teacher needs to be given the support that any new member of the department would get. The most direct kind of support is to give another person in the depart-ment the job of working out with the supply teacher a coherent programme of work — perhaps most easily based around a class reader or a collection of short stories.

Discipline

SALLY

'*Sally is in my 4th year. She is always late for the lessons, never has her books, constantly disrupts lessons by provoking others with personal insults and is intolerant of other points of view than her own. Her ability to read and write is very average, but not such that remedial help is needed. The problem is she isn't giving herself a chance to get any better. She'll occasionally half-start a story, half-attend to reading we're doing, but most of the time she is just contemptuous of my attempts to interest her in a variety of types of work.'*

FOUR BOYS

'There's a group of four boys in my 2nd year class who regularly cause two or three disturbances in every lesson. They are mixed in ability and motivation and just seem to set each other off. Even when separated in the room they find ways of operating so as to disturb one another and everyone else. Very little gets done. The rest of the class find them amusing and a useful distraction and expect them to 'perform'. I get on with them fine but I can't get them to really settle — they don't seem to take me or the work seriously for long enough to avoid trouble.'

MY THIRD YEARS

'My 3rd years are beyond me. It's chaos practically every lesson and I end up hoarse with trying to settle them down. It's a low band class but most of them could be doing a lot better than they are. But they never give it a chance. I can't try anything which involves talking, they just won't listen to me or one another: talking becomes a shouting match. So it's all writing, but they won't stick at that for more than ten minutes at a time. I've tried working from a course book but they say it's too hard and it's boring and so on . . . '

THE PROPER CLIMATE . . .

During the late 60's and early 70's English teachers gained a folk-loric reputation for being unconcerned about behaviour in the classroom. That was never the case. What was evident to English teachers then is true now: that establishing the proper climate for productive work in English lessons requires subtlety, good sense and a willingness to allow pupils to have a say in the rules. The proper climate has two main features:
> — a pleasant, relaxed relationship between teacher and class;
> — the provision of opportunities for both individual concentration and active collaboration between pupils.

Misbehaviour of the kind which makes individual concentration impossible or which destroys the stability needed for productive collaboration between pupils often pushes a teacher into monotonous and narrow versions of English in order to manufacture crowd control; giving endless written comprehension exercises or 'tests' of various kinds is characteristic of this insecurity.

Discussion of discipline shouldn't be left to disciplinarians in the school; any department which hopes to develop its work and give all children a fair chance to make progress needs to formulate a basic plan of action to deal with predictable problems, and to discuss openly ways of supporting one another in coping with and working with children who seem inclined to reject what is on offer in English lessons. If the issue is not discussed openly in the department there is a danger that the problems which individual teachers face will produce isolationist attitudes of the 'this-is-my-classroom-and-I'm-shutting-the-door' sort. Furthermore, new ideas for practice which need imaginative and confident classroom management are likely to remain merely ideas for some members of the department unless problems of control are aired.

ANALYSING PROBLEMS

Classroom control is a sensitive issue; discussion of it should be about ways of *analysing* and *remedying* problems and as far away as possible from *blaming* them on pupils and teachers; it should take place on the basis that *everyone* has problems at some time or another. Focussing on specific situations (like the ones described at the beginning of this section) is a good way to get discussion going on three key questions:
— what kind of behaviour do we expect?
— why does misbehaviour take place?
— what can be done about it?

What kind of behaviour do we expect?
It may be worth trying to discover what different people in the department regard as essential features of good classroom behaviour (that is, what children need to do in order to get on well with one another and with their work) so that expectations can be compared. What do people regard as acceptable/unacceptable in terms of such things as noise, movement around the room, horseplay, jibes and digs, rate of work and so on?

Why does misbehaviour take place?
There are a large number of possible explanations for misbehaviour which have more to do with the rules and structures of the institution as a whole than with the psychology of individuals. Some problems, however, may be specifically to do with the way English lessons are run. They may come down to such factors as:
— the department's policy on the composition of teaching groups;
— the way English lessons are timetabled;
— physical arrangements and organizational procedures in the classroom.
The most direct question is the hardest one for most teachers to

ask: is the work that pupils are supposed to be doing appropriate, interesting and worth doing?

What can be done about it?
Many of the causes of misbehaviour listed above can be removed by examining and modifying department policies. Other problems can be solved or eased by establishing a mutually supportive 'coping system' within the department and a clear policy for referring serious or long-standing difficulties to pastoral staff. The following possibilities for action within the department may be useful as short-term measures in particular circumstances when the normal combination of good humour/straight talking/interpersonal wizardry doesn't work:

— temporarily transferring a pupil or pupils to other classes for a cooling-off period;

— sending a pupil to work alone in a small space (the department's office? the stockroom?) under the watchful eye of a teacher otherwise occupied there;

— establishing a 'contract' with the pupil(s) for a change in behaviour and work over a specified period, perhaps with the head of department acting as overseer;

— pairing two simultaneously-timetabled classes together for a specified period so that work can be jointly planned and the pupil groupings flexibly organized;

— arranging (where timetable arrangements allow) for another teacher to work alongside the class teacher for a short period, both to help particular pupils and to offer the class teacher another assessment of the situation.

TED - D

First Year Teachers

HOW DOES IT FEEL?

'I stayed up until 11.30 marking, not that 11.30 is late, but I wasn't relaxing — just working. And then, when I got up at around 6.45 — I would feel as though I hadn't had a break. By the end of the week, you can't teach properly because you're so tired.'

'Most teachers are OK on "What book are you reading with your fourth year? Is it going down well?" etc. But if you get any closer than that they close up.'

'My problem is working against the kids' ideas of what English is about. If I do anything that's not writing stories . . . I can't have talking because "that's not English". I've retreated into more traditional ways of teaching — but even that's beginning to fail now.'

'There are times in the last term and a half when I've really enjoyed teaching, when a lesson — or even a whole day — has gone well. But the problem is bridging the gaps between the good days and somehow getting myself onto an even keel. I doubt if there's been a time in my life when I've been so up and down.'

'College did show me possibilities which aren't anywhere near being possibilities for me at the moment. One of the worst things is feeling alone in your ideas about teaching. I'm really glad I've seen their ideas working with other people's classes.'

These quotations are extracts from a discussion with a group of first year teachers. They give some indications of the pressures and shocks which first year teachers are likely to experience as they grapple with new and conflicting roles and responsibilities. Self-confidence can be at a low ebb and the department should do everything to ensure that the first-year teacher feels supported and encouraged. This is especially important in the first few weeks, when the demands of pupils, the department and the school can be so difficult to subdue and relate to an overall pattern.

THE DEPARTMENT'S SUPPORT

Some local authorities have special policies for the induction of new teachers, involving lighter timetabling, release for programmes outside the school and definite supervision within it. (See appendix for an outline of the ILEA scheme.) It's up to the head of department to ensure that these policies are adhered to — and to fight the still prevalent mentality which holds to the 'chuck-'em-in-the-deep-end' theory. Whether there is a formal induction scheme or not, the department can offer its own support in the following ways.

The teacher's friend

Many schools have a member of staff with general responsibility for the induction of new teachers. This person is often a senior member of staff who has an assessing as well as a supporting function. It is important that there is also someone in the department assigned to the role of supporting new teachers. The teacher who does this job should ideally be a sympathetic person who is reasonably successful in the classroom and yet has not been teaching so long that s/he has forgotten what it is like not to be coping. A teacher in this position may find it easier to help a probationary teacher understand which issues and problems are the result of his/her actions and practices, and which are created by the constraints implicit in department or school organization. (In departments which use a pairing system anyway, sharing problems and resources, the first year teacher won't feel as if s/he is being treated exceptionally.)

The department's resources

Make sure that the first year teacher is aware of all the department's resources and how to get hold of them. Many teachers in their first year find that their repertoire of teaching strategies collapses with disconcerting speed; most need help in choosing and using appropriate material. Inappropriate material (or inept use of appropriate material) leads to problems of social control which in turn can lead to pessimism about the potential of children. Detailed help can be given by the 'teacher's friend'. Lists and instructions are not enough; there needs to be extensive dialogue about the range of possible ways in which the department's material might be used. The probationer is most likely to see fresh possibilities for classroom work as a result of these informal exchanges.

A lighter timetable

Try to ensure a lighter timetable so that the teacher has a chance to consolidate experience rather than drown under pressure. Other possibilities that require adjustments to the timetable are as follows:
  — release the 'teacher's friend' so that s/he can work alongside the probationer for a period in the week;
  — arrange for the probationer to follow one of his/her classes through the day to get some idea of what other subject teachers offer and how the class responds;
  — arrange for first year teachers to observe each other — since it's often easier to learn from a peer than someone with more experience.

Difficult pupils

Discipline can be a focus of intense concern for first year teachers. Various suggestions were made in the previous section, such as offering a procedure for off-loading difficult pupils into other classes for short periods of time. But while there may be a range of strategies for dealing with the symptoms, the underlying causes need to be addressed as well, and this can only really be done by someone observing the lessons. The probationer needs to be aware that *all* teachers have discipline problems and that his/hers may just be an inevitable consequence of not yet being part of the furniture.

Class history
Make sure that the probationer is fully informed about the history of the class in terms of what they have read and done and also in terms of particular individual problems (crucial things like partial hearing for example). Some of this information can be put on paper, but it's a great help if the previous teacher of the class can talk it through as well.

Responsibility
Try to involve the new teacher as soon as possible in some area of responsibility in the department. It may afford satisfactions that are not being experienced elsewhere. Involvement in small planning groups is very helpful especially if it involves selecting or devising teaching material. An invitation to participate in extra-curricular activities (a drama production, theatre visits and so on) may be of particular value in giving a new teacher a chance to develop relationships with pupils outside the classroom.

Assessment procedures
Offer help and information about the procedures for assessment connected with the probationary year. Basically the probationer needs to know the following:
- most probationers pass; if things go continuously wrong sometimes a six-month extension can be recommended;
- teachers are informed that they have passed by the LEA, usually in the last term of the probationary period;
- the probationer is assessed by the head teacher's report, written by the end of the first term — usually based on a report by the head of department, which, in ILEA at least, the probationer has to see and sign; usually there is a visit from the LEA inspector/advisor.

Student Teachers

It is not uncommon to hear departments complaining about the disruption that students on teaching practice cause. This deficit view is unfortunate, for the student teacher can offer a great deal, not only as an extra pair of hands but as an importer of interesting ideas. The department should be able to see itself as helping students as part of a professional responsibility shared with the training institution — and, in the process, gaining a valuable perspective on its own work.

GUIDELINES FOR THE PRACTICE

Obviously there will be difficulties, but these can be minimised if the department has a clear idea of what the particular teaching practice system is and of what it can do to ensure that the practice runs as smoothly as possible. It is vital that clear guidelines are agreed with the training institution about the nature of the support and assessment the department is to offer. This is best done in a face-to-face meeting with the student's supervisor and the deputy head responsible for overall liaison. The main issues which need sorting out are as follows.

Timetable
How many periods a week are to be spent with whole classes? How much of this is for observation, sharing the class, or working with individuals or small groups? When the student is not actually teaching can s/he be involved in some departmental work — e.g. making materials, assessing books for class library use?

Classes
What kind and spread of classes does the practice require? From the department's point of view it is important that the advantages and disadvantages of having a student taking on classes are shared around as far as possible. This consideration needs to be balanced with the need to save certain classes (tricky ones; ones getting close to examinations; ones which have had students or supply teachers in previous terms) from the disruption which having a new and inexperienced teacher causes.

Curriculum
Does the student teacher (a) follow the classes' current programme; (b) a programme prepared at the college; or (c) collaborate with the class teacher to devise a programme? While there are possible differences in emphasis here, the student is likely to derive maximum benefit from the practice if the class teacher is closely involved in both planning and evaluation of the work.

Discipline
The department needs to know if the student is likely to need special help here. Legally the class teacher remains responsible for the class and should be on call within immediate reach should any crisis develop. The student teacher should feel free to make such calls rather than brave out an awkward confrontation.

Assessment
The teacher with special responsibility for students is usually expected to write some kind of assessment for the college. For the student's

sake it is important that there be some discussion about the relevant criteria for this kind of report. For example, on a first teaching practice details of classroom management may be less important than enthusiasm and personal relationships.

MAXIMUM HELP

Once the guidelines for the practice have been established, discussions about precise arrangements can be held with the student during a preliminary visit to the school. At this stage the student needs to get essential documentation about the structures and routines of the school and the department, a general idea of what materials and other resources are available, and an opportunity to see something of classes in action. On that basis the student and the head of department (or whoever takes this responsibility) can discuss how to match the student's own intentions and interests with what the department is able to offer. Subsequently the head of department, in consultation with other teachers, can draw up a timetable for observation, small group and whole class teaching.

Once the practice gets under way the department obviously needs to offer the same kind of welcome and support (including a 'teacher's friend', invitations to meetings and social events, and so on) as it would to a new permanent teacher — only more so.

Non-Specialist English Teachers

We all know the old canard that 'anyone can teach English'.
English departments can suffer by having teachers of other subjects
(or heads of year, or members of the hierarchy) foisted on them as
schools get smaller. This need not be a problem: these people
may quickly become excellently concerned and careful teachers of
English who can show the specialist English teachers a thing or two.
But what is fairly predictable is that:
- non-specialists will already have developed certain teaching
styles derived from their own subjects, which may not
always be appropriate to English;
- senior members of staff may either have rather out-dated
views of what English teaching should be, or may be constantly called away from lessons for pastoral or administrative reasons, and may want work that can be set quickly and
done quietly.

THE DEPARTMENT EXPECTS

The head of department ought to exert control (on behalf of the
department as a whole) over who teaches English. (See the section
'The Composition of the Team'.) If someone from within the school
needs to be used to make up the department's teaching strength,
clearly it is better to choose someone rather than have someone
chosen for you: making an offer is easier than exercising a veto.
Before a final timetable commitment is made it is worth establishing
a firm basis for the intending teacher's membership of the department.

Knowing the background
Just as you wouldn't start teaching Physics or French without some
preliminary reading about the discipline, so the head of English can
reasonably require intending non-specialists to do some reading
about English. A selection from the list at the back of this book
might be helpful, along with any other printed matter on the English
curriculum that the department might currently be considering.
Offering some background reading is one way of ensuring that the
English-is-easy idea is buried.

Joining in
A non-specialist English teacher should be expected to make some
contribution to the department other than turning up in the classroom. At the very least this means agreeing to come to relevant
department meetings; it could also mean getting involved with other

teachers in devising teaching materials, going on courses and feeding back information from them, and undertaking some minor responsibility for departmental organization. Involvement of this kind is the best way of turning a non-specialist into a specialist.

Establishing policies

On the other hand, a non-specialist teacher of English has as much right to support and guidance as a newly-qualified English specialist. Even an experienced deputy head can sink in a sea of vague suggestions and general remarks about what good English teaching is. The clearer the department is about its practice — such things as what goes on in each year, what standards are expected from written work, the use of group talk, the promotion of individual reading — the easier it will be for a non-specialist teacher to devise a suitable teaching programme and teaching style.

Available resources

As with first year teachers it is particularly important that non-specialist teachers are made aware of the range of materials which the department has. Otherwise they may be inclined to rely on the provision of a simple-minded course-book and a soporific class reader with no further questions asked. Pairing the non-specialist teacher with a full-time specialist who teaches the same year(s) is probably the most effective way of ensuring that good materials — and ways of using them — are made available to the non-specialist teacher.

Not So Brilliant

Not all teachers are brilliant; not all brilliant teachers are brilliant all the time. Lack of brilliance among classroom teachers is a subject about which it is impossible to say anything without falling into yawning chasms of over-generalization and unprofessionalism. It is also a subject of urgent concern to many departments.

The focus of this section has been on ways and means of making a department a developing and mutually supportive group of teachers. It has assumed, on the part of teachers, confidence, tirelessness, commitment, enthusiasm, sensitivity, openness, skill, efficiency, a capacity for change, a sense of purpose, an ability to cope with the demands and peculiarities of the school system. We none of us have all those qualities in equal proportions and on constant call. There are any number of individual reasons to explain why we don't — and some of these reasons (to do, perhaps, with personal and domestic circumstances) may be quite out of the reach of any efforts the department makes to ensure that people feel good about their work. However, having said that, there are causes of lack of brilliance which *are* amenable to the department's efforts to improve the quality of teaching.

STRATEGIES FOR HELP

So what departmental strategies can help? Most of these ideas have already been raised in one way or another in other sections, but it's worth mentioning them again in this context:
— offering teachers special responsibilities for areas of the department's work or for a particular project;
— suggesting attendance at an in-service course;
— looking again at the timetable and room arrangements;
— setting up pairs or small groups of teachers to design units of work together;
— organizing mutual observation of lessons between pairs of teachers;
— operating a temporary system for off-loading difficult pupils.

These are all strategies within the normal scope of the department's work — which is the best, and least threatening, context for one teacher to be encouraged to re-think his/her practice. If it comes to the point where the head of department feels that these normal strategies are not making any difference to the practice of an individual teacher — or simply that the teacher does not want to participate in the department's work in this way — then that's the time for the head of department to talk gently with the person concerned. Consulting with the head would take the business a step further; a further stage would be to ask for the advice and assistance of an LEA inspector/advisor. At this point things are becoming serious. These questions have to be asked: have we exhausted all the informal measure available to the department? are the children in these classes getting a really bad deal? what will be the effect on working relationships of calling on help from outside the department? is it likely to make a positive difference where our own efforts have apparently failed?

This is a tricky business — but then a head of department shouldn't be in the position of carrying the can for a failing colleague without at least informing the head of the school of what is happening.

APPENDIX

THE ILEA INDUCTION SCHEME

Every probationary teacher in the ILEA is entitled under statutory arrangements to be 'free of teaching duties for the equivalent of one half-day per week to take part in a systematic programme'. Specialist and multi-purpose teacher centres each offer a series of 8 half-day induction sessions; arrangements for these are notified to schools in the preceding year so that they can be taken into account in planning the new teacher's timetable. The remaining 22 half-days are intended to be taken up by an induction programme organized within the school; this programme may include a variety of activities which the teacher, the department and the school as a whole reckon to be helpful. The school is compensated for the loss of teaching time incurred in the induction programme by an increase in its authorised staffing of ·1 for each probationer released. An extra staffing allocation of ·05 per two probationers is also available for the duties of the 'teacher tutor' who is designated to support probationers in school.

The Syllabus

The Syllabus

The Worry Of It

The English syllabus is a great worry. People are constantly asking for it, losing it, not following it, following it too slavishly, criticizing it, defending it, thinking about it, writing it, thinking about changing it. The syllabus is a description of the department's curriculum, 'a programme of hours' as the OED has it; it is also a justification of why the department does what it does. As both description and justification it hovers uncomfortably between being a list and being a work of philosophy; as a correlative of the department's state of mind it hovers uncomfortably between being a stick and being a carrot.

Every department in every school is supposed to have one. The British education system is supposed to be based on the principle that each school decides what and how it teaches; and, by tradition, the responsibility for detailed decisions about what and how in secondary schools is devolved onto subject departments. (That's the theory anyway; any school or department which has tried to make decisions about what and how which swim against the tide knows it's not quite as simple as that.)

So every department is supposed to have one. The head wants you to have one, and would like a copy of it to put in a file, as a buried talisman of efficiency. The advisor/inspector wants you to have one too, and will periodically ask you to produce it; or even suddenly ask you to produce it — with the air of a policeman, doubtful of your ability to control the vehicle, asking you for your driving licence.

What manner of thing is this syllabus and how do you make one?

IDEAL AND REALITY

An English syllabus ought to be the department's own agreed collective statement of its principles and practices. It ought to represent what the department (or at least most of the department) believe their English teaching to be about; it ought to describe what the members of the department (or at least most of them) actually try to do in the classroom. As well as saying WHY and WHAT it ought to say WHEN and HOW. It ought, that is, to be a combination of honest manifesto and working manual which can

60

genuinely be used to describe and justify what the English department is doing.

That's the ideal, and that may not be what the department's syllabus actually is. The syllabus may, in fact, be no use to anyone; when read it may crumble to nothing, like an ancient parchment exposed to air. It may be useless for any of these reasons:

— It is not an agreed collective statement but was composed by one or two people in the department with no reference to the others. It may be splendid but it doesn't correspond to the range of teaching experience and style within the department.

— It is out of date, like a 1952 AA book, bearing little relationship to the current views and practices of the department's personnel.

— It is merely a collection of general remarks and good intentions which nobody feels inclined to dispute. The authors of the syllabus may have had in mind particular classroom practices to enact their intentions, but they are not described. The spirit is there, but not the flesh.

— It is merely a list of possible themes and topics that should (or can) be covered in each year. The authors of the syllabus may have had good reasons for making their choice, but the reasons are not articulated. Something of the flesh is there, but not the spirit.

THE DIFFICULTIES

There are good reasons why many English departments do not have a syllabus which the department members themselves regard as real and useful. The process of agreeing and making a syllabus can be an arduous and frustrating affair, especially if there is an effort to involve everyone who teaches English in the discussions. It tells you again (in case you had forgotten) how elusive the business of English teaching can seem when you try to work it out. There is a lot to think about, and Murphy's Law says that in any discussion of teaching the hardest questions get asked first. Working on a syllabus can illuminate again the problems of making the connections between theory and practice, between what you would like to do and what you actually do do; and it's common for departments to feel embarrassed at the homespun quality of the connections they make. It can reveal again what is easier to forget: that there can be sharp differences of opinion on matters of policy even among people who drink together and support the same causes. It can also take a long time; the syllabus can't be knocked out in three lunchtime meetings if it is to represent the department's real thinking. Agreeing the syllabus may also seem not to have an immediate pay-off; there are other things to be done, for tomorrow and for next week, which are more pressing or for which there is more direct reward.

Why Bother?

So why bother with the palaver of collectively agreeing and writing up a real and useful syllabus? If it's just a matter of pressure from the head on the department to produce a typed document by the beginning of the next term, then the H.O.D. can be trusted to adopt a suitable procedure: it may be four-square resistance; it may be asking some smart-alec in the department to knock out something over the holiday; it may be judicious use of scissors and paste on a document from another school.

But there are of course some good reasons why the department should brace itself and aim to produce, for its own sake, a real and useful syllabus, a collectively agreed account of what, why, when and how. At the risk of stating the obvious, it's worth spelling out these good reasons.

SEVEN GOOD REASONS

1. There is security and satisfaction in knowing where you stand, in having formulated a description of what you do and why you do it. The creation of a framework which makes individual lessons coherent has a particular value to inexperienced members of the department.

2. Knowing where you stand helps you to hold a course against pressures which threaten to keep the departmental boat turning in circles. These pressures may come
    — from within. 'The easy life' is an attractive one. 'The easy life' for English teachers is making it up as you go along, ad hoc-ery, the avoidance of any commitment to a particular way of working lasting more than a week. (Actually 'the easy life' is not easy at all: it's a real strain to have to continually invent lessons out of nothing.)
    — from children. They may come to your English lessons with expectations (perhaps derived from their experiences in other subject lessons) which your lessons do not meet. Those children who say, in one way or another, that they prefer filling in blanks and doing dictations, may say so quite forcefully; their demands for 'real English' can be hard to deal with and easy to cave in to if you haven't given yourself a chance to work out what 'real English' really is.

- from other teachers. English teachers frequently find themselves under attack from other colleagues for 'allowing them too much freedom' or 'not teaching them to write a letter' or whatever. The accumulation of remarks like these can have an insidious effect, so that eventually you start to hear them in your own head.
- from heads of schools, governors, parents, employers. These groups have legitimate reasons to make their views on English teaching felt, but the interests they represent may sometimes contradict what you see to be the interests of children.
- from the news media. In recent years the media, especially the press, have used education (and sometimes English teaching in particular) as an arena in which to act out guilt and confusion about social and moral values. The arena used to be religion. Teachers need to be sure of their ideological position on educational practice (and specifically on language and language development) in order to understand the ideological position which generates and amplifies unreasoned media coverage.

3. English teaching has notoriously weak boundaries. It has a tendency to absorb (or have thrust upon it) responsibility for both content-areas and processes which no other subjects want to deal with but which, at the same time, everybody thinks are vital. The current examples might be race or 'visual literacy' or 'life skills'. The syllabus can be a map of the territory the English department actually wants to occupy — including, if it wants to, race or 'visual literacy' or 'life skills'.

4. One of the trickiest jobs a department has to do is to get the best out of part-time, non-specialist teachers of English whose commitment to developing their English teaching is limited by their commitments elsewhere. Most of that job has to be done by discussion and example, but it helps a great deal if there is something written down that these teachers can refer to and use. In the absence of a coherent framework provided by the department some of those teachers who teach 'only a bit of English' are likely to rely on their own hunches — or, possibly worse, insist on the false security of the illusory 'course' which coursebooks pretend to provide.
    (Detailed departmental documentation of what it does and why may also be an intimidating weapon to wave in a battle with a head who believes that *anybody* can teach English off the top of their heads.)

5. Teaching is a profession marked by a low level of job satisfaction. That's to do with the conditions of the work. One of those conditions is the lack of opportunity for serious discussions with the people you work with about the intelligibility and the usefulness of what, routinely and yet under strain, you do every day in the classroom. Collective departmental discussion about what you do and why you do it is a way of remaining intellectually alive and of sustaining an interest in working with young people. Schools should be places where teachers as well as pupils learn.

6. The primary value of the process of agreeing and making a syllabus is to the current members of the department themselves. Where the process is carried through successfully there will clearly be substantial benefits to those teachers and to their pupils. But, in addition, other people will have a genuine interest in seeing an authentic and carefully formulated statement of what the department thinks it's about. Those people will include
    — inspectors/advisors;
    — school governors;
    — parents;

- the head and the curriculum overseer;
- teachers in other departments;
- teachers in contributing primary schools;
- teachers in local FE colleges;
- English departments in neighbouring schools;
- prospective newcomers to the department;
- students (and their tutors) who come to work in the department.

7. The list of interested parties should also include the pupils. Some subjects use textbooks which may give pupils an idea of where the work they are asked to do is coming from and going to. Other subjects may communicate an air of coherence to pupils through practical work in which something visibly grows. Children often have difficulty in establishing a rationale for the work they are asked to do in English and in seeing plausible connections between one bit of work and the next. Mostly they have to take it on trust that the rationale and the connections are in the teacher's head. Some kind of map of even just the forthcoming term's work in English tends to reduce the strain on that trust.

TED - E

Five Levels of Questioning

The business of making a real and useful syllabus needn't mean an intensive slog of full-scale meetings in which the department starts (boldly) with the 1st year and finishes (limply) with the 5th year. It could well be a slow process of accretion which involves department sub-groups looking at aspects of current practice as a prelude to forging an overall direction. The most appropriate starting point and style of working will depend on the department's history, its complexion and the ways in which it operates. (More of this later.)

Whatever the starting point and the style of working the department adopts it's as well to be aware of the different levels at which discussion about English teaching needs to take place. What follows is a crude outline of the different levels of questioning which should inform the compilation of the syllabus: roughly, 1) WHY, in broad terms 2) WHY, in terms more specific to English 3) WHAT 4) WHEN 5) HOW. No hierarchy is implied by the order here. The levels of questioning overlap and are intimately linked; in fact the making of the connections between the five levels is the centre of the department's work in agreeing a syllabus in which principles and practice cohere. That's the hard bit. Otherwise principles and practice can easily come adrift from one another.

LEVEL ONE: WHY? (THE NUTRITIONAL VALUE)

What kind of child would we ideally like to see emerge from five years of English teaching?

Answering such a question will involve looking at English teaching in relation to broad educational aims and at the social and political context in which schooling takes place. It means the department articulating the ideas it has at the back of its head about children, culture and learning. These have to be formed in general terms. A department might identify, for example, a wish to encourage children to:
- take responsibility for their own actions and their own learning;
- develop a critical consciousness about themselves and the society in which they live;
- work co-operatively with others.

It is clear that a department with broad educational aims of this kind could well find their views to be in conflict with the school's current — though perhaps inarticulate — notion of what it is about. The brand of English teaching which identifies aims of this kind has oppositional elements built into its function — and these need to be discussed and thought through.

Questions about children, culture and learning are heavy matters and since they inevitably involve talking about issues of race, sex and class, they are almost bound to be controversial ones. For some departments they won't provide the most sensible *starting point* for syllabus discussions. But they can't in the end be ignored; nor can agreement about the answers be assumed.

LEVEL TWO: WHY? (THE INGREDIENTS)

What role does English teaching play in the development of children's use of language?

Answering this question involves a focus on the components of English teaching and on the development of the child as a skilled user of language. It means a consideration of ideas about the nature of language and language development and a consideration of the kinds of context which most effectively support it. Among the issues for discussion here are:
- the varieties of function within the modes of talking, reading, writing;
- teachers' attitudes to children's language;
- notions of correctness and appropriateness;
- what children need to know *about* language;
- the relationship between speech and writing;
- what writing is for and how it gets done;
- the nature of the reading process and of comprehension;
- what literature can do for people and how it does it;
- the linguistic demands of adult life.

The answers teachers propose to the first level of questioning (what kind of child?) will obviously have a bearing on their attitudes to issues such as these at this second level. Those teachers who believe, for example, that the major function of schooling is to encourage children to regard themselves and value themselves as active learners are likely to respond to a view of the reading process, for example, as an active business in which readers *make* texts mean something. So in considering attitudes to issues of language and its development we are getting closer to the ground, to the shaping of classroom practice. What discussion might produce here is a series of 'statements of principle' about reading, writing and talking out of which classroom practice should grow.

LEVEL THREE: WHAT? (THE RECIPE)

What is the proper stuff of English?

Answering this question involves consideration of the relationship between *content* and *process* in English teaching. It means looking at what the department sees as its rightful territory in terms of material and as its proper ways of managing that territory — in other words how English teaching goes about its business in ways distinct from other subjects. The agenda at this level will very much be determined by the department's views on issues at the second level, and will look directly at how these views on language and language development should take shape in the material and activities to be used in the classroom. In addition there may be areas of content suggested here by the department's views on issues at level one; a study of how newspapers report the news might be implied, for example, by the belief in the need to develop pupils' critical thinking.

So while the focus here is on 'what to do' in terms of topics, themes, units of work or items of literature, choice of content is not something to be made independently of either language process or value. The department needs to develop criteria for choosing content in terms of what pupils will do with it and what they will get out of it. The department might consider here for example:
- what kinds of literature pupils should be encouraged to read, and whether literature is something pupils should 'know about' or simply experience in quantity;
- the part that simply 'making things' (stories, poems, plays and so on), with no content strings attached, should have in pupils' experience of English;
- whether themes such as 'The Seasons' or 'Old Age' are to be introduced (for their intrinsic importance? for their social relevance? for their interest to pupils? for their power to stimulate talking and writing?);
- the extent to which children's own cultural interests should form the content of English lessons;
- whether the study of language as a topic in its own right should be included in the curriculum and, if so, in what form;
- whether the study of film and TV is rightfully 'English' and, if so, what form that study should take.

OTHER SUBJECTS

The problems involved in deciding on 'what to do' in English can seem particularly sharp in comparison with other subjects which have apparently clear parameters and solid substances. In geography they do glaciers; in biology they do rats; English has only Language and Life, and the problem of where to draw the lines. In fact the proper stuff of geography and biology is almost as elusive as that of English. Teachers of those subjects worry just as much about the quality of their content (is it worthwhile/illuminating/relevant/ interesting/appropriate/accessible?) and about whether the content is getting in the way of pupils' understanding of the subject's special processes (however these are defined). Discussion with other subject teachers about how they decide 'what to do' may be helpful in a general way; more directly the English department's decisions about content may be affected by an awareness of the content their pupils meet in subjects like social studies, careers or health education.

LEVEL FOUR: WHEN? (THE DIET)

How is one year's work in English different from the next?

Answering this question involves consideration of sequence, continuity and development in English teaching. It means looking at the logic and coherence of the department's 5-year programme of work, and at the match between (a) what teachers ask pupils to do in particular phases of that programme, and (b) teachers' expectations of the kind of performance pupils should be producing at different ages. It is a matter here of putting the intentions represented in levels 1-3 into an order of events. Discussion of the match between (a) and (b) will necessarily involve articulating some crude hypotheses about general linguistic, emotional and intellectual tendencies shared by most children at a particular age. Linguistic, emotional and intellectual development, as far as any one individual child is concerned, is not a smoothly linear business; we know enough about sudden spurts and odd delays, about uneven and inconsistent progress, about the 'plateau effect' and deterioration before breakthrough, to realize that any simple plotting of growth would be naive. Mixed ability teaching in English is founded on a reaction against naive and confused notions of development which have assumed, for example, that the test of a child's capacity to respond to a 3rd year curriculum which includes Shakespeare could reasonably be his/her ability to paragraph informational prose at the end of the 2nd year.

But however flexibly mixed ability teaching operates teachers still have to make broad decisions about *when* to do *what* with a class. Such decisions are inevitable, since it is impossible to move forward simultaneously on all fronts; they are also practical necessities if teachers are at least to avoid the nuisance of the 4th years complaining that they wrote their life stories last year or that they've already read *Of Mice and Men*.

CONTENT/PROCESS

Bearing the issues of level 3 in mind, sequence in content and development in process need to be considered together here. Coursebook series in which material is designed for no-one in particular and everyone in general tend to assume a conventional movement in terms of appropriate thematic content from, roughly, 'Animals' to 'Adventure' to 'Ghosts' to 'Parents' to 'Work'. This progression is related to a generalized notion of what children of a certain age are interested in as they move towards 'adult interests'. There is of course no reason, considering content independently, why that progression couldn't be reversed; it depends, as suggested in level 3, on what you want pupils to do with the material and what you hope they will get out of it. The same applies to the order in which items of literature are put. Given five Steinbeck novels (*The Red Pony, The Pearl, Of Mice and Men, The Grapes of Wrath, Cannery Row*), the conventional response would be to present them to children in that order. There is clearly some sense in that order, but we've all had experiences (*The Pardoner's Tale* with a 1st year, *Flat Stanley* with a 5th year) which overturn the conventional order. In other words, what is demanding or interesting is not so much to do with the material (within certain limits of tolerance) as in what pupils do with it: the language and thinking processes they are expected and willing to operate.

What development means in terms of language processes is a difficult issue — and would be even if there weren't substantial differences between individuals in rates and patterns of development. One of the problems is to avoid the 'hierarchy trap': assuming that because one particular skill (in reading, for example, 'questioning the author's intention') *seems* more advanced than another ('reading for literal meaning') it must therefore 'come later'. It may be more helpful to think in terms of establishing everything you would like to develop as early as possible in classroom activities. Then it becomes a matter of marking points in the 5-year span at which you say simply 'more of this', 'better at that', 'confident of this', 'getting closer to that'.

(Sorting out hypotheses, however crude, about development in language process is an essential preliminary to an informed departmental policy about the assessment of individual pupils' performance. What such a policy might entail and how it might operate is dealt with in 'Assessment, Exams and Grouping.)

LEVEL FIVE: HOW? (EATING AND DIGESTION)

What happens in practice?

Answering this question involves looking at the materials the department uses, at teaching strategies, at what pupils *do* and what they *learn*. This is the closest encounter, the level of questioning which really makes a syllabus useful; it refers to that stage of discussion which details what happens in the classroom when the department's broad aims, its ideas about language, its ideas about appropriate content and its ideas about sequence and development are translated into reality. It will be concerned, therefore, with such things as:

— ways of getting work going and of sustaining it
(is this worksheet interesting, demanding and sensible?);
— the kind of activity or activities to be encouraged in a particular unit of work
(how much emphasis should there be on redrafting in the unit on 'Writing Stories for Others'?);
— the patterns of communication in the classroom
(should small group discussion be the pattern for work on the poetry anthology in the 3rd year?);
— how pupils respond to being asked to work in particular ways
(what do they get out of writing a play with other people?).

WORKING TOGETHER

There is an assumption here that it is sensible for teachers within a department to share the materials they use, to pool their experiences of working in particular ways and to devise materials and plan strategies together. Most teachers in most departments would drink to that. For some departments this kind of shared work on what happens in practice doesn't happen in any systematic way. This may be partly because of the time that working together needs; it may partly arise from the unspoken belief that teaching (and perhaps English teaching in particular) is heavily dependent on individual inspiration and personal style; working together may also be discouraged by the system of pupil grouping and/or the timetabling.

Departments which have systematically worked together on what happens in practice know that it has immediate rewards. It reduces the pressure on each teacher to find, adapt and produce materials from scratch for their own classes every day of the week. It also broadens individual teachers' ideas of what can be done in the classroom. But it would be a mistake to see this level as strictly pragmatic. The syllabus-making process will not be served simply by swopping worksheets or by getting people to turn the handle together to make new ones. When a department works together on shared materials it creates the possibility of common ground for people to examine and evaluate their own practice — which is something very difficult to do on your own. So discussion at this level is a matter of looking analytically at what you do in order to find out why you do it — and in order then to work out how you can do it better.

EVALUATION

Any intentions which teachers formulate on behalf of their pupils are in a sense provisional; there is a need to continually evaluate the effectiveness of the practices which are to make those intentions operative and, by doing so, to re-examine the intentions. If a department decides, for example, that it wants to encourage understanding of the meaning of forms in literature in the 3rd year, and works out how that is to be done, it needs also to assess the effectiveness of the approach, albeit in an impressionistic way (e.g. by interviewing pupils, asking them to write reports, sharing a series of lessons with another teacher). Feedback from this kind of 'testing' could be used to revise the materials and/or the classroom procedures and possibly the intention itself (the idea may be wrong or have the wrong emphasis; the 3rd year may be the wrong time).

Can It Happen?

Setting out in this way the levels of questioning to which syllabus discussion can be addressed may make the business seem elaborate. In a sense it is; designing a real and useful syllabus covers more or less the full spectrum of the department's concerns. Getting the thing done needs calm waters — and most departments work in conditions of varying turbulence. So can it be done? A number of points are worth emphasizing here.

HOW MUCH TIME?

Syllabus-building ought to be a slow process if it's to be worth doing. Attempting only a bit at a time is good sense as well as practical necessity. If the department doesn't have a meeting period built into the timetable already, there is every good reason to press for it if you're embarking on syllabus-building. Even if the timetabler can only manage to do that for a miserable single period a week, that at least can be used for administrative matters which might otherwise clog up after-school meetings. It may also be useful to plan for a weekend meeting on the syllabus at an appropriate juncture, even if not everyone can make it.

PRACTICE-THEORY-PRACTICE

Part of the reason why any department would feel weak at the knees faced with syllabus-building as outlined here is the sense of the intellectual weight of levels 1-4 bearing down on level 5, classroom practice. There may be some people in a department who, though quite happy to tell you what they did with *Joby* and how it went, tend to find urgent business elsewhere if explicit discussion of the nature and function of literature is suggested at a meeting.

Every one of the issues raised as examples in levels 1-4 (as well as others not raised) is difficult to explore; books have been written about most of them, often with only a low degree of resolution of the issues. But while it is fair to say that many teachers come to a useful understanding of these issues by a pragmatic route, there is a danger in assuming that experience and commonsense will always lead to a useful understanding of them. The 'commonsense tradition', the hearty denial of the value of 'theory', is a strong one in English teaching. But commonsense is a volatile commodity and what it tells us is reasonable to do varies from year to year. Teaching by commonsense is not teaching without theory (since all practice implies a set of theories) but teaching without thinking, without articulating and analysing the assumptions upon which practice is based.

But, that said, it is the development of practice which is the aim — not the perfection of theory. Practice, analysed and examined, comes first and last; if that is established in work on the syllabus by always starting with and coming back to particular agreed problems at level 5, there is a good chance that the discussions will be anchored not only in classroom reality but in department reality.

WHAT WILL IT LOOK LIKE?

We have got used to the idea of a syllabus as a single, continuous, once-and-for-all-time wad of paper, with everything from general aims to the kinds of dictionaries available jostling for space on closely-typed A4 pages which fade with each new generation of photocopy. The single continuous document guarantees its own obsolescence; the feeling that if you change one thing you'll have to get the whole thing done again produces a disinclination to make any revisions at all. The single continuous document is also unlikely to meet realistically the information needs of the different groups of interested people outside the department. Parents, for example, will be more interested in a brief and accessible statement of overall aims and in examples of what you do in lessons than in lists of 3rd year class readers.

Both those considerations suggest the syllabus should be (wait for it!) *a ring-binder folder* instead of a stapled wad. The folder could have a number of separate sections — for example:
- a *short* statement outlining the department's philosophy for the whole age range;
- detailed statements of policy on particular areas of concern, like encouraging independent reading for pleasure or helping

pupils with spelling difficulty;

— descriptions of organizational matters, like the relationship between English and remedial provision, how cover work is arranged, and so on;

— outlines of general plans and agreed curriculum units for particular years, with annotated lists of relevant stock (and perhaps with the pupil materials for one unit included as illustration);

— titles of books and copies of articles on aspects of English teaching which the department has found useful, and which might form 'prescribed reading' for newcomers.

Other items (the special handout for parents on marking; examination syllabuses; minutes of meetings and so on) can be added to the folder at will, so that it becomes the department's reference book/history book/guide to the galaxy. The sections can be done in whatever stages are appropriate; particular pages can be extracted and revised when necessary, without having to unravel the whole thing.

WHO DOES IT?

Thinking of the syllabus as a series of unassuming sections rather than a seamless dissertation means that the H.O.D. can be relieved of sole responsibility for getting the syllabus devised and written. Subgroups can be set to work on a section with a variety of people (and not only the obvious people) responsible for organizing and chairing meetings, editing the section, and taking it back to the whole department.

Getting Discussion Going

Seeing the syllabus as a developing, re-negotiable manual-and-manifesto, rather than as a once-and-for-all wad, would seem to make the business less intimidating. This model suggests a series of excursions, led by different people in the department, starting from and coming back to problems which the department identifies. But issues at all five levels will be met on each excursion, and, at some point, discussion held on them in order to establish — and then to write down — what the department thinks. Assumptions which emerge in the course of excursions need to become explicit views: the framework of attitudes and principles which make bits of practice coherent. The suggestions which follow relate to the five levels outlined above; they are examples of ways of focussing discussion which have been used in departmental meetings or on in-service courses.

LEVEL ONE: What kind of child
1) Read together an article or an extract from a book which addresses the issues of childhood, culture and learning either in an educational context (like the Schools Council booklet *The Practical Curriculum*) or in a wider context (like Colin Ward's *The Child and the City* (Penguin)).
2) Ask everyone at a meeting to write down five qualities or virtues (self-discipline, confidence etc) that they think schooling should encourage. Start from there.

LEVEL TWO: Language issues
1) Collect a series of statements from articles or books on the particular issue on the agenda (the function and value of literature for example). Ask members of department at the meeting to put them into the order in which the statements have some 'bite' for them. Start by comparing the different orders people have.
2) At a meeting given over to a general consideration of writing, for example, give everyone three small filing cards and ask them to write down three conditions which they think help people to write successfully. Spread the cards out, organize them into categories and go from there.
3) Draw up a series of questions that the department has on a particular issue (like the nature of reading difficulty). Then invite in an outsider (someone from the Remedial department, an English teacher in another school, or an advisory teacher) to open the discussion using the questions as starters.

LEVEL THREE: The proper stuff of English
1) Ask everyone in the department to describe one unit of work they do which they feel particularly committed to: what kind and range of activity does it encourage? what do pupils get out of it?
2) Invite someone from humanities/social studies to talk to the English department about the kind of work their department does, perhaps focussing on a particular unit of work. Discussion about this may highlight what is considered specifically 'English' material and approach.

LEVEL FOUR: Development
1) If pupils' exercise books or folders are retained in school at the end of each year it is possible to look at the differences in the nature and the range of the written tasks they are offered over a period of time. By concentrating on a small sample of pupils it may also be possible to look at the ways pupils of different ages take up and respond to written tasks of a similar kind.

2) Try out a particular bit of work (perhaps a short story or a set of poems) with classes of different ages. By documenting in an impressionistic way what goes on it may be possible to use this evidence to start a discussion on the assumptions normally made of what demands are proper to make of pupils in a given year.

LEVEL FIVE: Classroom Practice

The starting point here is whatever currently raises itself as a problem needing solution — preferably something that catches the widest spectrum of departmental practice with a particular year. It may be, for example, that everyone uses a class reader with a 1st year, and that there is some doubt about what kinds of thing are possible and useful after the book has been read. The particular focus here may be an agreement to compile a booklet of activities for pupils based on an agreed book in order to investigate the possibilities. The sequence of events might be:

1) Children who have read the book are asked to tape a discussion about it so that the department can learn something of the way children respond to it without teacher intervention.

2) A department meeting is given over to a discussion of the book 'at adult level' to see what issues in the book and reactions to it are worth pursuing.

3) Activities based on the book are baldly outlined, tried out on a guinea pig group, and then fully formulated in a home-produced booklet.

The department might then on that basis construct a sort of map illustrating generally the kinds of things which can be done with a class reader and then proceed to develop pupil booklets on other agreed class readers; or move sideways to look at the provision it makes for independent reading — which it may agree the use of class reader is primarily intended to stimulate.

English and Media Studies

While many teachers would agree that the study of the mass media has a legitimate place within the school curriculum, identifying where that place should be is more of a problem. Separate Media Studies department are rare; in some schools aspects of the media form part of an upper school Social Studies syllabus or are included under an Art/Creative Design umbrella. But in the majority of cases, where work on the mass media is done at all it is done by English teachers, who take responsibility for it out of a conviction that the mass media stand squarely (or fairly squarely) in their field of interest.

Study of the mass media would clearly benefit from a cross-departmental approach, and the possibility that interested departments might jointly develop work in the area is worth investigating. This section is intended to help English departments to identify the nature of their current commitment to study of the media, and to suggest ways in which that commitment could be extended, either in collaboration with other subject departments or within the English department alone (which might include the possibility of the department setting up a separate media study course in the upper school).

APPROACHES TO MEDIA STUDY

What follows is an outline of different approaches to media study that English departments have adopted; they illustrate the variety of ways in which responsibility for media study has been interpreted in practice.

Model A: Just part of our work . . .
The 'media is integral' approach is reflected in the guidelines of many English departments. The media may be meant to be integral, but work on it is occasional and usually boils down to:
— a bit of newspaper comparison (at its most staid comparing editorials in 'The Guardian' and 'The Daily Telegraph'; at its most stimulating taking one day's papers and comparing presentation);
— some work on advertising slogans, with collages from the colour supplements;
— a number of films, chosen mainly for their availability and used as a stimulus for discussion;
— the writing of reviews of television programmes and a survey of viewing habits.

Model B: The 'let's-look-seriously-at-films' approach
Here teachers will have made decisions to order a number of feature films. Sometimes there will be a pattern to the ordering, sometimes

it will merely reflect current set books and what is cheap and available. Usually each film will have a worksheet for discussion, comprehension and creative writing. Recently schools have been able to pursue the same approach more cheaply and flexibly using video films, but the practice is still most likely to reflect the ethos of '60's film appreciation and memories of nights at the Paris Pullman.

Model C: The package trip

This occurs in a department where one or more members have taken an interest in a more analytical approach to media. They may have been on courses or attended BFI Summer Schools. They will have read some theoretical work in the field and will be keen to move away from the 'appreciation/discrimination' model which tends to characterize Models A and B. Working within existing English courses they will be constructing units of work to last between 3 and 6 lessons. These might include:

— a group of lessons based on an episode of a TV series like 'Grange Hill';

— a series of lessons based on BFI material (say the 'Star System' or one of their genre packs);
— a week spent on a newspaper simulation or on photoplay exercises;

— a home-grown exercise in documentary representation based on photos of the school.

These packages will tend to be rather random and rarely become a coherent part of the department's practice, although some departments ask one teacher to be in charge of these and insist that every teacher does at least one in each year.

Model D: The package tour

This occurs when the department decides to institutionalize the 'package trips' approach and put together a mini-course of units that would be used in Model C. These usually fit into schemes for broadening the 3rd year curriculum or as an option in a mode 3 CSE or CEE English courses. These can be excellent introductions to the media, and do not require a great deal of extra work. What is required however is some careful thought on how a unit might build up in a way that makes sense to the participants (see later).

Model E: The 'give-it-exam-status' approach

Here the mini-courses are developed to such an extent that they become full option choices in their own right, appearing separately on the upper school timetable. There are now a number of courses at CSE and O level, and if you shop around it's possible to find another school's mode 3 which fits your needs. Sometimes these courses are treated as 'leisure' options and no exam is attempted — or if it is success if hampered by the view that this is a 'non-academic' course. Before embarking on this kind of course you will need at least one member of the department with specialist recognition and a separate budget.

SOME PIECES OF ADVICE

Unless you already have plenty of specialist experience within the department, it would be wise to focus attention on Model C and build up from there, finding out which teachers have used the material and encouraging them to initiate other teachers. It's better not to insist on these 'package trip' units until everyone has had a chance to experiment a bit. However, the sooner you can look for some kind of structure the better. Once the department feels confident with the 'package trips', you can then encourage your experts to begin the 'package tours' and then the exam options. Wherever possible you would do best to carry the majority of the department with you. Too many excellent programmes fizzle out when the solo enthusiast leaves.

Once you have identified where you are now and how far you expect to go in the forseeable future you can begin to decide on strategy. You might find it useful to bear the following pieces of advice in mind.

1. Encourage your enthusiasts

Many departments will have at least one person who is interested in the media in some form. They may not have done much to bring their interest into the classroom, but might respond well to encouragement to attend courses and collect/devise materials — and perhaps to take specific responsibility for promoting this kind of work.

2. Get advice

Media Studies is a specialist subject in its own right. Teachers of English without particular expertise in the area will benefit from support and advice provided by agencies like the BFI Education Advisory Service, by advisory teachers with responsibility for promoting work on media, and by experienced teachers in local schools. Support and advice will be valuable on materials, syllabuses and equipment. But guidance will also be useful in finding a way into theoretical writing in the field. The theory can be off-putting in its apparent obscurity, but it has been the driving force behind the development of critical form of Media Studies and it needs to be acknowledged if you intend to go any distance.

3. Get properly equipped

Too many schemes for work on the mass media have been hit on the head by a lack of resources like:
- a 16mm film projector (and a room with a real blackout);
- a decent carousel slide projector;
- a small number of reasonable quality 35mm still cameras;
- a portable video-recorder and camera.

While items like these (and their associated software) aren't cheap, they are necessary to the development of active, interesting work. The school's media resources officer needs to be consulted on their purchase, use, storage and maintenance. (See also the section on audio-visual equipment in 'Teaching Materials'.)

4. Start early and small

It is a widely held belief that Media Studies begins in the 3rd year, and that work with classes below that must of necessity be lightweight and frivolous (collages, class newspapers and photoplays). In fact one of the reasons many pupils reject the more rigorous demands of work in the 4th and 5th year is a marked lack of any early experience. If basic visual literacy exercises are attempted with 1st and 2nd years as part of regular English work, not only are teachers surprised at the degree of visual sophistication displayed, but such exercises serve as an excellent basis for subsequent analysis in the middle and upper school. A particularly fruitful approach in the lower school is to use slides as a focus for analysis and discussion. Photoplays do not have to be mere aids to story-telling — they can be used to explore narrative possibilities, points of view and ambiguity.

5. Don't forget the still image

In the rush for the apparent immediacy of film and television there's a danger of missing out on the possibilities for analysis of the still image. Still photography contains all the essential elements of 'a representational practice'. Using 35mm cameras with black and white film to explore the process of editing, point of view, bias and so on, can be a far more fruitful exercise than embarking immediately on a study of 'Nationwide' or documentary film. Equally, newspaper photos and advertising images are far more accessible, in the first instance, than their television counterparts.

6. Don't be too ambitious

The 'it's-all-part-of-English' approach has tended to give the impression that it is possible to 'do the media' at speed. Once you begin to scratch at the surface of any aspect of the media it becomes clear that an attempt to 'do media' by spending a couple of lessons on advertising, a couple on newspapers, a bit of TV and a few films, is bound to encourage a belief in the essential superficiality of this area of study. To combine some basic theory on production and audience, some viewing and analysis, some practical simulations and possibly an attempt at making a simple alternative on, say, an episode of 'Coronation Street' would be a far better way to teach pupils about how television works than a whirlwind spin through TV genre.

To illustrate the final axiom here is how one over-ambitious teacher chose to introduce the 3rd year to the mass media in a half-term unit (Model D) of seven 1 hour lessons:

Lesson 1: Do 'Choosing the News' (a newspaper simulation)
Lesson 2: Visit the local paper.
Lesson 3: Look at 'Psycho' extract; work on suspense story-board.
Lesson 4: Discuss slides of advertisement and design an advertisement.
Lesson 5: Look at 'News at 10' and compare with 'The 9 o'clock News'.
Lesson 6: Plan photoplay and take pictures round school.
Lesson 7: Put sound track to photoplay and write essay on mass media for homework.

Plenty of excellent material here, but at no point will the class ever have the opportunity to get to grips with an idea. The concepts involved are numerous and complex — and in any other subject we would be calling for a careful and gradual build-up towards an understanding of them. A more productive strategy might be to focus on an issue like the representation of young people in the mass media. So an alternative course might look like this:

Lesson 1: Take a day's newspapers: extract stories about young people; attempt to categorize the stories.
Lesson 2: Plan and take a few b/w photos to illustrate the various categories and perhaps some alternative categories.

Lesson 3: Work on one story from 'Choosing the News' to show variety of stances and degrees of manipulation which are possible.

Lesson 4: Use photos from lesson 2 to write alternative news stories to counter dominant categories.

Lesson 5: Devise and stage a school incident, recording it with b/w photos and taped interviews.

Lesson 6&7: Use raw materials from lesson 5 to produce two radio news items and two newspaper reports, from different points of view.

A much more limited range of objectives, but a course which will give the participants a sense that they have begun to understand one or two important principles and which could therefore lead on to more elaborate work on television and film.

Examples of work on stories from 'Choosing the News' (English Centre)

English and Drama

This section looks at how a department might establish a relationship between work in English and work in drama. The curriculum issues here are complicated by questions of organization. Whether drama should be organized as a department separate from English is an old argument. It's enough to say here that while drama clearly is a special discipline, its links with English teaching are potentially very strong and direct — though in practice they aren't always seen to be so, even where drama is organized as part of English.

"YOU BE GRENDEL, I'LL BE HIS MUM"

A lot has happened since the days when drama meant the adventurous English teacher pushing back the desks on a Thursday afternoon and persuading the class to enact a scene from *Beowulf*. In most schools that is. There are still schools where 'pushing-back-the-desks-when-you-feel-like-it' is still the only recognizable form of drama to take place. The majority, on the other hand, will have institutionalized drama — and it may be taught, in some schools at least, by a separate Drama department which has, for example, double-periods with each lower school class, Theatre Arts/Drama exam options, an A level course (plus after-school clubs and street theatre for the dinner queues).

Between these two extremes — sporadic desk-pushing and autonomous Drama Empire — lie a range of possible set-ups, each of which may involve an uneasy or undeveloped relationship between drama and English work. It may be that:
— there are specialist drama teachers within the English department who keep their speciality to themselves and who seem mainly interested in mime and masks;
— there is one drama specialist (or even half a specialist) with no fixed allegiance who takes coffee with the P.E. department because she does a lot of movement work in the gym;
— all the drama on the timetable is done by a deputy head who simply takes each 3rd year class for one period (set against sex education) and whose emphasis in teaching falls somewhere between deportment and different ways of taking a dive on stage.

But whatever the situation — in terms both of the organization of drama and what goes on in lessons — it would be true to say that DRAMA IS A GOOD THING, and that the English department's first aim should be to get on good terms with whoever the drama teachers are and be prepared to put its weight behind the development (or protection) of specialist drama provision. Having done that you can then explore ways of making links and setting up collaboration between English and drama. That means getting up to date with what has been happening in the drama world.

TWO SCHOOLS OF THOUGHT

Crudely speaking there are now two main schools of drama teaching. **School A:** This is the school anyone who was keen on drama at college will recognize. It favours an approach which relies on small group improvisation of short plays based on ideas initiated by the teacher. These plays are usually intended to be presented to an audience of some sort. The lessons are usually one-off, so the emphasis is on ideas which are accessible and self-contained.

School B: This school sees drama as mainly process rather than product. More likely the whole class will be working together with the teacher in role planning and making changes on the run. The drama usually carries on from lesson to lesson and will attempt to explore more abstract and demanding concepts. Small group work will occur but will be concerned with developing the ideas in the drama. All the time the aim will be to deepen emotional involvement rather than improve techniques of presentation.

We are concerned here primarily with how English and drama lessons can enrich each other, rather than with what lies behind those two broad approaches to drama teaching. (The ideas are, of course, more sophisticated than their description here allows.) But obviously it is important for an English department which is keen to collaborate with drama teachers in the school to know what kind of approach they adopt.

Collaboration here means something active. In the end the best way for English teachers to connect with drama is to do it — possibly team-teaching with a drama teacher in the first instance as a way of building up confidence and expertise. Clearly School A lends itself to easier collaboration: one-off lessons can make something out of that cramped *Beowulf* stuff in the classroom; role-play link ups can mean that work in drama can influence writing in the classroom and vice versa. Those who aspire to School B will be less happy to collaborate on a one-off basis and they will see little value in the enacting of already defined narratives even allowing for the freedom of improvisation. On the other hand the School B lot will be far more productive on any long-term piece of curriculum development involving concepts (say, for example, as part of a unit on 'Arrivals' for a 1st year course). They will tend to require more commitment from the English teacher, but because they see drama as primarily a learning process the potential rewards in terms of language and social development would be much greater.

'THE SILVER SWORD', FOR EXAMPLE

Suppose the English department had decided to make *The Silver Sword* a compulsory class reader in the 2nd year. You may have a booklet of writing suggestions. In making contact with School A drama teachers you would probably quite quickly be able to devise a series of lessons: escaping from a prisoner of war camp, running a school on nothing, smuggling food, bluffing the Burgomeister and so on. These might in turn develop into a series of short plays for assembly. The enrichment would be reciprocal but drama would be *serving* English. To set up even a small scale initiative such as that could well be the beginning of a beautiful friendship.

School B on the other hand would only be interested in collaboration on a more equal footing, one which placed the drama experience on a higher level than the literary experience. They would probably embark on a piece of drama about a group of refugees — who may be in space or in Hackney or in post-war Europe. The aim would be to explore the concepts of inter-dependence and survival established over a number of lessons. The whole group would be confronted with problems both from within the group and from without. They may well be asked to write a diary, forge documents, work out duty rotas. There would be long debates about possible courses of action. All the time the drama teacher will be attempting to deepen and sustain the drama. Not much good for assembly, but a responsive English teacher could see a whole range of possibilities for capitalizing on the potential for language development thrown up by the experience — part of which might be to read *The Silver Sword*, but also Brecht's 'The Children's Crusade'.

MATTERS OF ORGANIZATION

In addition to the pushing of curriculum initiatives suggested above, an English department should be prepared to offer drama teachers support in matters of organization even if it's not directly responsible for them. Drama in schools needs a lot of support to survive and develop in these times. It needs recognition and resourcing as a specialism whether or not it's separately organized. Some of the important issues are noted here.

1. A reasonable space
Some drama work can be done in the classroom, but having access to a reasonable space is essential for most kinds of work to really get going. Contrary to what some deputy heads appear to think a reasonable space doesn't mean a converted cloakroom or the dinner hall from 11.30 to 12.30. A reasonable space means a large, private, defensible area with effective blackout, a minimal lighting system

and some storage facilities.

2. Reasonable time
No-one can teach drama in 30 minute periods. School A might be tricked into it; School B cannot function in much less than one hour blocks.

3. Reasonable group-size
Drama greatly benefits from team-teaching or half-class teaching. To teach full classes can force less confident teachers into the superficial 'games-and-then-your-own-plays' approach. Timetabling a team-teaching arrangement between English and drama teachers is an excellent way forward from the long-term in-service point of view as well as from the pupils' point of view.

4. Reasonable expectations on the productions front
If a school collectively wants to put on a full-scale production of *Oliver!*, there's no reason why it shouldn't. And there's no reason why the drama teacher should do all the work either. *Oliver!* is to drama teaching what the traditional school magazine is to English teaching. There are positive ways of finding audiences for classroom work which don't lead to the drama specialist's annual solo nervous breakdown.

5. Reasonable exam status
While some drama teachers prefer to run upper school courses which are uncertificated, there's nothing like a good exam to validate drama as a separate entity on the 4th - 6th year timetable and as a serious option for pupils to take. An English department might well want to support a drama teacher looking for a suitable exam to borrow or wishing to propose a tailor-made mode 3 syllabus.

Assessment, Exams & Grouping

Pupil Grouping
Internal Assessment Policy
Assessing a New Intake
Special Help: Reading and Writing
Special Help: ESL Pupils
Examinations

Assessment, Exams & Grouping

The kind of syllabus planning outlined in the previous section can't be divorced from consideration of the way pupils are grouped for English and of the way their development and attainment is assessed. This section looks at:
- forms of pupil grouping;
- internal assessment policy;
- assessing a new intake;
- the provision of special help for pupils with reading and writing difficulties;
- special help for pupils who use English as a second language;
- public examinations.

All these areas have a direct bearing on what happens in the English classroom, and all of them involve complex issues of both administrative and curricular kinds. A department's own thinking about them has to take into account arrangements in the school as a whole. In many schools, for instance, help for pupils with special language needs is organized not by the English department but by separate Remedial or ESL departments; and there are also considerable differences between schools in the amount of responsibility and freedom an English department is given to decide for itself what to do about internal assessment and public examinations. The size of the school and the nature of its intake may well be crucial factors in determining policies in all these areas. Our purpose here is simply to raise some questions about policies and procedures in each area and to offer some examples of particular practices which have been adopted in schools.

Pupil Grouping

The experience of English lessons, for both teachers and pupils, is conditioned to a very considerable extent by the form of grouping which the department uses. It affects not only the curriculum and the way it is resourced but also the way in which teachers view pupils and pupils view themselves. Because of the implications which different forms of grouping have for classroom work and for the ethos of the school as a whole, the issue can be a contentious one.

There are four broad kinds of grouping a school can use, though the divisions between them can be blurred in a school's particular arrangements:
- streaming, where pupils remain in the same 'narrow' ability group for all or most subjects;
- banding, where pupils are arranged in 'broad' ability strata within the limits of which departments can, if they wish, arrange their own teaching groups;
- setting, where departments can form ability groups of their own devising from within the whole year;
- mixed ability, where each group contains a full range of ability and stays together for all or most subjects.

"WE HAVE MIXED ABILITY FOR THE FIRST TEN MINUTES"

SCHOOL POLICY

Some schools take a policy decision on a single form of grouping which all departments are obliged to adhere to. In other schools departments are permitted to make their own arrangements, even if these run counter to the practice of the majority of departments. A combination of setting and mixed ability grouping is the most commoi pattern in these schools. But it is possible, for instance, for an English department to run mixed ability groups even in an otherwise streamed or (more likely) banded school, so long as classes in each year are timetabled for English together to enable the reshuffling to be done.

Getting classes on the timetable together is the key to flexible pupil grouping. It allows not only for a department to form groups as it wishes (including allowing for fluid movement between groups once they are constituted and for the efficient organization of a withdrawal system for special help), but also for direct and regular co-operation between teachers and for shared experience of special events like visits, speakers, films and so on. (If a department in a large banded school does not have sufficient staff, specialist rooms or stock to block timetable all the classes in each year, blocking matched half-years against another subject which wants to take half-years at a time is the next best thing; see the section on timetabling in 'Time, Space and Money'.)

ASKING QUESTIONS

In other words, it's not timetabling constraints which pose the problem; any form of grouping is possible for English provided that senior staff are willing to allow it to happen. Gaining that willingness can be difficult for all sorts of reasons. Perhaps the most powerful reason lies in the tendency in a school which has established streaming or banding as its single policy for this form of grouping to achieve a fixed and 'natural' status in the school's way of thinking.

To take one example: all teaching, whatever the grouping, ought to involve sensitive monitoring of long and short-term pupil progress. However, the use of a banding system, for instance, tends to obscure this need for responsiveness to pupil development because it creates the illusion of reliable ability levels; deviation from the common-sense norm ('you wouldn't expect that from a band 1 child') is regarded as stemming from deficiencies in the child rather than deficiencies inherent in the banding system. Children's abilities are not fixed; they fluctuate according to the way they see themselves in relation to the teacher and other pupils, the curriculum, the pattern of classroom work and, perhaps most importantly, in relation to the nature of a particular learning activity.

Any department ought to regularly ask itself questions about the form of pupil grouping it uses. The questions might be these:
— what sense does it make in relation to what we think about how the ability to use language develops?
— what effects does it have on the size of teaching groups and on the way staff are allocated?
— is it supporting or frustrating our work with pupils across the whole year, and what evidence do we have of its success or failure?
— who decides which pupils should go into which group?
— what criteria guide the selection procedure and what kind of evidence is used in reaching the decisions?

The answer to these questions won't necessarily involve changing the system — and in some schools the overall policy won't in any case readily permit a change in the direction a department wants to go.

PRESSING FOR MIXED ABILITY

While acknowledging the complexities of mixed ability teaching the Bullock Committee maintained that 'where it is practicable this is the form of grouping which offers most hope for English teaching' (15.12). We agree with this view and list below a number of assertions which we believe support the case.

For Pupils:
1) Mixed ability grouping avoids overt labelling of pupils and so helps to prevent pupils making limiting decisions about their own potential as learners.
2) Mixed ability grouping encourages co-operation as opposed to competition. Pupils who show different abilities in different modes of language can learn from one another and gain from each other's strengths.
3) All pupils have access to the same kind of curriculum and resources. Most research shows that 'less able' pupils do better in mixed ability classes and that able pupils maintain their level of performance.

For Teachers:
1) Everyone teaches the same kind of class in a given year. This means that opportunities for co-operation — developing common practices and sharing the real problems of teaching and learning — are maximized.
2) The move to mixed ability teaching can provide a department with an exciting change of direction as teachers are forced

to re-examine their assumptions about the nature of English teaching. This often leads to the creation of coherent units of work offering a framework within which new and fruitful patterns of communication in the classroom can develop.

3) Teachers are invited to see pupils as members of a class possessing constellations of different qualities rather than as a homogeneous group with certain shared characteristics. This means, among other things, re-considering the criteria by which they judge pupils' performance in English and communicate that judgement both inside and outside the classroom.

TACTICS

There is no one guaranteed tactic which a department keen to move to mixed ability grouping can use to persuade senior staff who aren't keen on the idea. But various combinations of the following tactics have been found successful in different circumstances:
— drawing up a brief paper outlining why mixed ability grouping would be appropriate to the goals of English teaching in the school and to the department's current state of development, and suggesting how the department intends to deal with the implications of mixed ability grouping in terms of materials, teaching approaches and assessment;
— drawing up an additional paper which outlines the results of research reports on mixed ability teaching;
— approaching teachers in other departments and teachers with pastoral responsibilities who might take a similar view and then convening a cross-curricular working group and/or referring discussion of it to a heads of department meeting;
— inviting the head and other senior staff to a department meeting at which the issue is discussed, perhaps with the help of teachers from neighbouring schools who use mixed ability grouping;
— suggesting a three year trial period during which the attitudes and performance of pupils in mixed ability groups can be sensitively monitored;
— making positive suggestions about how the timetable can be modified to allow mixed ability teaching to take place in English without incommoding other subject departments.

Winning the argument is the thing; but it is also important that the department also establishes and wins its claim for what it needs to make mixed ability grouping work — perhaps including:
— fixed and properly equipped rooms;
— additional funding for new materials;
— the use of extra staff for withdrawal or support teaching in the classroom.

Internal Assessment Policy

Assessment looks at both the pupils and the curriculum: it involves interpreting evidence of how the pupils and the curriculum are getting on together and suggesting how they might get on better in the future. In this sense it can be a small business ('this child needs help on using a dictionary') or a large one ('there's something wrong with the way we're approaching literature'). It also takes us from relationships within the classroom to realities in the world outside school. A full consideration of the kind of assessment policy which a department might evolve for itself would need to look in detail at a range of classroom issues (including, for example, responding to pupils' writing) and at the nature of judgements made about children and language outside the classroom (in relation, say, to non-standard forms of speech). This section simply outlines some general ideas for an agreed departmental system for gathering information on pupils' performance and making it available to others. In any given school the procedures which a single department adopts would obviously have to fit into the whole school assessment policy — including such things as the nature and timing of reports to parents.

THE FEATURES OF A SYSTEM

What are the characteristics of a useful departmental assessment system?

1. Modesty
The assessment of language performance is an extremely messy and complicated affair. The real difficulties of it have long been obscured by the aura of authority carried by the sealed-papers-and-silence style of traditional public examinations and by the considerable confidence of those in education and outside it who believe that legitimate judgements about children's uses of language are easily come by and can be readily expressed as grades on an absolute scale. Objective, comprehensive and reliable assessment of language performance is not possible. That's not to say that there aren't ways of seeking descriptions and judgements which are a great deal better than others and ways of expressing them which are a lot more helpful than others — simply that the use of any set of procedures in a department needs to be accompanied by an awareness that the descriptions and judgements it delivers are partial and imprecise — and may be misleading.

2. Coherence
An assessment procedure shouldn't be just stuck on top of what happens in different teachers' classrooms. An agreed policy for

describing and judging pupils' performance in English won't make much sense unless it is based on an agreed set of syllabus aims (what do we want them to achieve?) and on some necessarily rough ideas about development (by when do we hope, in general terms, these things will be achieved?). Seeing one pupil's performance in this perspective is not easy, but unless there is some effort to do so, to identify and agree the criteria by which judgements are made, then individuals teachers' assessments will tend to hang in mid-air and be very difficult to relate to one another. (See the discussion of the issue of development in 'The Syllabus'.)

The effort is worth it not only so as to make the assessments intelligible in terms of the intentions displayed in the syllabus but also because it leads to a focus on the classroom practices which are supposed to fulfil those intentions. Assessing pupils means assessing the work they've been asked to do and the help they've been given. Considered from that point of view it has a direct value for the department in calling attention to what's having the desired effect and what isn't.

3.   Informativeness
There is no point in having an assessment procedure which makes no difference. Assessment implies communication and an intention to make changes. Apart from giving the department some general evidence about how its intentions are being fulfilled in practice, the assessment procedure needs to provide positive and detailed information on the progress and the current strengths and weaknesses of individual pupils. The most effective use of this information is that made of it by a teacher in deciding on new ways of helping individual pupils to develop their experience and use of language in the classroom. Obviously — and very importantly — this includes a teacher who is taking over a class from another teacher. The most significant use of it, and the one needing the greatest care, may well be in making decisions about pupil grouping and about the provision of special help.

People outside the department — including pastoral staff, parents and potential employers or F.E./H.E. institutions — will also want to have access to information about individuals pupils, though their uses of it won't be the same as those of English teachers. These different audiences have to be taken into account and need to be given an explanation of the system and the criteria used. It is the pupils, however, who have the greatest interest in information about themselves — and they need to be given access to it.

4.   Efficiency
The procedure the department decides upon needs to be carried out

with some thoroughness by everyone. That means that it must be a procedure which is tailored to the department's circumstances and which can be carried out in the time that teachers have available to them. Perfection isn't possible if you've got five full classes to consider; a carefully designed and sensitive procedure which is also elaborate and time-consuming isn't likely to do its job.

GETTING THE INFORMATION

We describe here the main methods which departments use to collect information about pupils' performance in English. These methods are often used in combination.

CONVENTIONAL EXAMS

The use of regular end-of-term or end-of-year internal exam papers of the conventional sort (where pupils write a single story or essay and answer a set of questions on a passage) is now less common than in the past — though some teachers and senior staff in schools clearly still like them for their convenience and familiarity. Those teachers who have given them up have done so because they believe that the limited, random and artificial nature of the sampling provides quite inadequate information about the full range of language performance.

Their scepticism has been reinforced by research into the conventional methods of public examining in English. The reliability — as well as the validity — of these methods has been seriously questioned. Public examinations are conducted with considerable care by experienced examiners who have the time and resources to design questions and tasks which are pre-tested before final drafting and to standardize and scrutinize the marking of the papers by a paid team. Since few English departments who use conventional exams could claim to conduct them with this kind of care, their use if particularly unfortunate where performance in them is converted into a supposedly accurate percentage or grade which forms the sole measure of achievement in English. (See also 'Assessing a New Intake' for comments on the use of standardized tests.)

CUMULATIVE ASSESSMENT

The use of informal assessment procedures based on systematic observation and analysis of pupils' work in its natural context has been developed with great skill by a number of departments. These procedures build on what teachers do anyway in looking closely at what happens in classrooms — but pay deliberate attention to the choices pupils make in their work and to the strategies they use in class, in an effort to understand what they are trying to do when

TED - G

they talk, read and write. Assessment of this kind will be particularly concerned to take into account the opportunities that classroom activities allow to pupils to show what they can do.

Some of the teacher's observations may be made as simple notes on a record sheet during class, though these would serve as reminders of what goes on rather than as a complete account of it. Some use may also be made of audio and video taping as a way of making evidence of pupils' choices, strategies and responses available for analysis. Experience shows that it is extremely helpful for individual teachers to examine some of this evidence with others in the department so that ideas can be shared. Some departments have been able to develop this form of classroom research as a regular joint activity.

It is clearly unrealistic to attempt to monitor everything and everybody in a class in this way. Some particular issues (like small group talk or responses to poetry) or some particular children can be the focus of attention at any one time.

ASSESSMENT 'OCCASIONS'

While keeping the focus described above on pupils' work in its natural classroom context, some departments have chosen to limit more deliberate kinds of assessment to certain times in the year or to particular units of work. In this case close attention can be given to pupils' performance in carefully prepared reading or talk activities which have special significance in a sequence of lessons because they allow pupils to demonstrate an important range of skills. The method applies most often to major pieces of writing, which can then be retained in a 'best writing folder' and to which pupil and teacher can add comments. Selecting and retaining writing in this way (in some departments, regularly throughout the secondary years) can give valuable information — as well as pleasure — to pupils as well as teachers.

PUPIL SELF-ASSESSMENT

A number of English departments have had considerable success in involving pupils in describing and commenting on their own work. This invitation to pupils has a variety of interesting effects, not least being that their comments can feed directly into the work which takes place in lessons. Successful practice has often begun on a small scale with pupils simply keeping a record of books read and of writing and oral work done, using record sheets, a specially printed booklet or an exercise book acting as a journal. This has led to more ambitious schemes which involve pupils in evaluation of their work in a particular unit or on a regular basis throughout the year.

Establishing a climate conducive to the process of self-assessment
is not without its difficulties. Pupils clearly benefit from discussion
of what self-assessment means and from seeing examples of comment-
aries written by others. A simple set of questions like those below
may provide useful guidance for a written commentary on work done
over a period of time which can then become the basis for discussion
between pupil and teacher.

PUPIL ASSESSMENT

Please write about yourself and your own work. These are some questions to
help you do this. You do not have to write answers to all the questions and
you may add anything which you feel is not covered by them. Please be as
honest as you can — and be fair to yourself.
1. How have you been getting on with your work this year in English?
2. What do you think you have got out of English so far?
3. How much effort have you put into written work, discussion, drama,
   reading, writing about the books you have read, homework?
4. Is there anything special *you* have done this year in English?
5. What work have you done which you have found particularly interesting
   or enjoyable?
6. Have you found any of the work difficult?
7. Is there anything new or different you would like to do in English?

RECORDING AND STORING

The next step is to consider how the information about pupils gained
by individual teachers is going to recorded in a permanent form and
made available as a statement to others. Over-elaborateness in the
design of a storing system is a distinct danger here.

There is a good case to be made for the idea that the best place for
much of the information is in teachers' heads (and in their personal
record books); anyone who wants it can ask for it and can then be
given an appropriate selection from it. Where 'best writing folders'
are used or where pupils are asked to keep work diaries or to write
self-assessments, these can be retained as they stand, with only minor
administrative labour required to allow other people to have access
to them and to understand their context.

SUMMARY STATEMENTS

Having 'raw data' available in these ways is very useful. But there
would still seem to be a need for teachers to present at least some
of the information they have in a summarised form — and to do this
on a small number of occasions in the year.

There are two broad possibilities for the form such a summary can
take, both with some advantages and disadvantages.

Profile sheets

One possibility is a printed profile sheet or card in grid or tabular format, which lists particular aspects of language use, normally sectioned under reading/writing/talking. The boxes or columns can be filled in different ways (using short phrases; ticks/crosses/question marks; a code of numbers or symbols; shadings or hatchings; etc.) to express the extent to which the behaviour referred to occurs in pupils' work. The advantages of using a format of this sort are:

— it acts as an aide-memoire in calling attention to particular aspects of language;

— it can be filled in and updated fairly quickly;

— it is fairly easy for a reader to scan in order to see what a pupil can do now and what s/he needs help with.

The problems in designing and using formats of this kind are considerable:

— the aspects of language use need to be selected and phrased with great care so that they make sense in terms of both language and classroom practice;

— separating aspects of language use in this way discourages a view of the relationships between them;

— any coding system will be an insensitive tool for saying what needs to be said about pupils' performance and offers an invitation to box-filling without thinking;

— there is no opportunity provided for teachers to give reasons and to make predictions and suggestions for the future.

Just words

These are serious problems. While it might be possible to design a more sophisticated and complicated profile sheet (with space for a written commentary) to take some account of these problems, the alternative form of summary — using just words — may be a better tack to take. A simple printed sheet with space for an extended written statement and for updates of it has a number of advantages. The most important of them is that words are flexible: they can describe the particular features of a pupil's performance (including attitudes, progress and possibilities for the future) with sensitivity

and make clear the relationships between different aspects of language use. The objection that a blank page provides no guidance on what to write about can be met by the use of a set of questions referring to key aspects of language use. These questions need to be carefully formulated so that they relate to the aims specified in the department's syllabus and reflected in common classroom practice. An example of a set of questions follows.

QUESTIONS TO USE WHEN COMPLETING RECORD SHEETS

Reading
What kind of reading performance generally on a suitable text?
What kind of attitude to reading a shared class text?
What use of books to get information when inclined to do so?
What kind of attitude to independent reading?
What habit of independent reading (in school or at home)?
What type(s) of material read independently?

Writing
Is writing usually regarded as useful, important, enjoyable?
What kind of commitment to a writing task?
Interest and ability in particular form(s) of writing?
Willingness to experiment with form/style?
How is writing presented: does it allow for easy reading?
What kind of control of spelling, punctuation, syntax?
What kind of control over larger units (paragraphing, overall shape)?

Talking/Listening
Natural qualities as talker/listener as seen in class?
Takes a constructive part in whole-class or large group talk activities (involving description, exploration, debate)?
Takes a constructive part in small group or pair talk activities (involving description, exploration, debate)?
In a supportive context, can present/maintain/support/develop/modify ideas (including responding to others doing so)?

ONE MODEL

We give here an outline of a model for a departmental assessment procedure to illustrate one way in which methods of gaining information and ways of making it available could be related.

1.   Teachers write down a detailed set of notes on a printed sheet about the performance of each pupil in the 1st - 4th year at the end of the first term (or early in the second), with an update at the end of the year only where there is something significant to add.
2.   These notes are based on what has been observed in normal classroom work; the writing of them is aided by a checklist of questions which are to do with aspects of reading/writing/talking and with general approach to work in English — and which are clearly linked to agreed targets described in the syllabus.
3.   The writing of the notes is further helped by devoting a couple

of department meetings beforehand to looking closely at examples of pupils' work in order to establish some agreement on criteria for assessment.

4.   The notes are accompanied by:

(a)   examples of each pupil's writing done in the first term and in the third term (with brief indications of how these pieces emerged), and

(b)   a written response by the pupil to some questions about what s/he thinks about her own work in English up to now.

5.   The notes and accompanying material go in a ring-binder folder for the class, which has a front-sheet recording major units of work (themes/topics/class readers) done in each term.

6.   This folder is then:

(a)   available for anyone in the school to look at;

(b)   used as the basis for discussion at a parents' evening;

(c)   discussed with pupils at the end of the year, and

(d)   passed on to the next teacher who takes the class (who then adds new sheets for the subsequent year).

7.   Finally, a department meeting in the summer term looks at the information on a few pupils in each of the first three years to see if there are any points of possible interest to the department as a whole (in terms of new materials/emphases/strategies which are needed).

Assessing a First Year Intake

A department which has investigated the business of assessing children's performance in language will be aware that any assessment system is imperfect and will want proper control over the uses made of information and judgements about individual children. This is particularly important when the information may directly affect pupils' prospects of employment or further education after school. But it is also critical during pupils' school career where the information is used to decide (in schools that operate streaming, banding or setting) which ability grouping a pupil should go into or to decide (in all schools) whether a pupil will receive special help with reading and writing or special ESL tuition.

While decisions of this kind can be made throughout the pupil's secondary schooling, those which are made at the outset are often the most influential. For this reason the question of assessing the language performance of pupils in a new 1st year intake is considered separately here, although policy in this respect ought to be closely related to the department's assessment policy for pupils at other stages. Obviously, information about new pupils is valuable to teachers of 1st year English classes (and others) whatever uses are made of it to allocate pupils to classes and to organize special help.

WHAT GOES WRONG

There are three main things that can go wrong in the gathering of information on the language performance of a 1st year intake.

1.   The English department is not involved.

In some schools pastoral staff or teachers in a Remedial department take charge of the business. They may, of course, do it sensitively and efficiently as part of an overall analysis of the educational background and intellectual ability of new pupils. But there is some danger that information on language performance will be lost (or not discovered at all) amid information of other kinds, or that the English department's perspective on language use will not be represented. At the very least, someone in the English department needs to be consulted about the procedures adopted.

2.   There is heavy or exclusive reliance on standardized tests.

To provide evidence for judgements about performance in reading or, less usually, in writing, standardized tests may be given at the end of primary school, at the beginning of secondary school, or both. (See appendix for the banding procedure which is used in primary/secondary transfer in ILEA.)

Over-reliance on standardized tests is extremely unwise, because:
— to varying degrees, the tests currently available make use of limited samples of language, depend on assessment techniques which bear little or no relation to the actual processes and the real uses of reading and writing, and use content which is dated and/or culturally biased (see appendix for a description of ILEA's 'London Reading Test');
— the different quotients or 'ages' which tests produce have no extrinsic meaning, are not directly comparable with one another, and suffer from built-in statistical errors, sometimes so large as to make the figures useless as ways of distinguishing between levels of performance even in the task the test defines;
— scores on the tests are easily distorted by the 'practice effect', by the circumstances in which the tests are conducted and by inexactness in their administration and checking.

We would argue, then, for the utmost scepticism about the results of standardized tests. A secondary school which compiles a list of 'reading ages' from transfer-profiles without taking into account what tests were used or what they actually involve — or a school which assembles disoriented 1st year pupils in the hall on their first day and gives them a reading test which wasn't appropriate or reliable twenty years ago — and then proceeds to allocate pupils to classes and define special needs on that basis, is getting it wrong.

3. **Insufficient use is made of the knowledge of primary school teachers.**

This may partly be due to the design of the transfer-profile, which may invite primary teachers to do no more than tick some boxes or make some brief general remarks on performance in different aspects of language. But it may also be due to lack of liaison between primary and secondary schools beyond the administrative level. Where no opportunities have been created for primary and secondary teachers to discuss aims, methods and content in the curriculum, to look together at examples of children's work and to hold joint meetings with parents of transferring pupils, the passing of information on individual children is likely to seem, to both parties, a purely clerical affair. Experience shows that contact of these kinds between primary and secondary teachers tends to produce useful, detailed information which goes beyond the usual 'reads fairly well and is quite enthusiastic'. It thus helps to avoid the secondary school 'starting again' syndrome about which primary teachers rightly complain. Where a secondary school receives pupils from a large number of

primary schools, managing liaison of a fruitful kind with all of them, is, of course, difficult. (See also the section on primary/secondary liaison in 'The Department and the School'.)

A POSSIBLE SEQUENCE OF EVENTS

The suggestions which follow on organizing the gathering of information on new 1st year pupils are based on successful experience in ILEA schools where English teachers have been closely involved, usually with reading teachers or pastoral staff. They refer to schools which have mixed ability classes in the 1st year, so that the main intention in gathering information is to identify pupils with special needs and to provide information useful to 1st year teachers in designing their teaching programmes. The procedures described here take time, effort and organization — and are worth it.

BEFORE THEY COME

1.   The teachers involved might go through together the transfer-profiles received from the primary school in the summer term, in order to identify the needs of particular pupils or to note where further information about language performance is required.

2.   If a parent and prospective pupil visit the school in the summer term, they can be asked about the pupil's reading habits at home during the course of the interview.

3.   A visit to main subscribing primary schools by two teachers can be fruitful. The primary class teacher can provide detailed information about the capabilities and attitudes of individuals; the visit can also offer an insight into teaching materials and methods. In addition, there is the chance to talk with some of the pupils themselves and to collect some samples of their work.

4.   Pupils can be provisionally allocated to groups and plans for providing special help drawn up on the basis of the information gained so far (though other criteria will also apply).

THE FIRST WEEKS OF TERM

5.   In the first few days of the new term pupils can be given the opportunity to produce some free writing and to choose books in English lessons. The piece of writing could be short and based on a personal topic like family/old school/particular interests; the selection of books for choice should be as varied as possible. The aim of these sessions is to provide a relaxed atmosphere in which the pupils can provide a sample of their best writing and to show something of their reading interests and behaviour.

6.   As soon as possible, two or three teachers can then 'interview' all the new intake, withdrawing pupils from lessons for a short time.

The interview should be informal and relaxed. The intention is to find out as much as possible from the pupils themselves about their reading and writing. A list of questions to generate discussion is helpful — for example: is there any kind of writing you like doing in school? what do you feel about your spelling? do you like reading to yourself? if you like reading books, what sort do you choose? It is possible to use the sample writing done in class and a book brought from class as a basis for discussion. It is also possible to ask pupils to read aloud and to note particular features of the reading on an impressionistic basis — though this needs to be carefully handled.

7.   At this stage it is useful to compare notes with 1st year English teachers (and perhaps Humanities teachers) to see if the impression about pupils gained from the interviews can be confirmed or enlarged.

8.   Not until at least the third week of term, if at all, should there be a more formal test of the pupils' reading. The test should be one designed for silent reading, should be in continuous prose, and possibly involve cloze deletions; it is important for the test to be able to 'discriminate' well at the lower levels of performance. There are few tests available which will fulfil these requirements. The purpose of giving a test at this stage is not to make decisions but to encourage a second look at pupils whose scores don't match up to information already gained.

USING THE INFORMATION

9.   By now, there should be some useful information available — and it shouldn't disappear. The most convenient way to distribute the information is to write up a summary language profile sheet on each pupil. These can be collated for each class, and distributed to everyone who teaches 1st year classes.

10.   Discussion on any necessary re-organization of classes can now take place, and the full pattern of special help can be fixed (including referrals for specialist advice). By the end of the first term an update of information on special cases can be provided, involving comments on progress made or further information revealed over a period of time.

11.   A final event in the sequence could be to invite as many as possible of the children's primary teachers to visit the secondary school, possibly towards the end of the first term or early in the second. The occasion might be to see a display of work or some special classroom project, but a normal English lesson would do. The intention would be partly social in the sense that 'old friends' could meet, but there would also be opportunities for the primary teachers to comment on the progress, or lack of progress, of children they knew well. It is also helpful in maintaining secondary/primary links between teachers on a personal level.

Special Help: Reading and Writing

Every comprehensive school has a number of children who are in need of extra help with reading and writing. Even if not directly responsible for providing this help, an English department ought to be closely involved in planning the system of support and monitoring its effectiveness.

There would seem to be two main issues to clarify:
    a) How do we *define* and therefore *select* those pupils who are in need of help?
    b) What particular forms of organization would seem to be both practical to the school and fruitful for the children?

WHICH CHILDREN NEED HELP?

Deciding which children are in need of extra help demands careful thought. As suggested earlier, information from primary schools, pooled observations by teachers, profiles of individual pupils as readers and writers based on interviews, all have roles and might be used in combination. A screening test is not enough on its own, although it may have a role in calling attention to pupils who might otherwise have been missed.

There seem to be two categories of pupils in need. The first is a small group of pupils with acute learning difficulties who cannot cope with the whole school curriculum without substantial extra help. The second is a wider group who need some degree of extra help with reading and writing. Our impression is that the first group consists of 5 to 10 pupils a year in a 6 to 8 form entry school, and that the second group can be as large as 30% to 40% of the intake. Of course these numbers will vary considerably from school to school.

We need to say that our definition of children who need extra help involves caution in the use of the term 'remedial' since this is often used to imply some kind of innate deficiency in the pupil. This judgement is frequently based on the results of inadequate assessment procedures which themselves reflect narrow and misleading definitions of what learning involves. The vast majority of children who are poor readers and writers do not suffer from any unusual motor, visual, auditory or psychological problems; the vast majority of them would achieve much more than they do if ordinary curriculums and classrooms were managed differently.

WHAT KIND OF HELP?

The Bullock Report was concerned to blur what it saw as an unhelpful distinction between ordinary teaching and remedial teaching: 'There is no mystique about remedial education nor are its methods different from those employed by successful teachers everywhere. The essence of remedial work is that the teacher is able to give additional time and resources to adapting these methods to the individual child's needs and difficulties.'

The Report insisted that there should be a basic minimum of human and material resources to help children with reading and writing difficulties make progress. No system has any chance of working effectively unless there is proper staff provision to give children extra help. While an English department which has thought through its programme will be trying seriously to take account of the needs of the 30% - 40% group of pupils in its mainstream practice, it has a responsibility also to argue within the school for the additional time and resources which the Bullock Report calls for. For the group of pupils with acute problems there needs to be specialist help on an individual basis, and probably in a one-to-one ratio. This help may come from both within the school and from outside agencies. For the larger group, there are a variety of alternatives discussed below.

In principle, however, we do not consider that the approach to the language development of *either* of these groups should be different from the approach to the language development of the majority. Whatever the form of organization adopted we believe that teachers ought to work with individuals and small groups as they do with whole classes to help pupils create meaning in the texts that they read or write in the context both of the children's interests and of the school's curriculum.

ORGANIZATIONAL PATTERNS

There are three main organizational patterns for providing extra help in the first three years:
- a Remedial department which takes a special class (or classes) for most of the week, and which offers pupils a special curriculum;
- small group or individual teaching of pupils who are withdrawn from a few lessons per week for 'booster' sessions with either a remedial specialist or an English teacher;
- a support teacher who works in the mainstream classroom with another teacher, for some key lessons (including some

or all English lessons).
In the 4th and 5th year, either the patterns above are continued or
'extra English' or 'extra reading' appears as a choice for certain
pupils in their subject options.

Clearly no one system has proved to be wholly successful — and
indeed what happens in reality may not be so clear-cut. What follows
are descriptions of the organizational patterns in four ILEA schools;
they illustrate the variety of special measures which schools adopt
in their different overall contexts.

SCHOOL A: REMEDIAL CLASSES IN YEARS 1 & 2

10 form entry. There is a separately staffed and organized Remedial
department. In the 1st and 2nd year there are two remedial classes
of 20 pupils each. The pupils are assigned to these classes on the
basis of primary profiles and a short reading test administered at the
time of the pupils' interview in the summer term before they come
to the secondary school.

Each of the four teachers in the Remedial department takes a class
for the bulk of its timetable during the first two years. In the 3rd
year the pupils from these classes become the responsibility of
subject departments. All subject departments (with the exception
of P.E. and Design) operate setting in the 3rd year; former pupils
from the remedial classes are generally placed in the bottom set for
all subjects.

Those 3rd year pupils who still have reading difficulties are withdrawn
from their English sets for special help provided by English teachers;
the decision to withdraw is made on the recommendation of English
class teachers, but no pupil is required to attend these sessions if
s/he does not wish to. This extra help is given to about 20 pupils per
year in a special room in groups of 4-6. The maximum time available
is 3 periods per week (i.e. 195 minutes), but in practice no pupil is
withdrawn for more than 2 periods (i.e. 130 minutes). Sometimes
the room is used by more than one group at a time; this is possible
because the work on reading is done entirely on an individual basis.

There is no withdrawal system in the 4th and 5th year, but in English
the bottom set is kept to a maximum of 15 pupils.

SCHOOL B: WITHDRAWAL BY SPECIALIST TEACHERS

8 form entry. All departments teach mixed ability classes in years
1-3; thereafter in examination sets. In the first week of the 1st year
information on pupils' reading is collected through interviews and
observation by English teachers and from a group reading test; an
average of 100 pupils (out of 240) are regarded on this basis as in
need of some special help with reading. Some pupils with apparently

severe learning difficulties are referred immediately to the Schools Psychological Service.

There is no separate Remedial department; two full-time and three part-time teachers, attached to the English department, are responsible for the teaching of reading. All the teaching of those pupils offered special help is done on a withdrawal basis in a large classroom adjoining the library, in groups of up to 10 per teacher. Some pupils come once a day, others three times a week; each session is 50 minutes. They may be withdrawn from any lesson, but not normally from practical subjects or from English.

The numbers of pupils withdrawn drops to about 50 in the 2nd year and about 30 in the 3rd year. The decision to cease withdrawal is made by the reading teacher. A small number of pupils continue to receive extra help in the 4th and 5th year through a special 'support option' and through withdrawal from CSE English groups.

SCHOOL C: WITHDRAWAL BY ENGLISH STAFF (PLUS HELPERS)

6 form entry. English is taught in mixed ability classes throughout the school but most other departments organize their teaching in sets from the 1st year. There is no Remedial department; the English department is responsible for the assessment of and provision for pupils with reading difficulties. After four weeks of the 1st year, the English class teachers compile lists of pupils who may benefit from extra help. These lists are based on their own observations and on their discussions with colleagues in other departments who teach the 1st year classes; there are rarely more than 6 pupils per class on these lists.

Each 1st year English class teacher is timetabled for three extra periods per week (i.e. 135 minutes) to be available to work with these pupils; the timetable is arranged so that these periods normally coincide with 1st year Humanities. These extra periods are usually given over to further work on material used in normal English lessons, which themselves depend heavily on extensive individual reading.

In addition, the 1st year English team is supplemented by a group of 6th formers and parents who work with individual pupils (and pairs of pupils), sometimes in normal English lessons, sometimes withdrawing from them. These helpers are under the general direction of the member of the English department responsible for the provision of special support.

This system continues in a slightly modified form into the 2nd year: where possible, the class has the same English teacher, but the extra timetable provision drops to two periods and no more than three helpers work with the English classes. In the 3rd year, one member of the department withdraws pupils for some or all of the Humanities time (i.e. up to 225 minutes per week); approximately 12 pupils receive help in this way; there is no extra timetabling for 3rd year English class teachers and there are no helpers.

SCHOOL D: SUPPORT TEACHING BY I.S. STAFF

6 form entry. Integrated Studies (English/History/Geography/RE) accounts for just under half of the teaching time for 1st and 2nd year classes. The course is taught in mixed ability groups; one of the IS team acts as the group tutor. The teaching is organized on a team basis with four teachers for each of the 3-class units; the sessions are whole mornings or afternoons.

One member of each IS half-year team takes responsibility (in rotation) for poor readers in the 3-class unit. Work with these readers takes place in the normal IS setting; since IS teaching is largely based on small group activity and makes use of study areas in the library and elsewhere, there are regular opportunities for close-contact teaching. Decisions on which pupils to give special attention to are made and reviewed on the basis of the team's experience. In addition, the 'silent reading time' in registration periods (i.e. 3 x 30 minutes per week) is used by this 'floating tutor' to encourage and monitor independent reading, particularly among less confident readers.

Separate subject teaching replaces IS in the 3rd year. One English teacher runs 'support groups' of 3-4 pupils who are withdrawn from English, History or Geography lessons (for around 120 minutes per week). Those pupils from these groups whose reading and writing cannot fully meet the demands of subject teaching in the 4th and 5th year are timetabled for 'Learning for Life' in the 4th and 5th year (which occupies two options blocks, amounting to 360 minutes per week). This is in addition to normal English classes. 'Learning for Life' is the responsibility of the pastoral/careers team.

SOME GENERAL OBSERVATIONS

Having described the operation in four schools of three main systems for organizing extra help in the lower school (and their extensions into 4th and 5th year), it may be helpful to make some general points about them.

THE REMEDIAL CLASS

The remedial class is often considered to be an effective teaching context because of the possibility that children can get expert help from committed teachers using materials and approaches tailored to their needs and able to win their confidence and respect. Good progress has been noted in language development generally where a successful Remedial department has worked closely with the English department in devising a rich curriculum for the class.

On the other hand, there are significant disadvantages to organizing things in this way. Many teachers do not favour the idea of a remedial class and may be very unhappy about having to operate in this context. A Remedial department often becomes isolated from the mainstream of the curriculum and children grouped within it often manufacture a poor image of themselves and their prospects. The haphazard way in which children are 'screened' on entry to some secondary schools which use this system casts doubt upon the accuracy of placement in a remedial class; and while transfer to other classes is possible theoretically, it may be rare or difficult to organize in practice. Once a child is classified there are many different kinds of pressure to maintain the status quo. The closer children move to exam years, the more this applies. Also, if transfer does take place after the 2nd year, children are often unprepared for mainstream teaching and regress. Truanting at this stage is symptomatic of a loss of faith. Finally, while it is true to say that many teachers who teach remedial classes have become expert at doing so, it is also true that there are some who find themselves with a class of children with a variety of learning problems and without much support to

113

help formulate ways of coping with them in the classroom. Equally, the idea of 'special remedial expertise' can be a discouraging one for colleagues, who may tend to see children who are experiencing learning difficulties as outside the scope of their own expertise. For these reasons many schools have moved away from this form of organization — a movement that is reflected in current educational thinking as exemplified by the Warnock Report.

WITHDRAWAL GROUPS

This is a common method of giving pupils extra help. It permits pupils with similar needs to be taught together for some periods in the week without separating them off entirely. The flexibility of it allows for small groups and for greater concentration on individual pupils, and can lead to a more direct connection between the provision of special help and the normal curriculum. It thus encourages a generally positive relationship between specialist reading teachers and subject teachers and, especially where subject teachers and pastoral staff become involved in teaching groups themselves, spreads interest in the nature of reading difficulty more widely through the school.

Clearly, a withdrawal system demands a high level of organization. Staff and pupils alike need to know precisely when and where sessions will take place, what the work will be, who should know about work done and progress made. There are problems attendant on the staffing and timetabling of groups which have to be resolved if the system is to be effective. A great deal of discussion is needed to decide the cut-off point for help and the amount of help which can be made available at any stage. Careful planning and negotiation is needed between the organizing teachers and subject teachers to ensure that the withdrawal pattern is reasonably satisfactory; pupils themselves need to be involved here where possible, so that they don't find themselves timetabled for withdrawal from all their favourite subjects. It may be more convenient in some respects to withdraw pupils from English — but possibly less productive. These problems have been minimized in schools which have, to some extent at least, managed to allow for an acceptable withdrawal pattern in the construction of the timetable. (See also 'Special Help: ESL Pupils.)

Where staff other than specialist teachers are involved in withdrawal group teaching, the provision of appropriate materials and of some kind of in-service programme is essential if they are not to be left with nothing but good intentions to go on. Perhaps one of the best ways of offering support to these teachers is to give them the opportunity to observe and work for a while with one or two children alongside someone with greater expertise and experience in working in this way. The need for this kind of support is probably even greater where parents and 6th formers are used as helpers. While some schools have made considerable efforts to make use of volunteer helpers with good results, experience shows that such a scheme is best begun in a small way. (It is important, also, that the presence of volunteer helpers is not used to conceal major deficiencies in the staffing of withdrawal groups.)

SUPPORT TEACHING

This is a form of team-teaching in which two colleagues work together in the classroom so that additional help can be given to some pupils. Some schools have found it a powerful way of using extra staffing for remedial help because it allows pupils in need of help to be given access to the full curriculum 'as it happens'. It also means that isolationist and 'experts only' attitudes are discouraged, and classroom demands are more manageable when there are two teachers to cope with problems and evolve strategies to help all pupils in the class.

Support teaching is often operated in conjunction with a withdrawal system, or may be seen as appropriate to a particular section of a subject syllabus and so might be run, for example, for the first term to introduce all pupils to the demands of the English curriculum.

While many teachers have found the experience of this form of organization very positive, it also presents considerable problems: of finding colleagues who are compatible, of clearly defining roles, and of structuring the right kind of classroom situation for the method to be efficient and effective. A high level of commitment and flexibility is required from everyone involved.

Special Help: ESL Pupils

An English department's work may well be affected by the presence in the school of numbers of pupils for whom English is a second language. Many pupils in both primary and secondary schools in ILEA (as in other areas of the country) are using English as a medium of instruction and communication in school while using another language — their first language — at home and in the community. In the *ILEA 1981 Language Census* (RS 811/82) a total of 44,925 pupils — 16.1% of the ILEA primary population and 11.5% of the secondary school population — were identified as using at home a language other than, or in addition to, English. 131 different languages were recorded in the census, the twelve most common being (in order of number of speakers) Bengali, Turkish, Greek, Spanish, Gujerati, Punjabi, Italian, Urdu, Chinese, French, Arabic and Portuguese.

We should be clear that we are not talking here about pupils — most obviously pupils of Caribbean origin — who may speak a dialect with its own rules and style as well as standard London English, but about pupils whose home language has no relationship, even of an indirect kind, with English.

ILEA PROVISION

To meet the needs of newly-arrived pupils for whom English is a second language some LEAs have established full-time reception/language centres. ILEA's policy has continued to be to admit newly-arrived pupils directly to schools. The advantages of this policy are spelled out in ILEA Report 9519, 'The Teaching of English to Pupils Whose Home Language is Not English', 1979:
'(a) Children can attend schools in their immediate locality.
(b) Parental contact with schools is easier.
(c) Children come into early contact with members of their own ethnic group who already speak English.
(d) Children have many incidental opportunities to hear English spoken and to detect meaning through context.
(e) The children are placed in many social situations where they have to start using the English they are learning in order to communicate.
(f) The appropriate relationship between language learning and the school curriculum can be more easily pursued and early emphasis can be placed on the child's general learning.'
The report notes that there are also acknowledged disadvantages:

'(a) Children do not spend their whole time with specially trained teachers.
(b) The demands upon teachers are increased if they are to make adaptations in their teaching appropriate to the needs of ESL pupils in their classes.'

While ILEA has a commitment to placing ESL pupils in ordinary schools, special support for them is provided by divisional Language Centres or by specialist ESL teachers within schools.

DIVISIONAL LANGUAGE CENTRES

In the ILEA there is at least one Language Centre in each division for teaching ESL at secondary level. Pupils are referred from their secondary schools as being in need of ESL help and are admitted on a half-day basis. Some groups attend 4 half-days a week and others 5 half-days. At the Language Centre they are taught in groups according to their knowledge of English, not their age. This can mean that pupils aged 11 and 16 may be in the same teaching group. The maximum number per group is 15 and the same teacher usually teaches them every day throughout their stay. The Language Centres generally run 4-5 term courses for their pupils by which time most pupils are thought to be proficient enough to return to their mainstream school on a full-time basis. For some pupils there will be continuing support in their schools from one of the Language Centre staff working there for two or three sessions per week.

ESL DEPARTMENTS IN SCHOOL

These have been established in secondary schools which have a large number of ESL pupils. Departments vary considerably from school to school — from one department with a substantial capitation, a suite of rooms and three full-time teachers, to another, dealing with a similar kind and number of pupils, which has two part-time teachers, no permanent space of its own and finance only on request from the small Remedial department budget.

Most schools with ESL departments operate a withdrawal system (after an initial 'settling in' period for pupils within subject sets or mixed ability teaching groups). A special timetable is devised which allows for pupils to be withdrawn from mainstream lessons for special teaching alongside pupils at the same level (though perhaps of different ages). The frequency of these withdrawal periods can vary from 2 periods to 10 periods in a 30 period week depending on staffing and the pupils' needs. The groupings here will range from pupils who are at an early stage of learning English to those who are competent and confident users of English but who require continued support as they face the demands of public examinations designed for native English speakers.

117

THE ENGLISH DEPARTMENT'S ROLE

Whatever the nature of provision for direct ESL teaching, the English department, because of its special interest in language and learning in the school, needs to be involved in some way in supporting this teaching and in helping to develop the relationship between ESL provision and subject teaching. (In some schools the English department is, in fact, responsible for arranging or co-ordinating ESL teaching.)

It is only by ensuring time for real exchange of information between subject teachers and ESL teachers that ideas about ways of improving classroom experience for ESL pupils in subject lessons and about ways of focussing the work they do in special English lessons can come to fruition.

INFORMAL MEETINGS

A useful starting point might be meetings and exchanges of classroom visits between ESL and English teachers; this can be particularly valuable where pupils attend a Language Centre the location of which prevents casual conversation between teachers of the sort that's possible in schools. Initial meetings of an informal sort can allow both ESL and subject teachers to discuss how they arrange their work and the practical difficulties they meet.

ASSESSMENT

From this base the next step could be to look at the system used to assess ESL pupils and to discuss how subject teachers can best have access to it. It is easy for subject teachers lacking understanding of ESL learning both to overestimate competence on the basis of fluent colloquial speech or to underestimate it through being misled by 'obvious' mistakes in spoken or written English. The most positive way of building up a useful picture is a combination of a record of a 'structured interview' and an analysis of a clearly defined piece of writing. The information on an assessment sheet could also include details of first language use, the length and nature of prior ESL learning, and the extent to which English is used by the pupil outside the classroom.

LANGUAGE AND LEARNING

Consideration of a positive and sensitive assessment procedure can usefully fuel joint discussions towards policies which take into account the presence of ESL learners in subject classrooms and which minimize the distinction between 'learning the language' and 'learning the subject'. The aim is to ensure that ESL learners derive

the maximum benefit from their experience of subject teaching. Discussion could focus on any of these possibilities:
- the provision of special materials for pupils in the early stages of learning English;
- ways of setting up oral group work around shared tasks or practical operations which support language learning;
- analysing teaching materials for the language demands they make on ESL pupils and working jointly on the design of materials which take their needs into account;
- the provision of models and close support when a written response is called for from semi-fluent writers;
- the use of available subject textbooks in the first language as a support for groups of ESL learners in subjects like Maths or Science;
- arranging for an ESL specialist to act as a support teacher in some subject lessons where staffing and circumstances permit;
- ways of identifying progress in ESL learning.

ISSUES FOR THE SCHOOL

Such discussions of language and learning for ESL pupils in subject classrooms would provide a valuable framework for the school's decisions on the extent and nature of timetable provision for direct ESL teaching. These decisions may be severely constrained if this is the responsibility of a Language Centre (or, perhaps, peripatetic teachers). If the teaching is internally organized, however, the decisions will be about the balancing of direct teaching with integration into the normal timetable, and about how to make a withdrawal system work with maximum effectiveness and minimum fuss. Faculty timetabling with consistent blocking can allow 'vertical' as well as 'horizontal' withdrawal without too much mess since it makes it possible to avoid clashes with 'practical' and/or 'linear' subjects; it is especially helpful where ESL staff are part-time or where there is also withdrawal for remedial teaching. It also offers opportunities for ESL staff to work alongside pupils in subject classrooms rather than always with extracted groups.

There are of course larger questions which the school as a whole needs to consider in relation to ESL pupils and which the English department may have a special interest in raising:
- the working of the pastoral system and communications with parents;
- the involvement of ESL pupils in general school activities;
- examinations policy and specific help towards optimum

performance by ESL pupils;
— the provision or the encouragement of mother-tongue teaching.

THE CONTENT OF ENGLISH

These are specific issues within a general consideration of the extent to which the whole curriculum reflects the diversity of cultures present in the school. Paradoxically, the sharpest edge here may be addressed not to, say, Home Economics but to English itself. For ESL pupils English lessons can seem like a game the rules for which are frustratingly difficult to grasp, and in which the fullness of the language may appear especially inaccessible. The English department's answer — if it is based on the assumption that the diversity of languages in a classroom can be welcomed as a resource rather than seen merely as a problem — might suggest changes in the content of lessons as well as changes in teaching strategies. There might, for instance, be a proposal to develop work on language variety and language use, or on a study of common patterns in storytelling which includes literature from other languages and, where appropriate, in other languages.

Examinations

The examinations system has always exerted a powerful effect on what is taught in English lessons — not only in examination classes but throughout the school. In addition, the existence of the dual system of GCE and CSE and the division between A Level and other 6th form examinations have had important implications for the grouping of pupils and for the allocation of staff.

Dissatisfaction with the impact of the examination system on curriculum and organization in schools has a long history and has grown increasingly intense among English teachers in recent years. Although there have been a number of positive innovations in examining over the past fifteen years, the rate of change towards an examination system which is flexible and coherent, which bases assessment on pupils' best work in all aspects of English, which puts the emphasis on the provision of useful information, and which promotes sensible practice in English lessons — the rate of change towards such a system, despite the persistent efforts of teachers and others, has been extremely slow.

CURRENT DEVELOPMENTS

We describe here the state of progress on developments in different parts of the examinations system in September 1982. We hope this description will soon be out of date.

A COMMON 16+ EXAM

The idea of a single examination to replace O Level and CSE has been debated for almost twenty years. Currently, regional consortia of GCE and CSE boards are engaged in formulating syllabuses for the proposed common 16+. It seems likely that joint English syllabuses will be on offer in some areas in the near future, whether or not an official decision is made to institute a single certificate. The design of these joint syllabuses will vary from area to area, the differences being mainly to do with:
  — whether language and literature are separately examined and certificated;
  — whether some assessment of oral language is included;
  — the extent to which the assessment of writing and response to literature is based on coursework folders or assignments.

A particular cause for concern in the current negotiations has been whether the target for the examination should be only the top 60% of the school population. There has been some discussion of the possibility of a certificate for the remainder of the population based on profile assessment.

17+ / 18+ EXAMS

At present it seems unlikely that there will be major changes to the A Level system, though it is worth keeping an eye on the various GCE boards (particularly AEB and JMB) for modifications in method: of examining and in the choice of literary texts, and for the development of A Level syllabuses which include study of language or communications as well as (or instead of) literature.

The life of CEE continues to be extended from year to year on a pilot basis, with certificates issued in CSE grades. English is one of the few subjects in which there has been significant take-up of the examination. The future of CEE will depend on a decision on how its present 'general education' emphasis relates to the 'vocational education' emphasis in other new courses for the post-16 age-range. There has been rapid development in the F.E. sector of vocational courses with a communication component (organized by the City and Guilds Institute and the RSA in particular). Some of these courses are increasingly filtering into schools. The positive experience of many teachers using CEE English has shown that it is possible to combine its 'general eduation' emphasis with the best of the communication courses.

EXAMINATION PATTERNS

In the absence of a sensible national framework for assessing achievement at 16+, 17+ and 18+, English departments can do no more than put together less than satisfactory combinations from what is currently available (including mode 3 options). We give below the examination schemes for 5th and 6th years used by two departments. The departments differ not only in size and organization but also in their notion of what makes a worthwhile set of examination targets for their pupils.

SCHOOL A

General

School A is an 8 form entry mixed school. English in the 4th and 5th year is taught in mixed ability groups with O Level Language, O Level Literature and CSE as the possible targets. The 6th year has compulsory English; all students follow a one year common course which leads to certification in either CEE, the RSA/ILEA Practical Communication Profile or O Level Language. A Level English is offered separately.

The system used was gradually introduced within a stable and unified department over a period of four years, beginning with JMB O Level Language (Syllabus D) at 5th year and with CEE in the 6th year. Despite the extra planning and co-ordination which the full system involves, the department is satisfied that their efforts are being reflected in a more purposeful and ambitious approach on the part of the whole range of students. The department is especially concerned with literature and, in particular, wants its courses to encourage wide and independent reading. It is committed to the principle of assessment by coursework.

5th year courses

Exam work begins in the final term of the 4th year, with three options in mind:
1) JMB O Level Language (Syllabus D).
This is a 100% coursework exam in which the candidate submits a folder of 12 pieces of writing. There is no precise specification for types of writing except that there should be a variety.
2) London O Level Literature (Syllabus B).
A selection of authors is set, rather than specific books. The final paper invites candidates to draw on their reading experience to respond to general questions relating to authors studied.
3) LREB CSE (Mode 3 Syllabus)
This is the school's own unified language/literature syllabus in which the literature element is assessed wholly by coursework and in which there is an option system allowing for work on media studies and on communications/language study. Personal and 'functional' writing is examined by final paper.

The elements of these three syllabuses allow for common work which can be used whatever exam(s) pupils are eventually entered for. For example: work on literature can be used for either the O Level Literature final paper or for the CSE literature coursework folder; personal and 'functional' writing tasks can be a preparation for either the CSE final paper or be used in the JMB O Level Language folder. By matching three different syllabuses in this way, decisions about entry can be left until almost halfway through the 5th year and considerable scope can be given to mixed ability teaching.

6th year courses

In the 6th year, students are timetabled together for compulsory English regardless of the success they achieved in the 5th year exams. The one year common course consists of a number of units, including a literature unit, a writing workshop and a communication studies unit. The organization of these units is flexible enough to provide for the requirements of three exam options:

1)   JMB O Level Language (Syllabus D).
This is re-offered in the 6th year for students entered for the exam
in the 5th year who wish to improve their grade and for some students
with CSE certificates at grade 2 and below.
2.   LREB CEE (i.e. former MREB syllabus).
There is an emphasis in this syllabus on literature and personal
writing, but substantial weighting is also given to performance in a
group oral test and to an individually chosen 'depth study'.
3.   RSA/ILEA Practical Communication Profile.
This is an assignment/workshop-based, profile-certificated scheme.
The checklists of skills form a 'template' which can be laid over an
existing course for an analysis of skills involved in the assignments
and for certification.

All students are entered for at least one of these exam options at
the end of the one year course. At present there is a very small
degree of common work with students undertaking a two year A
Level English course, the AEB English Literature Alternative
Syllabus (753), which includes a component of internally-assessed
coursework for which the school chooses the texts. Some students
transfer from this A Level course at the end of the first term. On the
other hand there are students who, after completing the common
course, then undertake the two year A Level course.

SCHOOL B

General

School B is a 5 form entry mixed school which groups pupils in
ability sets from the beginning of the 3rd year. O Level Language
and Literature are offered to those in the top set in the 4th and 5th
years, though fairly easy transfer is possible from CSE groups up to
the third term of the 4th year. In the 6th year English is offered to
anyone who wishes to take it. Apart from a small A Level group,
there is a group formed to take or re-take O Level Language; another
group is given a communication skills programme as part of a City
and Guilds Foundation Course.

The department feels that the 4th and 5th year system works fairly
well, although there is some worry that the forms of examining used
in the O Level Language syllabus and in the CSE final papers restrict
the range of language work undertaken. The 6th form provision
reflects the problems of a school with small 6th form numbers and a
full range of ability, but the department sees possibilities of development through further links with F.E. and with local schools.

5th year courses

There are three possible examination targets:

1)   London O Level Language
This exam has two final papers: one is a multiple-choice comprehension test; the other has an essay and a summary/directed writing exercise.

2)   Cambridge O Level Literature (Plain Texts)
The final paper in this examination permits the use of set texts in the exam room; the questions place more emphasis on understanding and response than in some other literature papers.

3)   LREB CSE (Syllabus A)
In this syllabus the literature element is assessed through a coursework folder; there is an oral test which accounts for a small percentage of the marks; comprehension and personal/'directed' writing are assessed in final papers. (The department at one time also ran its own Mode 3 CSE syllabus with a ceiling of grade 3 intended for weaker candidates, but falling rolls made this arrangement impractical.)

6th form courses

In the past the school has encouraged students with specific vocational plans to go from the 5th year to F.E. college. As a result, 6th form numbers have been smaller than is usual for a school of this size. The provision for non-A Level students is:

1) London O Level Language

A repeat course is offered to those who achieved low grades in the 5th year and to those who gained CSE grade 3 or above. The level of success achieved by 6th form candidates is poor.

2) City and Guilds Foundation Courses

For some years the English department has been keen to introduce CEE for students with CSE grade 3 or below, but deficiencies in 6th form provision as a whole meant that students' remaining timetables would have been difficult to fill. Recently the school has decided to solve this problem by offering a choice of vocational courses in conjunction with the local F.E. college. The City and Guilds scheme involves students spending two days at college doing the vocational element of their choice, one day a week on work experience, and two days in school doing the 'Communication', 'Optional Activities' and 'Careers and Personal Education' elements. Assessment is by a combination of teacher-assessed assignments and multiple-choice end-of-course exams. The English department has responsibility for five lessons a week communications skills teaching; they are expected to provide some assignments which link broadly with the vocational choices students have made and to prepare them for the multiple-choice exam in communication skills.

Students who stay on for two years and have gained CSE grade 1 or an O Level pass take London A Level. There are usually 7 or 8 of these in the group, but experience shows that one or two always drop out, so the average group is usually 4 or 5. As this is small for an A Level group, first and second year 6th form groups combine for work on practical criticism and, where possible, they also combine for work on the same set text.

POINTS TO CONSIDER

The job of making an adequate pattern from the range of examination syllabuses available involves a fair amount of planning and a fresh look at the department's resources and teaching approaches. It is likely that an examination pattern will work well if the department feels that it matches, at least to some extent, its particular aims and intentions for upper school students, and that it satisfies the needs of students for appropriate courses and certification — and does this without penalizing pupils lower down the school and without making impossible demands on teachers. These organizational points might be considered when thinking about putting a new

syllabus into the pattern:
- the weight of administration it may involve, in terms of any internal standardizing, contact with moderators and attendance at meetings organized by the examining board and/or with other schools in a consortium;
- the need for special course planning to take into account any assignments/projects, oral tests, the completion of coursework folders, or mock exams;
- the difficulties which may be posed by possibly having students in the same class undertaking more than one exam target;
- the maximum group size to allow teachers and students to work effectively on the course, and the minimum size needed to justify the staffing cost against other demands;
- the number of periods needed to make the course effective and how these periods can best be arranged on the timetable.

ADMINISTRATION

The administrative work connected with public examinations can be time-consuming — and it requires absolute exactness so as to prevent the possibility of heart-stopping mistakes in the interpretation of syllabuses, in the selection of set books, in the compilation of entries and so on. Every teacher needs to have a clear picture of what the demands and the procedures of the exams actually are so that these can be taken into account in planning the year's work; this is, of course, particularly important where the department is undertaking a new syllabus or where new teachers are involved. As a minimum, everyone ought to be provided with copies of the relevant documents for reference, but it's also helpful to have a department meeting early in the year to discuss the syllabus requirements and to assemble the procedural nuts and bolts into a working machine.

WHAT THE SYLLABUS REQUIRES

A double-check is needed to ensure that this *is* the right section of the right syllabus for the right year and that any changes from the previous year are clearly marked on individual teachers' copies. Check also that you've got copies of any additional instructions on the syllabus which the examining board has issued, copies of the Chief Examiner's Report and copies of relevant past papers. All these carry information about what the examination expects of the candidates — sometimes more explicitly than the written syllabus itself. Any doubts and queries which remain can best be cleared up by writing to the examining board; retain the written reply.

Detailed investigation of the syllabus in this way not only reduces anxiety and the chance of teachers making mistakes in emphasis but also makes it more likely that they will be able to squeeze out of the written syllabus every bit of possibility for fruitful work which it allows.

WHAT THE PROCEDURES ARE

It may be worth compiling, in consultation with the school's examinations secretary, a chart which indicates (if only approximately) what has to be done when: when entries have to be in the hands of different boards; when standardizing meetings for teacher-assessors take place; when orals have to be completed; when coursework assessments have to be sent in; when exam sittings take place. The department's own plans for what it needs to do can then be cast around these fixed dates: meetings to decide who is going to be entered for which exams; the arranging of internal standardizing meetings for coursework assessment; contacts with moderators; the organizing of mock exams and the marking of them. (The completed chart would probably be of help to candidates as well as to teachers; some departments also provide candidates with a leaflet which details exactly what the examination requirements are.)

ANALYSING RESULTS

Assume that you are given the figures below without any further information than that they show the examination results in English for one 5th year in a 7 form entry school. What can you read from the figures?

	GRADE							Total candidates
	1	2	3	4	5	U	Ab.	
CSE								
	14	8	24	27	20	18	19	130

	GRADE							Total candidates
	A	B	C	D	E	U	Ab.	
O Level Lang.	2	5	10	12	8	17	1	55
O Level Lit.	4	2	10	8	9	8	1	42

Examination results do not provide anything like a complete picture of the achievement of students; nor do they by any means accurately reflect the quality of what goes on in English lessons. The tendency to play crude number games with examination results and to use them as the sole criterion for judging a department's work is a common one, and needs to be resisted. This is particularly important now that schools are obliged to publish their examination results (though this in effect simply means making them available to interested parties who ask to see them). There is widespread misunderstanding about what examination results actually *mean*, about different modes of examining, and about the relationship between examinations of different types. (The persistence of the idea that grades A - C at O Level represent a 'pass' is a case in point.) An English department needs to play its part in ensuring that examination results are given no more significance in school and outside it than they deserve and, in particular, that any analysis of overall results is done in relation to the school's intake and to its examination entry policy.

WHAT HAPPENED?

Nevertheless, all English departments are concerned about the results they get — because they are important to students and their parents and represent some form of public statement of achievement. Considering its overall examination results, trying to understand them in the context of the school and of the department's practice, is an important exercise for a department to undertake, largely so as to plan for the future. Where results are disappointing, this may be because:
- there has been some modification in the way the examining board arrives at results;
- a particular element of the examination has caused unusual difficulty for the school's candidates, despite apparently adequate preparation;
- teaching approaches, in relation to the syllabus as a whole or to certain parts of it, need revision;
- the policy on entering candidates needs re-thinking;
- the syllabus itself is inappropriate.

Most examining boards will provide (at substantial cost) a general report on the performance of a group of candidates where the school feels that the overall results in a subject are unexpectedly poor. (This is a different matter from requesting a re-assessment and/or profile report on the performance of individual candidates whose results are unexpectedly poor.)

129

APPENDIX

ILEA PRIMARY/SECONDARY TRANSFER BANDING PROCEDURE

To provide.information for the balancing of the intake of secondary schools, pupils in their last year of primary school take a verbal reasoning test, anonymously. The raw scores are sent to the Authority, which uses the scores to inform each school of the approximate number of pupils it could expect to find in Band 1 (i.e. the top 25% of the ILEA population), Band 2 (the middle 50%) and Band 3 (the bottom 25%). Since this is a group rather than an individual test, each primary school uses its own observation and diagnostic procedures to assess which band a given pupil should be allocated to, using the verbal reasoning test as an indicator of the numbers of pupils within each band.

THE LONDON READING TEST

The London Reading Test is of ILEA's own devising and has been in use since 1978. It provides a common denominator in the transfer of information from primary to secondary schools about pupils' reading performance. It is not part of the banding procedure, but is a screening device based on the level of difficulty of lower secondary school text books. It consists of two cloze passages, the second being slightly more difficult; and a third passage, accompanied by various types of questions, which discriminates more sharply. A copy of the test is available from ILEA Research and Statistics Branch, EO/ER/GP/1, County Hall, London SE1.

EXAMINATION BOARDS

GCE

The Associated Examining Board (Wellington House, Station Rd., Aldershot, Hampshire, GU11 1BQ).
University of Cambridge Local Examinations Syndicate (Syndicate Buildings, 17 Harvey Rd., Cambridge CB1 2EU).
Joint Matriculation Board (Manchester M15 6EU).
University of London Examinations Board (University of London, 66-72 Gower St., London WC1 6EE).
Oxford and Cambridge Schools Examination Board (Oxford Office: Elsfield Way, Oxford OX2 8EP; Cambridge Office: 10 Trumpington St., Cambridge CB2 1QB).
Oxford Delegacy of Local Examinations (Ewert Place, Summertown, Oxford OX2 7BZ).
Southern Universities' Joint Board for School Examinations (Cotham Rd., Bristol BS6 6DD).

CSE

Under present arrangements (except in special circumstances) schools can only use the syllabuses of its local CSE board. The ILEA area is served by:
London Regional Examinations Board (Lyon House, 104 Wandsworth High St., London SW18 4LF).

Other Boards

Royal Society of Arts Examinations Board (18 Adam St., Adelphi, London WC2N 6AJ).
City and Guilds of London Institute (76 Portland Place, London W1N 4AA).

Time, Space & Money

Time
Space
Money
Secretarial Help

Time, Space & Money

Whatever forces help to shape the nature of English teaching in a given school, there is no doubt that the timetable, accommodation and capitation can play a vital part in determining the infrastructure within which English teachers operate. They are in a sense the key areas which have a bearing on a teacher's everyday working conditions and sense of professionalism. As such there is an especially crucial role for the head of department in holding out for the maximum material support for the teaching of English. There is plenty of evidence that heads regard English as a 'soft' area to be squeezed into the remaining niches after the needs of the 'harder' subjects have been met — so English departments need to exert muscle if they are to assert their central role in the curriculum. Good English teaching depends on continuity of classroom use if books are to be effectively stored and displays maintained and respected; also the efficient sharing of resources and ideas requires ample areas for storage and a space for departmental meetings. The way the timetable is constructed can make or break the department's work; it needs to satisfy some key requirements for good practice and professional needs. For example, it should ensure for the English department a reasonable amount of inviolable marking time, block timetabling where necessary and a fair distribution of double-periods in the morning and afternoon. A fair share of the school's overall capitation is essential if a department is to have the range and quantity of books and other materials it needs.

Time

THE BREAK-THROUGH

'I think the big break-through in the department came a couple of years ago when we managed to get all the classes in each year timetabled together. It has simplified everything from an administrative point of view and it's meant that co-operation between teachers is really on the cards rather than being just a theory. The only thing against it is that there aren't enough 'English' rooms to go round.

We also decided last year to give up a free period each so that there could be an extra teacher to float with the first year classes. It's been very valuable for the first year class teachers to have another person available for at least part of the time — and it makes you realize how inflexible things are in the classroom when it's just you and 28 kids.'

A SEAL OF GLOOM

'Timetabling a small department like ours really shouldn't be much of a problem: we don't ask for much. But somehow every July we get the same mess for the following year: classes split between teachers, classes in the same year spread all over the place instead of blocked, single periods instead of doubles. It puts a seal of gloom over the end of term, thinking about what you're coming back to.'

OUTSIDE OUR CONTROL?

The timetable is the concrete representation of the department's priorities and concerns: or it should be. For some departments the production of the school timetable in an inexorable process over which they have little or no control; for many the process begins with optimism ('next year we'll get it right') and ends with recriminations ('not again!').

The attempt to exert some control over how the timetable comes out needs to be based on some understanding of the process by which it is made. While understanding the complexities of timetabling *is* difficult, it is not as difficult as some timetablers would wish to make out. With a little logic and persistence much of the process can be followed quite readily — and thus interventions made at the right time and in the right way. What follows is some advice on how to make the timetable a positive statement of the department's intentions — *or* some advice on how the department might learn to love the school's Timetable Boss and get at least some of what it wants and needs.

THE OVERALL PATTERN

Clearly the way English teaching is timetabled can't be considered separately from the school timetable as a whole. The school timetable is the result of policy decisions made at some point by a combination of senior staff, individual departments and the whole staff about how pupils should be grouped, about the subjects they should meet and how much time they should spend on each of them, and about the pattern of the school day. These decisions are partly based on practical considerations (staffing, school roll, number of sites and so on) and are further interpreted by the timetabler in the light of constraints imposed by such factors as the availability of specialist rooms and resources, the hours which particular part-time teachers are able to work, the need to co-ordinate with any schools and F.E. colleges with whom there are consortium arrangements.

THE CURRENT ARRANGEMENTS

The most important thing to remember at the outset is that virtually all timetabling is based on the existing timetable. It is therefore important to make a study of what is happening *now*. Look particularly at the way the 6th form courses and the 4th and 5th year option systems are blocked. Look at where the games afternoons are, how the Technical Studies/Home Economics blocking is done. Then look at how the English department fits into to all of that. If the TT Boss is approachable get an explanation of the priorities well before s/he embarks on the process. Many timetablers are more than willing to hold a meeting for interested staff on how the timetable is put together. Apart from being very useful, discussion with the timetabler about priorities (and constraints and conflicting demands) can warm any timetabler's heart.

CHANGES IN THE PATTERN

But neither policies nor practical considerations are forever fixed:

they are, of course, subject to change. Some changes in the current timetable may be proposed as the result of a decision to introduce a new form of pupil grouping (a 'Basic Skills' group in years 4 and 5?) or a new course (a 'Social Education' course in year 3?); others may be proposed on the grounds of expediency (a music teacher leaves and isn't replaced, so double-periods of music are no longer possible for years 1 and 2).

Teachers in the English department need to have a voice in discussions about the current overall curriculum pattern and in decisions about changes to it — a voice not only as individuals within the whole staff but as members of a subject team with a central role in the school. Changes in the overall pattern won't necessarily affect English teaching directly, and they shouldn't be seen from an exclusively departmental point of view. But it is wise to be alert to the possible consequences of changes and to consider the degree to which they might support or interfere with the department's own preferred arrangements. The important questions to ask about a proposed change are:
- is it going to make any difference to the nature and size of groups which English teachers meet?
- is it going to make any difference to the scope of the department's curricular work?
- is it going to alter the amount of time which English gets?

HOW MUCH TIME?

The first two questions receive some attention elsewhere in the book. The question of how much time English gets needs a mention here.

In a survey carried out for the Bullock Report it was found that the average time spent on English by secondary pupils was 200 minutes per week (i.e. roughly 15% of the actual lesson time in a school week). The survey was done prior to 1975. However, there has been a tendency in some areas in recent years (to some extent reinforced by suggestions made in the 'common curriculum' debate) to cut down the amount of time given to English to around 10% of the week. Whatever the motives for this policy (and there could be a number) it should be resisted. 200 minutes per week is not a magic figure, but it does seem to represent the minimum allocation necessary for English teachers to provide classes with the range of activities which constitute the full potential of the subject. Where there is an integrated studies course in which English plays a part (see 'The Department and the School'), the amount of time this is given should not be significantly less than the aggregate for contributing subjects if they were timetabled separately.

CONSULTATION

It is invariably the head of department who acts for the department in the timetabling process itself, from the point where initial claims are made to the completion of the whole timetable. At the sharp end of this process the head of department may on occasion have to make some unilateral decisions. Many schools do not allow for genuine consultation to the bitter end. Nevertheless any head of department committed to harmony and collaboration will appreciate that the timetable can cause resentment and downright animosity, which may diminish with time but is of course enshrined in a teacher's daily experience for three terms. So the advice is: wherever possible *consult, discuss* and *agree*. This can improve the climate for the decisions which have to be made unilaterally. Prior to the timetabling period it is worth circulating everyone with a form which gives them a chance to assess their existing classes, make an initial decision about whether they want to take them on, and also to note any further thoughts for the next year.

It is important for everyone to realize that at this stage their requests must be viewed as provisional. It has been suggested that as the timetable takes shape that teachers should have the right to *one* flat refusal, but after that should be prepared to take what they are given. The crucial thing is for people to be kept informed at every stage. If they feel in touch then they will accept the less than satisfactory with good grace. *What is to be avoided at all costs is the situation where the department receive timetable slips on the last day of term which bear no resemblance to what was originally agreed.*

Finally some English departments will be in the position of having deputy heads, heads of house and teachers of other subjects teaching part-time. If this looks like causing conflict the department should insist that the needs of the full-time specialists ought to come first.

PRIORITIES

Timetabling is about priorities. Deciding between alternative courses of action on the basis of an order of importance is at the root of the whole process. A good timetabler will have worked out the list of priorities for the school upon which s/he bases each decision; that list provides a framework for discussion and negotiation. An English department ought to do the same, taking particular care to ensure that the preferences of individual teachers and the needs of the department as a whole are considered together.

About the middle of the year the department can have an excellent discussion trying to put the following into an order of importance. Of course some of them may not allow for such linear construction, but the exercise is instructive and the end-product, whatever the qualifications, can be of tremendous assistance in making difficult decisions. Here's a discussion list:

— block-timetabling complete or half years so that pupil grouping can be flexible and teachers can co-operate
— preferences for continuity with classes
— equitable spread for each class (e.g. one lesson per day per class?)
— double lessons where required
— exam classes to be taught by English specialists
— 1st year classes to be taught by English specialists
— extra teachers for 1st year classes (or for special ventures)
— balance of individual teacher's timetable (in terms of age/ability/exam target)
— the use of English teachers on related courses (e.g. film study, drama, integrated studies)
— teachers taking English with their own tutorial groups
— a proper rotation of A level teaching
— teaching as far as possible in specialist rooms
— built-in time for meetings

SPECIAL ISSUES

This is just a sample list. Each department will have its own special issues: perhaps a need for block-timetabling and generous staffing in the 6th form to allow a compulsory common course to operate; perhaps a need for specially equipped rooms to be available for particular years so that drama, media or library work can take place. Departments in schools which operate on split sites will have particular problems to cope with, which may mean, for example, giving higher priority to *where* teachers teach than to who they teach. English departments which are responsible for the timetabling of withdrawal groups for remedial work or ESL teaching will want to try as far as possible to build these arrangements into the mainstream timetable rather than play jigsaw puzzles after the whole thing is finished.

Once the department's own list is drawn up in a rough order of priority then if something new does come up the department can decide how important it is by placing it in the order. A list like this can help enormously when planning strategy.

HOW IS IT DONE?

The way the actual timetabling process is approached is a function of how the school operates. What follows is a collection of hints for diff-

137

erent stages of the process.

THE STAFFING ALLOCATION

Begin by extracting as early as possible from the TT Boss a list of the department's staffing allocation (i.e. how many teachers will it have and how many periods a week will they teach?). From this work out how many *teacher periods* there will be (i.e. a unit that commits one teacher for one period). This is *not* the same as *class periods* (i.e. the unit which presupposes that each class is simply matched to one teacher). Work out the number of teacher periods you will need to cover the needs of each year. Make sure this tallies with the teacher periods available; if not begin immediate negotiations to increase staffing. (The way the department is staffed was considered in general terms in the section on 'The Team'. Departmental staffing allocation is an area of constant tension in many schools — and it is an area in which the LEA inspector/adviser expects to be closely involved.)

INDIVIDUAL TIMETABLE

Based on consultations with the department both as a whole and as individuals the head of department should draw up a proposed timetable for each teacher. Try to make this as tight as possible, while ensuring that each teacher gets the right free period allocation.

You should end up with a list that looks a bit like this:

HOD: Upper A level (3 periods), CSE/O level (3 periods), 4B (4 periods), 2L (4 periods), 1X (4 periods) = 18 periods.

2 i/c: Lower A level (2 periods), CEE (3 periods), 5K (4 periods), 4C (4 periods), 3R (4 periods), 1st year support (3 periods) = 20 periods.

THE DEPARTMENT TIMETABLE

The next stage is to see how the preferred arrangements for individual teachers mesh as a department timetable. Using a 'visual planner' like the one below, put together the classes that *must* be taught simultaneously and classes that *can* be taught simultaneously.

By filling each teacher's provisional timetable on the planner it will be possible to see how the blocks of periods fit together. It may be, for example, that there simply aren't enough periods in the school week to fit everything in, or that it's so tight that there's no room for a department meeting or for using teachers as floating support for particular classes because they are occupied elsewhere. It's possible to see at this stage what demands are being made on rooms the department has sole or major use of.

Generally, the fewer periods it takes to put on the department timetable the better — and the more your TT Boss will love you. Make any necessary changes by consultation now. (The use of a 'visual planner' may seem a mystery; there's a little exercise in its use at the end of this section.)

NAME OF TEACHER	NO. OF PERIODS AVAIL.	TIMETABLE PERIODS 20 period week; 3 periods of English per class 1 2 3 4 5 6 7 8 9 10 11 12 13 14 15 16 17 18 19 20
A	18	1st yr U6'A'
B	18	1st yr 6'O' 4th yr
C	16	1st yr 4th yr
D	8	6'CEE etc.
E	18	2nd yr 3rd yr
F	12	2nd yr 3rd yr 4th yr
G	6	2nd yr 3rd yr

Hand the visual plan to the timetabler, together with the finished allocation of teachers to classes. All that person has to do is to arrange the pattern into the school week — although there may be some difficulties caused by things like constraints on the number of available periods to play with by fixtures like Games times, or by conflict between this pattern and that of another department over a shared teacher, or by what's going to emerge for a particular class's timetable if teachers in their departments get their way.

PROVISIONAL TIMETABLE

The next stage is to get a provisional timetable for the department arranged for the school week. Some TT Bosses omit this stage, but they should not be allowed to do so. Pass it around and get comments. From what comes back decide which complaints can be dealt with *within* the existing framework, i.e. changes that can be made by juggling with the department's timetable without affecting any others, and which complaints require a fundamental change. The case for this must be made *fast* and coherent, preferably with a suggestion as to how it can be changed (this means looking at the overall timetable). Expect the TT Boss to suggest changes for other reasons; once again the crucial thing is not to agree to anything until consulted. Some things just won't pan out within the department's time and might mean liaising with other departments; but if something is worked out with another subject *make sure everyone knows*, especially the TT Boss.

RELATIONSHIP WITH TT BOSS

Very nice people can turn very nasty and inflexible if under pressure and doing the timetable is not an easy job. A preliminary chat-up by the head of department, which combines sympathy, awe and some naive assumed stupidity can work wonders. The TT Boss will have plenty of other people who don't take the trouble. Try to avoid abandoning the simple rules of diplomacy:

— try not to be *too* demanding;
— try to predict problems and conflict of interests *before* they emerge. (Many a good idea can flounder because the TT Boss can get away with saying 'Yes that's all very well but what you don't understand is . . . ');
— wherever possible have an alternative. So instead of 'Move it or else!', try 'I know that if 4th year English is moved from Friday period 6 it causes problems for the Technical Department, but I think it can be done by moving Home Econ. here, which leaves Tuesday morning free for Tech. Drawing which frees the Technical block here . . . ';
— avoid bother by negotiating liaisons with other departments before seeing the TT Boss. If two departments go together and present the TT Boss with a fait accompli all

the better. (Amateur psychology suggests that the accompli
should not be too fait when presented.)

APPENDIX

THE VISUAL PLANNER: AN EXERCISE

An exercise using the visual planner to test the mesh of provisional
individual timetables.

Suppose that your preferred arrangements for six teachers (A, B, C, D, E, F) to
teach English in years 1-5 (each with 3 classes simultaneously timetabled) are as
follows:

YEAR 1	YEAR 2	YEAR 3	YEAR 4	YEAR 5
A	A	D	F	F
C	B	C	A	E
E	C	E	B	B

To simplify the situation assume that there is a 10 period week, and that each
class has 3 periods of English. Enter your arrangements into the planner below
starting from the left. The 1st year periods are already in.

PERIOD	1	2	3	4	5	6	7	8	9	10
Teacher A	1st year	1st year	1st year							
Teacher B										
Teacher C	1st year	1st year	1st year							
Teacher D										
Teacher E	1st year	1st year	1st year							
Teacher F										

So: what is the problem? What changes in the arrangements will be needed to
make them fit into the week?

Space

ONE CONDITION

'I've been out of full-time teaching for a couple of years, but I'll be going back to regular English teaching next year. I only have one condition: I must have my own room. Everything else is negotiable — but I'm just too long in the tooth to plod around corridors with cardboard boxes and then spend the first five minutes of every lesson re-arranging the furniture.'

PLANS . . .

'We've spent most of a year sorting out elementary physical arrangements for the rooms we're teaching in. Two of our three teaching rooms were re-furnished with tables rather than desks; useless huge cupboards with doors hanging off were swopped for unwanted sets of old wooden lockers for storage; we converted two odd broom-cupboard spaces in the corridor into places where three or four children could work. Nothing's finished yet, but we've got plans . . .'

MINIMUM REQUIREMENTS

The nature of the department's accommodation (both teaching and administrative) has a direct effect on the morale of teachers and pupils. There is considerable variation in the quality of accommodation for English in different schools, even where the overall quality of the school buildings themselves is roughly the same. Some of this variation may be explained by details of school layout and overall policy. But the rest of it can only be due to differences in what the department has been prepared to press for and organize for itself.

We are not concerned here with what ideal tailor-made accommodation might look like, but with the minimum necessary to establish an efficient working environment for an active department. In comparison with the kind of accommodation which science or design teaching needs, the minimum requirements for English teaching (as for most other subjects) are comparatively simple and inexpensive. Each of the requirements suggested below should be attainable, given at least some flexibility in the way accommodation in the school is arranged:

- a department base in which teachers can work and talk;
- a conveniently located stockroom big enough to contain the the bulk of the department's materials;
- exclusive or major use of a number of classrooms (preferably in the same area) furnished and equipped so that the full range of English activities can readily take place;

— regular use of one large room (with blackout) which can be used for occasional classroom drama work that needs extra space and for the screening of films and television programmes to more than one teaching group;
— limited rights over available small rooms or spaces in which small groups of pupils can work (and preferably including at least one small room well-insulated enough for tape-recording to take place).

These are minimum requirements for a department which is responsible for 'English only'; extra specialist accommodation is needed for a department responsible for full drama provision throughout the school or for organizing special reading or ESL tuition.

Some further suggestions follow on the value of a department base, on claiming permanent teaching rooms, and on furnishing the English classroom.

THE DEPARTMENT ROOM

A spare classroom or a small room is an indispensable feature of an English department's resources. It is a place where teachers can meet, consult, mark and prepare and share in a way that helps to build up a department's morale and sense of unity. It gives teachers an instant audience for their classroom successes and failures and this informal contact can develop into a kind of seminar-on-the-run which enables teachers to exchange theory and practice in a way that might become smothered in a more formal meeting.

What goes into the room will obviously depend on its size, but handy items include:
- kettle, coffee, cups . . . ;
- extensive wall-shelving for books and pamphlet boxes;
- secure cupboard for small audio-visual equipment;
- filing cabinets or storage drawers;
- pinboard;
- trays or pigeon-holes or personal shelf-space for each member of department;
- a typewriter;
- equipment for designing teaching materials;
- a telephone . . .

As well as being the department's social and administrative base, if the room is large enough it can also double as a storage space — particularly for teacher-produced material, audio-visual software and other non-book items which can easily get buried in a stockroom. If some teachers in the department are obliged by the timetable to be nomadic, they can at least use the department base to store boxes of materials which have to be carted from classroom to classroom.

FIXED ROOMS — AND SUITES

Anyone who has endured the business of teaching classes in a variety of different rooms during the week knows the value of having a room you can call your own. It is a perk which some schools, by a curious piece of logic, award only to senior staff in a department, who are thu able to arrive in the staffroom at break carrying just a bunch of keys. Meanwhile less experienced teachers shuffle their belongings over break from the Small Dining Room to Home Economics 3 and find, after a matter of weeks, that their teaching programme is reduced to what is easy to carry and set up.

If having any kind of fixed accommodation is of major benefit to individual teachers, it is an enormous boon for the department as a whole to have exclusive use of adjacent classrooms along the same corridor. While recognizing the problems involved here, it is worth saying that any department that has managed to secure this kind of arrangement reports a radical enhancement of the department's moral and effectiveness. The following are some of the key advantages:
- heavy equipment (everything from class libraries to film projectors) can be moved easily from room to room;
- one classroom can be fitted with black-out facilities which means that elaborate negotiations don't have to be made with

the Geography department;

— co-operative teaching and team teaching are much easier to
organize, while class sharing can become integrated into the
working style of the department;

— sudden disciplinary problems can be more effectively dealt
with by 'fostering' the miscreant with a colleague;

— the compactness of the physical arrangements makes it
much easier to offer instant support to student teachers and
teachers in the first year;

— 'interference' with other departments on account of noise
level from talk and drama is reduced to a minimum;

— displays and particular kinds of furniture arrangements can
be preserved;

— if there is a stockroom nearby the borrowing and returning
of books can be efficiently managed (and if there doesn't
happen to be a stockroom handy, the classrooms themselves
can be used to store teaching materials).

OBJECTIONS?

In some schools exclusive use by the English department of adjacent
rooms may seem an impractical proposition. There may even be difficulties in establishing the next best thing: exclusive use of fixed rooms

which aren't in the same area. This may be because the school is too crowded, because it operates on a split site, or because curriculum design makes it an inefficient arrangement. These are important objections. However, it may be that an answer to them can be found in careful timetabling which takes room availability into account at an early stage so as to ensure maximum occupancy of the number of rooms claimed. (Blocking half-years together on the timetable rather than whole years makes this easier — if to do so fits the department's staffing and its policy on pupil grouping.) It may also be possible to negotiate shared use of a suite (or a set) of rooms with another department with similar accommodation requirements.

There is another, perhaps less common kind of objection to a department's claim for territory: that pupils, not subjects, should be given permanent homes. There are obvious advantages in an arrangement which allows pupils to stay in the same room (or general area) for some proportion of their day. However, a number of schools which adopt this policy still manage (by ingenious timetabling and by using subject teams as pastoral teams) to give subject teachers at least semi-permanent accommodation.

THE CLASSROOM ITSELF

LAYOUT

Many English teachers would much prefer not to have desks in rows but are prevented from experimenting with alternative arrangements because of the time taken to restore the classroom furniture for the 'transmission' lesson that may follow. Eventually the energy required to keep shifting the furniture will defeat attempts to change the relationship between teacher and taught by changing the spaces between them. With a suite of rooms used exclusively by English teachers arrangements can be made so that alternative arrangements can, as far as possible, be respected. It will also mean that tables, instead of desks, can be used, thus giving greater flexibility and more space. Here are some possible arrangements which have particular applications to drama and group work.

1. This layout is especially valuable for group work, as all the pupils are facing one another, and there is plenty of room for books, papers and other material.

2. The second arrangement lends itself particularly well to classroom discussion, as all the pupils can see one another and not just those in their own group. The layout is particularly convenient for drama, necessitating only a minimal amount of furniture moving, but it is less satisfactory for group work. The block in the middle is necessary only if the classroom is too small to accommodate all the desks around the walls.

3.   The third arrangement allows all the children to face the wall
     when writing. The desks are far more likely to fit the perimeter
     of the room when arranged like this. Again, this layout is con-
     venient for drama. For discussion and talk the chairs can
     simply be turned round. This layout creates a very workman-
     like atmosphere when reading or writing is going on, and the
     teacher has a good view of what is happening. It is easy for
     the teacher to talk to individuals without disturbing a whole
     group.

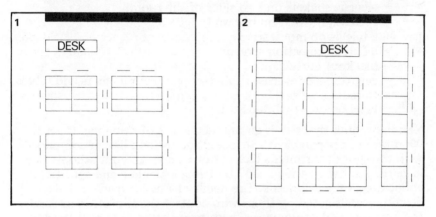

FURNITURE AND EQUIPMENT

Most teachers have to work in rooms which are pretty spartan. The
provision of proper furniture and accessories can lead to a quieter
and more productive atmosphere; our experience is, also, that the
nicer a room is the less inclined pupils are to make a mess of it. A
room needs to be designed to allow teacher and pupils to carry out
a full range of activities in English; for example, if there's no means

of storing and displaying class library books, it's unlikely that children will be given adequate opportunity to pick a book they want to read. Among the items we think are important are the following:
— display racks for books;
— pin-boards for wall displays;
— decent lockable cupboard space, preferably of the sort that can take storage trays;
— a mobile book trolley or storage tray trolley;
— a filing cabinet;
— electric sockets on two sides of the room;
— speaker(s) fitted on the wall;
— a television monitor;
— a fitted projection screen;
— blackout curtains;
— carpet . . . or at least rubber-tipped feet on chairs and tables to reduce noise;
— blackboard or whiteboard.

You may think that this is an unrealistic list of demands. It isn't. What do your department's teaching rooms look like in comparison with those of departments like Art or Science in your school: how have they got what they need? By being articulate and specific about their subject's needs. The needs of English teachers have been underestimated by those who control the allocation of funds for furniture and equipment. There may not be sufficient funds available for every department to get what they need; but you should claim your share. And then once you've got it (and you won't get it all or all at once) make sure the department makes use of it.

Money

LARGESSE

'It's the largesse system here. The head never tells us how much we've got for the year, so I just spend as much as I can before the inevitable summons to the office. She tells me off, I claim financial incompet- ?nce and ask for another £200. By March things can get pretty tense. I find I put off ordering things during the year because it's all such a nuisance, going cap in hand.'

NO TIME AT ALL

'One of my responsibilities as second in department is looking after the money. As there's so little of it, looking after it takes no time at all. Whenever I go into the science prep-room they're always deep into calculations about how much they've got left and what they're going to buy next. We don't have that kind of problem.'

A FAIR SHARE

This section is concerned with departmental capitation and with steps which can be taken to ensure that English is getting a fair share of the overall departmental allocation. Senior staff in schools can't be blamed for whatever inadequacy there may be in this overall allocation, but departments often complain of the apparent unfairness (or mysterious- ness) of the system used to divide up what is available. As with time- tabling, there's a good case here for a concerned English department to press, through the HOD committee, for a definite and open set of pro- cedures. Achieving the first step — the publishing of figures showing who gets what — will almost automatically produce a willingness to ensure that a fair distribution of money takes place if it doesn't do so already; nobody in a school likes *obvious* inequities.

A BUDGET SURVEY

What kind of financing do English departments get? They vary of course in the extent of their responsibilities. Drama, Remedial, ESL may be part of them, and if there is extra responsibility beyond main- stream English the department must obviously receive additional funding. The same applies to a department which runs special prog- rammes or courses or to a department which buys its own major items of audio-visual and reprographic equipment. As far as 'English only' departments in ILEA are concerned, evidence from a survey in 1979- 80 showed that the average expenditure was £1.70 per pupil if the department did not have to pay for consumable stock from its allow- ance, and £2.20 per pupil if it did. Average expenditures for different sizes of school looked like this:

Without Stationery	With Stationery
500 pupils x 1.70 = £ 850	500 pupils x 2.20 = £1100
700 pupils x 1.70 = £1190	700 pupils x 2.20 = £1540
900 pupils x 1.70 = £1530	900 pupils x 2.20 = £1980
1100 pupils x 1.70 = £1870	1100 pupils x 2.20 = £2420
1300 pupils x 1.70 = £2210	1300 pupils x 2.20 = £2860

However, the often enormous difference in allocation between schools of the same size can make the averages misleading. For example, the lowest allocation for a school of 1000 pupils was £1200, £500 below the no-stationery costs average, whereas the highest allocation for the same size of school was £3460, which is £1760 *above* the same average.

It's worth saying, too, that the average 1979-80 no-stationery figure of £1.70 per pupil was by no means high. A calculation done on the basis of 1979-80 figures and applied to departments with different curricula and policies on books showed that £2.20 per pupil was a more reasonable figure for book provision (tightly organized and with no frills).

An English department looking for an increase in its capitation might get it simply by casually asking for it. On the other hand, it may be necessary to look at the allocation system as a whole. The main factors involved are outlined below.

THE CAKE

A school's annual capitation allowance is calculated on the projected roll for the coming session; the school then decides how to allocate the money. Some LEAs (including ILEA) operate an 'alternative use of resources' scheme (AUR) which allows a school to make decisions on how the capitation allowance is used; it can, for example, buy some extra staffing or ancillary help, or allocate funds to minor works or to develop particular school facilities. A certain amount of the capitation will also need to be set aside to cover general school expenses (on office equipment, pooled audio-visual hardware, stationery and so on). Since these broad decisions will determine the amount of money available for spending by departments on books and other resources, it is important that the English department plays its part in making them.

Once the total sum available for departments to spend has been calculated, it is then divided up among them. It has to be said that in some schools this division is done arbitrarily. A tradition has perhaps been established that such-and-such a department has this much, that department has that much, and there seems no logic or plan behind it. Thus if the global budget is 10% up on last year, every department receives 10% more, regardless of their possibly changing requirements and burdens. It makes more sense to have a system under which all departments submit estimated budgets for the coming year so that the division can be based on discussion of need rather than on precedent.

ESTIMATING YOUR SLICE

Even if the system of estimated budgets does not operate in the school as a whole, an under-financed English department might well find it useful to submit a reasoned account of its needs. There are a number of factors to take into account in discussion of a budget submission within the department.

1. The department teaching (or pupil) load.
   Obviously the more pupils you teach and the oftener you see them, the more costly it is to run the English department. Normally, the English department has the heaviest pupil-loading in the school and this is a strong argument for the department to demand its fair share of the spending budget. The *pupil-loading* is calculated by multiplying the number of teaching groups by the number of pupils in each group and by the number of periods taught. So, for example:
   1st year: 4 groups x 28 pupils x 5 periods = 560.
   The aggregate for all years is the department's pupil-load; the

figure only becomes interesting when compared with that of other departments.

2. The need for books and resources in particular areas.
    The department may consider, for instance, that the 3rd year desperately needs new readers, and must calculate how much is needed and make a case for it in notes attached to the estimated budget.

3. The need to make up depleted stock.
    However tightly organized there will be a certain amount of depletion of stock. Unless usage of a set of books or a particular resource is being discontinued, then this depletion has to made good.

4. Examination book requirements.
    The department will have to calculate how much money to spend on examination texts for the session after next.

5. The requirements of special areas which come under the English department umbrella.
    For instance, if remedial work or drama is within the English department's sphere, then a separate estimate will have to be made for them after consulting with the teachers with special responsibilities for those areas.

6. Money required to fund new aspects of department's work.
    A new exam syllabus may require new books, or a change to mixed ability teaching might well lead to a change of policy on teaching resources.

7. Percentage of money to be spent on consumable stock.
    File paper, exercise books, carbons, banda paper, stencils, glue . . .

8. Amount of money to be spent on hardware.
    Does the department need a new record-player or video-tape machine? Does it wish to combine with another department to buy an expensive piece of equipment?

9. Individual allowance for English teachers to spend on resources as they think fit.
    Does the department grant a small proportion of the overall budget to individual teachers to spend? If so, how much?

OPTIMISTIC?

The cost of items under headings 2-9 may very well exceed even the most optimistic assessment of what the department is likely to get. As suggested in the section on 'Teaching Materials', particular priorities need to be identified and purchases planned on a long-term basis. However, these kinds of decisions should be notified in the budget submission so that the department's self-restraint is made known. It's also helpful to include a simple breakdown of where last year's money went as support — with an appropriate allowance for inflation — for next year's claim. (That's the strongest argument for the maintenance of fairly detailed records of departmental expenditure.)

HOW MUCH TO EACH?

Once departments have submitted their estimated budgets, the decision needs to be made on how much each department will actually get. In some schools the head makes this decision unilaterally; in others, the head tables proposals for discussion at an HOD or full staff meeting. Whoever makes the decision, the criteria by which it is reached need to be clarified.

PUPIL-LOADING

The simplest way of making this clarification possible is to take the pupil-period load of each department to a projected norm to show what each would get if percentage of the school's total pupil-period load was the only criterion. Thus, if the English department teaches 8000 pupil-periods, which works out at 16% of the school's pupil-period load, then by this criterion the department could expect 16% of the overall departmental allocation (i.e. 100% of norm).

However, an analysis of a school's current allocations in terms of pupil-periods and percentages of norm might in fact look like this:

	Pupil period load	Allocation	% of 'norm'
English	8000	£2000	100
Art	4500	£2400	213
Science	6500	£2700	166
Domestic Science	750	£2000	1064

Now, if a department is receiving ten times the norm, then inevitably some departments will have to receive well below the norm to compensate. Thus further analysis might reveal:

History	5000	800	64
Modern Languages	6000	500	33

OTHER FACTORS

But it would not be reasonable to suggest that Domestic Science, in this example, should operate on 100% of norm. Pupil-period load obviously cannot be the only criterion. Some subjects are a great deal more expensive to run than others — and this has to be taken into account. (Some schools apply a factor of x2 or x3 or x4 to the pupil-load of departments which consume very expensive materials.) In addition, the special needs of a department in a given year must be considered: a Drama department, for instance, may suddenly need a new set of lighting equipment which it would be impractical to buy over a period of years out of its normal capitation.

EXPECTATIONS: NEGOTIATIONS

There are, of course, competing demands on the school's overall departmental allocation. These can only be resolved by open dialogue on the needs of the various departments. The use of the pupil-loading formula cannot settle the arguments, but it can at least give departments a reasonable basis to negotiate on. Departmental expectations are very much part of this process. It may be that some English departments have had the expectation that they will operate with shoddy books, incomplete sets, little hardware and no money for extras, while other subject departments in the same schools have had the expectation that they will have the tools to do the job properly.

That said, an English department must strike a balance between pushing its own claims (based on reasoned costings) and recognizing the genuine needs and difficulties of other departments. While a Science department, for instance, may not need a great deal of help in getting its due share, smaller departments (perhaps Drama, Remedial, the Library, if they are financed independently from English) may need all the support that English teachers can give.

Secretarial Help

Ancillary help for English departments (on both typing and duplication and on the ordering and administration of stock) was the subject of a specific recommendation in the Bullock report. It suggested that, where assistance with typing and duplication was provided centrally (through the school office and the media resources centre), a further 20 hours of administrative assistance should be available to the English department for every five forms of entry in an 11-18 school (and pro rata). Not much notice has been taken of this recommendation. In many schools even typing essential to the department's work only gets done as a favour. This is clearly unsatisfactory. Getting 20 hours administrative assistance plus typing and duplication time for a five form entry school may not be a possibility. But it would not be unreasonable, for example, for a department of 6 or 7 teachers to expect around 10 hours a week total secretarial time.

THE BENEFITS

Given a suitable place to work — and a clear brief — an English department secretary can begin to identify with the work of the department and make an invaluable contribution to the life of the department. The benefits of good typing are self-evident but a key advantage is having someone to assist in the administration of the department. The following tasks can be done by such a person:

1. Book and stationery requisitions: head of department or teachers in charge indicate titles in catalogues and give a rough list. The assistant does the rest.
2. Overseeing book borrowing from class libraries.
3. Maintaining stock levels for examination set books.
4. Accessing new stock (perhaps in conjunction with pupil helpers).
5. Dealing with inspection copies.
6. Typing class lists, teacher-produced materials, writing by pupils and so on.
7. Filing letters, catalogues, documents, assessment sheets, exam papers and so on.
8. Helping to organize a resources index and bank of materials, including duplication.

A justification of secretarial assistance along these lines may be enough. But it might also be useful to co-operate with other major departments (perhaps Humanities) in presenting the proposal so that a full-time person can be shared between departments. If the climate is very hostile a department might consider spending some of its own capitation to buy in secretarial help, if only for a year as an experiment. It may be possible to show that having someone to monitor distribution and loan of books results in considerable savings.

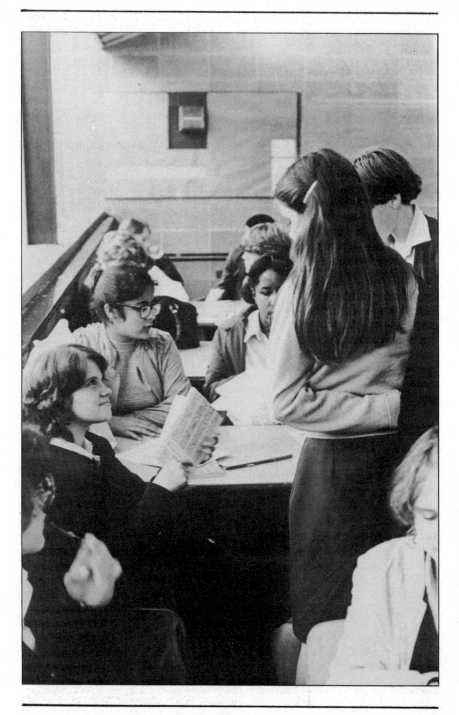

Teaching Materials

Teaching Materials

Ideas in Action

Issues to do with the nature and availability of teaching materials are at the sharp end of departmental policy and practice. Questions like 'what materials can I use with my 3rd year?' and 'when and in what quantity and state will they be available?' are of immediate and direct concern to all teachers. For many new, non-specialist or unconfident teachers they are of pressing concern. Finding, adapting and making learning materials takes up an enormous amount of teachers' time and energy.The frustrations involved in getting hold of stuff which the department has (somewhere) are a major source of friction in the department; the feeling, looking round the stock-cupboard, that there is nothing here that I can *use* is a demoralizing one for anybody.

Paradoxically, the business of the department's teaching materials can have a low priority on the agenda of departmental discussions; it can seem a banal and trifling matter. But, in the day-to-day running of the department, teaching materials represent the department's philosophy and approach: they are the department's ideas in action. The way in which teaching materials are selected and organized not only tells us something about the department's views of English teaching but also something of its assumptions about teacher behaviour. Clearly the question of materials is also related to matters such as finance, the size of school, the timetable, room allocation and geographical layout. Every department will be different in these respects; these issues are considered elsewhere. This section is concerned with general principles and descriptions of systems in the selection and organization of teaching material.

Basic Materials

What basic materials do all English teachers need to have in their

possession (or at least easy access to when required) in order to run a lesson?

'Basic materials' means materials in addition to those the teacher chooses to work on for a particular period of time. What are regarded as 'basic materials' will vary from department to department depending on philosophy. The list might include, among other things:

— a class library of paperback books for independent reading. The collection needs to be sufficient in range and quantity to allow individual pupils to find 4 or 5 books at any one time which they are interested in reading (the organization of class libraries is dealt with in detail later in this section);
— a collection of dictionaries, easy thesauruses and punctuation handbooks, not necessarily of the same kind, but enough so that groups of say 4 pupils can have immediate access to them when they're writing;
— a set of short-story anthologies which can be used to fill unplanned hiatuses in lessons or as occasional planned relief;
— a folder of photographs which can be used to stimulate imaginative writing when a writer is stuck;
— a collection of reference books (an atlas, books of lists/facts/records) to raid for odd bits of information.

Teaching Approaches

What kinds of material does the department want pupils to engage with and how are these resources going to be used in the classroom?

As pointed out in the section on devising a syllabus, departmental discussion of philosophy and teaching approach sometimes stops short of considering what materials and uses of these materials are implied by the department's general views. In other cases departments may find that there is a serious mismatch between, on the one hand, the kinds of classroom content and activities they have committed themselves to and, on the other hand, the stuff they've actually got in the cupboards. It's a question here of considering: (a) the resource implications of the approaches the department is committed to (and thus seeing what kinds of materials are missing) and (b) looking at the materials the department has got (and thus seeing what *uses* of them can be made — and whether any ought to be chucked).

To illustrate:

The problem: 3rd year literature. The department has recently extended mixed ability grouping into the 3rd year. In previous years the 3rd year sets have made heavy use of class novels (on average two novels per class per term), with particular novels having been designated as suitable for particular ability groups. In talking over the issue of literature and the use of class novels in the 3rd year, the department has decided the following:

1) to reduce the use of class readers to one longish (or 2 shortish) novels per class per term;
2) to make a list of 8 class novels which are appropriate for mixed ability classes and which are going to be used only with the 3rd year;
3) to produce a pack of worksheets on each of the 8 novels suggesting follow-up work of different kinds;
4) to break up some sets of books previously used with the 3rd year but not considered suitable for class reading with mixed ability classes into 'group-reading' sets of 6 copies. The idea here is to give these to groups of pupils to read together and then work on together to make a 'presentation' to the rest of the class.

The resource implications of these decisions.

1) Since there are not 8 books which fit the class reading bill, more will have to be considered and bought in.
2) Since teachers will now be using the same books arrangements will have to be made for planning who uses a book

when and for how long. In addition, these 3rd year class readers cannot be used with younger pupils.
3) A decision needs to be made about the design and production of the class-reader worksheets. (See the section 'Teacher-Made Materials' which follows.)
4) The group-reading sets will have to be sorted out and an end-of-term swop around organized.
5) Some of the old class readers are not suitable for group-reading or anything else. The set of *King Solomon's Mines* could be sold off as scrap.

Finding and Ordering Materials

What system does the department have for
(a)   finding out what published material is available;
(b)   examining it and deciding whether to buy it;
(c)   ordering it?

In some departments the person charged with responsibility for stocking the department is given (or takes) a free hand to decide what to buy. That system *may* work — provided that the person responsible is thorough, knowledgeable and tuned in to the department's needs. But there are drawbacks; it would seem to make sense to adopt more of a shared approach to decision-making. There still needs to be someone (or two people in a larger school) to initiate and oversee the process. Some suggestions follow for how the process might be organized.

FINDING OUT ABOUT MATERIALS

There are various sources of information about what materials are available from publishers of non-net educational books. (There is a separate section on class libraries which has information on publishers of net paperback children's books; for the distinction between net and non-net books see appendix.)

(1)   Other schools
An easy way is to ask teachers at a neighbouring school if you can drop in and look round their stock. They may laugh; but it is potentially a fruitful point of contact with people actually using the stuff (and may open up other possibilities for co-operation).

(2)   Publishers' catalogues
The major publishers of educational material issue annual catalogues which are sent to all schools in the country, usually in the New Year. The first problem is to ensure that these catalogues are getting

through to the right person. Some envelopes are marked 'for Head of English', but some catalogues come in a bundle for a range of subjects. It is not unknown for these to end up in the office bin or to be flung onto a staffroom table and promptly lost under a pile of marking. You need to make sure that you're getting catalogues from at least the following 20 commercial publishers who produce substantial quantities of material for secondary English teaching. That's not to say, of course, that other publishers' catalogues are not worth hunting for too. It may also be worth scanning Drama, Remedial and Humanities/Social Studies catalogues for appropriate material. For a full list of publishers of educational books, including non-commercial ones of interest to English teachers, see *What Every English Teacher Needs to Know About Resources and London* (English Centre).

Edward Arnold, 41 Bedford Square, London WC1 8LL. 637-7161.
Blackie & Son, Western Cledderns Rd., Bishopbriggs, Glasgow G64 2NZ. 041-772-2311.
Cambridge University Press, PO Box 110, Cambridge CB2 3RL. 0223-312393.
Cassell & Co., 35 Red Lion Sq., London WC1R 4SG. 831-6100.
Evans Brothers, Montague Ho., Russell Sq., London WC1B 5BX. 636-8521.
George G. Harrap & Co., 19-23 Ludgate Hill, London EC4M 7PD. 248-6444.
Hart Davis Educational, Box 9, 29 Frogmore, St. Albans, Herts AL2 2NF. 0727-72727.
Heinemann Educational, 48 Charles St., London W1X 8AH. 637-3311.
Hodder & Stoughton Educational, Mill Rd., Dunton Green, Sevenoaks, Kent TN13 2XX. 0732-50111.
Holmes McDougall, Allander Ho, 137 Leith Walk, Edinburgh EH6 8NS. 031-554-9444.
Hutchinson Educational, 24 Highbury Cresc., London N5 1RX. 359-3711.
Longman Group, Longman Ho., Burnt Mill, Harlow, Essex CM20 2JE. 0279-26721.
Macmillan Education, Houndmills, Basingstoke, Hants RG21 2XS. 0256-29242.
Methuen Educational, 11 New Fetter Lane, London EC4P 4EE. 583-9855.
John Murray, 50 Albemarle St., London W1X 4BD. 493-4361.
Thomas Nelson & Sons, Nelson Ho., Mayfield Rd., Walton-on-Thames, Surrey KT12 5PL. 98-46133.
Oxford University Press, Clarendon Press, Walton St., Oxford OX2 6DP. 0865-56767.
Schofield & Sims, 35 St. John's Rd., Huddersfield HD1 5DT. 0484-30684.
Ward Lock Educational, 47 Marylebone Lane, London W1M 6AX. 486-3271.
A. Wheaton & Co., Hennock Rd., Exeter EX2 8RP. 0392-74121.

(3) Reviews in journals
Educational publishers send their new books to a number of subject journals. For substantial review coverage of new teaching materials it's worth subscribing to:
Teaching English:
published 3 times a year by the Scottish Curriculum Development Service, Edinburgh Centre (Moray House College of Education, Holyrood Road, Edinburgh);

The English Magazine:
published 3 times a year by the English Centre.
The Use of English (published by the Scottish Academic Press, 33 Montgomery St., Edinburgh), the newsletter which accompanies *English in Education* (the journal of NATE, 49 Broomgrove Road, Sheffield S10 2NA) and the *T.E.S.* also carry reviews, as well as publishers' advertising of forthcoming material.

EXAMINING THE STUFF

Just getting hold of the titles (plus price and ISBN) of material of certain kinds may be enough — if it's just a question of odd copies for departmental reference or material that you're fairly sure about. But in most cases it is essential to handle and examine the stuff if you don't want to end up buying 30 copies of a pig in a poke. Members of the department need to see and talk over the material where possible. There are a number of possibilities:
1) borrowing copies from a neighbouring school that already has them;
2) sending off to the publishers for inspection copies (which you can then retain free if you're going to order a certain number, or buy if you're not);

3) visiting exhibitions of publishers' materials. For English
teachers there are two major annual exhibitions: at the
annual N.A.T.E. conference, held at Easter, and the London
School Books Exhibition, held in March. Publishers also
organize their own exhibitions locally at teachers' centres
and elsewhere, and the larger individual publishers have their
own travelling reps. who come into schools on an irregular
basis, and showrooms attached to their head offices (which
are mostly in and around London). (For information on the
permanent displays available for ILEA teachers, see *What
Every English Teacher Needs to Know About Resources and
London.*)
4) Foyles Educational Bookshop (37 Upper Berkeley St., London
W1) is one of the few places where you can buy educational textbooks off the shelf.

CRITICAL QUESTIONS

A departmental meeting which examines inspection material can be a
fruitful one. To focus the discussion when it's a matter of a big investment it may be worth making explicit the kinds of critical questions
which can be asked about a piece of teaching material:
— the kind (and the readability) of source material used;
— the print-size, layout and graphics;
— the nature of the activities (if any) the pupils are to engage in;
— the assumptions made about classroom organization;
— the expectations about levels of performance within a class;
— the extent to which the material recognizes that its potential
    readers are of both sexes and from a variety of cultures;
— the cost, in relation to the possible use of the material and
    the physical durability of the book.

Those are very general questions. Much more detailed ones could
be drawn up and presented as a checklist to guide the department's
selection of, say, poetry anthologies or class readers — items which
will be an important focus for classroom work and which represent
a considerable financial investment. (See appendix for examples of
checklists on different kinds of material.)

It is very likely that the department's budget will not stretch to buy
everything the department wants in any one year. This may be especially frustrating when you're trying to build up resources from a state
of real inadequacy. Clearly a department can't go from being poorly
stocked to superbly stocked in one year. It becomes, in that case, a
question of priorities, of deciding on a pattern of resource-building.
For example:
— is this collection of resources on the American West going to

be used by a lot of people or just by the one Western fanatic who suggested it?
— does every pupil reading *Of Mice and Men* as an exam text in the 5th year *really* have to have a personal copy?
— can we manage for a year with just a half-set of this beautifully illustrated poetry anthology?
— do we have an adequate stock of single copies of material which teachers can pillage for ideas?

But, before you cut items from your list of things to order, consider whether you could make a claim for more money for the department: if there is a need for particular materials because of a change in policy or the development of a new course, then cost what you need and submit a request for extra funds.
(See the section on capitation in 'Time, Space and Money'.)

ORDERING THE STUFF

At some point somebody is going to have to sit down and write out the orders. That's a dull clerical job that can be shared or rotated. Some points to bear in mind:
— where the order is being made through the LEA system by someone new to the job, the school secretary needs to be consulted on the correct procedure (the ILEA system is explained in an appendix);
— if you don't have the publisher's catalogue the hunt for price and ISBN (International Standard Book Number) can be speeded up by using the current *Books in Print* in the school or local library, or by phoning the publisher if it's new material;
— if materials (like exam texts) are urgently required for September, the ordering will need to be done early in the preceding Spring term, since delivery through the LEA system can be very slow;
— the main requisition can wait a bit longer (depending on when the capitation year ends), but it's worth thinking about the difference it makes to staff morale to be starting off with some bright new things to try;
— when you need material really urgently (like A level set texts or a particular play) it may be possible to get it quite quickly through a local bookshop (or through a distribution agency like 'Books for Students'). Normally you lose the LEA discount if you buy this way, but it may be possible to negotiate a discount with a bookshop (say 10%) if you agree to use it regularly;
— it's sensible to keep a copy (marked with date and premises

code) of any requisition you put in and to keep a track of how much you're spending;
— what is delivered may not be the same as what was ordered. Check the contents of a delivery against the advice note and against the original order. Orders for books which are 'temp. o.s.' ('temporarily out of stock') or 'rp' (reprinting) may have to be made again after a certain period of time. Check that you haven't been charged for them the first time round.

Audio-Visual Resources

What use does the department make of audio-visual materials?

Audio-visual materials of all kinds — films, videotapes of educational television programmes, slides and filmstrips, audiotapes of schools radio broadcasts and of book and play readings — are a major resource for English teaching. There are practical obstacles to their use — they can be expensive to hire or purchase and equipment can be troublesome — but the major problem may be of sorting out how they can be integrated into classroom work rather than regarded as isolated bits of light relief. Teachers can very easily manage the practical business of setting up and operating the hardware; the department's real task is to encourage exploitation of the possibilities of the software so as to persuade people that it is worthwhile wheeling out the hardware more than once in a blue moon.

A few LEAs (including ILEA) employ media resources officers to provide teachers with practical help and advice on the use of teaching materials, particularly (but not exclusively) audio-visual materials; their active involvement in the department's work can prove very valuable in this area.

AVAILABLE MATERIAL

The first problem is getting to know what is available to buy, hire or record.

Film. There is a wide range of feature and documentary films available for 16mm hire (and increasingly on video-cassette). Some of the major catalogues to look out for are:

BBC TV Enterprises: Guild Sound & Vision Film Hire Dept., Woodston Ho., Oundle Rd., Peterborough PE2 9PZ.
British Transport Films: Melbury House, Melbury Terr., London NW1 6LP.
Columbia-Warner: 16mm Booking Dept., Film Ho., 142 Wardour St., London W1V 4AH.
Concord Films Council: 201 Felixstow Rd., Ipswich, Suffolk.
Connoisseur Films: 167 Oxford St., London W1R 2DX.
Contemporary Films: 55 Greek St., London W1.
Harris Films: Glenbuck Ho., Surbiton, Surrey.
National Film Board of Canada: 1 Grosvenor Sq., London W1X 0AB.
Rank Film Library: PO Box 20, Great West Rd., Brentford, Middlesex.
United Artists: Mortimer Ho., Mortimer St., London W1.

The British Film Institute (81 Dean St., London W1V 6AA, 437-4355) provides a wide range of services to schools: film and film extract hire through its own distribution library; hire and sale of film-slides and study material; and the information services of its Central Booking Agency.

Some LEAs have their own free film libraries; the one provided by ILEA is particularly extensive. (The English Centre publishes a catalogue listing and annotating films in the ILEA Film Library of particular interest to English teachers).

Television. In addition to their normal output, the BBC and the ITV regions produce a number of educational programmes every year of potential interest; some of them are invaluable. The programme notices are sent to all schools well in advance so that programme notes and pupil booklets can be ordered. Videotaping of the programmes selected is more or less essential to full use of them.

The ETV branch of ILEA's Learning Materials Service now makes programmes straight onto videocassette; they can be hired by ILEA schools for long-term use at a nominal fee.

Radio. The BBC Schools Radio broadcasts programme is sent with the TV schedule, and is a valuable source of material, particularly of prose, poetry and play readings.

Audio-recordings. Tape material sometimes accompanies English source books and anthologies produced by mainstream educational publishers; this can often be valuable in its own right. Tape readings (usually on cassette) of stories and extracts from novels can provide powerful support for inexperienced readers (see the section on class libraries for some suggestions here). 'Spoken word' recordings and specially designed tape programmes concerned with broadly social studies topics and with background to 6th form literature work are produced for example by:

Argo: 115 Fulham Rd., London SW3.
Audio-Visual Productions: 15 Temple Sheen Rd., London SW14.
Caedmon: Teakfield Ltd., 1 Westmead, Farnborough, Hampshire.
Educational Productions: Bradford Rd., East Ardsley, Yorkshire.
Exeter Tapes: University of Exeter, Northcote Ho., Queen's Drive, Exeter.
Oxford Audio-Visual: Ely Ho., 37 Dover St., London W1.
Topic Records: 27 Nassington Rd., London NW3.

Slides and filmstrips. Packs of various kinds, sometimes with an accompanying tape commentary, are produced by a number of agencies including the ones below. They often deal with art/humanities/social studies topics; they are sometimes less useful to English teachers as they stand than as edited and re-organized to form a collection of images and image sequences. Items in the BBC's 'Radiovision' series (filmstrips which accompany schools radio programmes) are sometimes of immediate interest to English teachers. Filmstrips can easily be mounted as slides — which makes the material easier to play about with and to use. Some major publishers of slides and filmstrips:

Centre for World Development Education: 128 Buckingham Palace Rd., London SW1.
Concordia Films: Concordia Publishing Ho., 117-123 Golden Lane, London EC1.
Educational Audio-Visual: Butterley St., Leeds.
Educational Foundation for Visual Aids: 254 Belsize Rd., London NW6.
Focal Point Filmstrips: 251 Copnor Rd., Portsmouth.
Gateway Educational Media: Waverley Rd., Yate, Bristol.
Mary Glasgow Publications: 140-142 Kensington Church St., London W8.
National Art Slide Library: Loan Service, Victoria & Albert Museum, Cromwell Rd., London SW7.
The Slide Centre: Portman Ho., 17 Brodrick Rd., London SW17.
Visual Publications: The Green, Northleach, Cheltenham, Gloucestershire.

MAKING USE OF AUDIO-VISUAL RESOURCES

The second problem is to get some clear sense of what you've got on this tape or in this slidepack — and, consequently, of how it can be used. After it has been bought or recorded, much good audio-visual material tends to sit on the departmental shelf because it takes more effort to get to know it than it does to flick through a book. Fairly detailed summaries of the material are of great help here in simply calling attention to what the department has got; the summaries might be done by people who have had a go at using the material themselves and can suggest ways of exploiting it in the classroom. For some audio-visual material (TV or audio versions of a play, for instance) classroom uses will be obvious; but the successful use of some kinds of filmstrip/audiotape packs and some kinds of TV programmes takes thinking about. At this stage, then, the department might give meeting time over to looking at a programme or piece of material together to discuss where and how best to use it, as a prelude perhaps to formally integrating it into an agreed unit of work. Since audio-visual material (with the exception of hired films which have to be used when they arrive) is capable of flexible use, it is possible to try out material in different ways to see how it goes best (whether, for example, to show an ETV programme on 'writers at work' in a series of 10 minute chunks or all the way through).

EQUIPMENT

The nature of the department's use of audio-visual resources will obviously depend to some extent on the availability of equipment: the practical end of the business has to be faced. Whether the school or the department is responsible for buying audio-visual hardware, the following equipment represents the minimum necessary to make serious use of audio-visual resources:
— video-cassette recorder (preferably with built-in timer) and colour monitor;
— 16mm film projector with separate speaker(s) (preferably fed through an amplifier);
— a good quality radio-cassette recorder (preferably with separate speaker(s));
— cassette players with headphones (preferably usable with a group listening unit);
— a carousel slide projector (assuming that filmstrips are made into slides).

Teacher-Made Materials

What use does the department make of teacher-produced material, and what provision does it make for such material to be produced successfully?

In recent years English teachers have increasingly taken to devising and producing their own teaching material. There are a number of reasons for this:

- some teachers have felt that commercial publishers are not providing material that meets the needs of children in mixed ability classes, children with reading difficulties, and children in inner city areas with different cultural backgrounds;
- some teachers have seen the business of making materials in terms of devising whole curriculum units to give coherence to a subject that has often suffered from piecemeal improvisation;
- some have seen teacher-produced materials as the instrument through which pupils can be deliberately encouraged to work in ways that publishers' materials may not invite. Teachers may wish, for example, to develop small group collaborative work or to encourage extended writing — and so design materials to these ends;
- interpreting other people's teaching strategies, even in well-designed publishers' materials, can be a rather alienating business. Many have found that the investment of time and thought in producing their own material increases their commitment to using it successfully and their interest in observing how pupils respond to it.

Teacher-produced materials *can* make the match between (a) the pupils' needs and interests, (b) the teachers' wish to make the work coherent and 'their own', and (c) the teachers' desire to encourage particular ways of working in the classroom. Taking responsibility for designing successful materials can have a powerful effect on the confidence and expertise of individual teachers. Even more importantly, the collective production of home-made materials can be a very powerful way for teachers in a department to work together. The discussions and decisions involved in making a unit of material which enacts department policy can be extremely fruitful, both in terms of what people learn from one another and in terms of the satisfaction it produces ('we've made this').

FIVE QUESTIONS TO CONSIDER

But there are a number of questions to consider before a department gets seriously into the business of producing home-made materials; for they are not of necessity always better than published material — they can often be worse in terms both of content and presentation.

1. DOES IT ALREADY EXIST?
Time for teachers is very valuable and making materials is very time-consuming. Care should be taken not to expend hours of work prod-

ucing something from scratch that already exists in published form
(or could be adapted fairly easily). There is a wide range of attractive and useful material on the market — which can be selected from
and messed about with in various ways. There is also the possibility
that a department in a neighbouring school may have home-made
materials which you could take over (or at least look at). Some
teachers feel a sense of guilt about relying on 'ready-made' material,
feeling that they must produce their own original material all of the
time: that's a feeling to be resisted.

2. WHAT FUNCTION IS IT TO SERVE?

Teacher-produced materials can obviously perform a variety of
functions. For example:
- a sheet which just carries source/stimulus material (print and/
  or visual material);
- a worksheet which describes activities to accompany existing
  published material (like a short story);
- a worksheet which carries both source/stimulus material and
  the activities arising from it;
- a booklet which offers a 'map' or a set of starting points for
  a curriculum unit using existing material (like a booklet map-
  ping out a 4-week unit on 'Animals');
- a collection of materials and activities to accompany a novel
  or an anthology of poems;
- a booklet which is intended as a self-contained unit, complete
  with the source/stimulus material and the accompanying activities.

The different forms that teacher-produced material can take clearly
have different practical implications — in terms, that is, of design,
production, cost and copyright problems. (See the appendix to this
section for information on copyright.) But they can also have different implications for teaching approach and classroom organization.

To illustrate:
We can take as an example two different functions which teacher-
produced materials might have in a series of lessons on 'Animals'.

(A) Class A is introduced to the topic through a teacher-led discussion on pets. Then the class reads a short story featuring pets. Subsequently the pupils are all given the same worksheet describing an
activity (perhaps writing an account of personal experience) which
all pupils undertake. The same process is repeated in different ways
in subsequent lessons as the class moves through aspects of the topic.
In this case the series of worksheets simply provides written confir-
mation of what the teacher announces as the activity; the worksheets
spell out the activity and act as a reference point for pupils. The
pupils take on the activity as it comes to them, working in parallel

with one another at roughly the same pace.

(B)   Class B is introduced to the topic through a questionnaire which invites pupils to declare their attitudes to animals. The issues raised are then aired up in a general class discussion. Subsequently the pupils are given an A4 booklet in which information and activities on different aspects of the topic are presented. The booklet offers a number of ways into the topic and styles of working on it. The pupils are asked to work in pairs and select a page of the booklet they want to work from; they can call on other duplicated material if required. In this case the teacher-produced booklet acts as the teacher's agent in setting up and supporting a range of different activities in the classroom.

Obviously the form of the material does not *determine* the teaching approach and the organization of the classroom. It is possible to take material designed to fulfil one function and use it in a different way — simply, for example, by conducting a whole-class lesson on one page of a booklet designed to involve pupil choice of starting points and activities. Nevertheless it is helpful to think clearly about what the preferred function of the teacher-made material is to be before getting deep into production.

3. DOES IT MAKE SENSE?

Whatever the intended function of the material, the critical matter is the intelligibility and 'workability' of any activities which the sheet or booklet proposes the pupils should undertake. Coursebooks in English have been regularly criticized for the kinds of activities which they expect pupils to do and for the unimaginative, incoherent, and occasionally absurd ways in which these activities can be framed.

Teacher-produced worksheets or booklets are not immune from problems to do with the way activities are framed and worded for pupils. The problems are illustrated below in wordings taken from two different worksheets of activities based on the poem 'The Hangman' (a long narrative poem which tells the story of how a mysterious executioner steadily depopulates a town).

WORKSHEET A	WORKSHEET B
Is the activity worth doing?	
Make a list of the first four people to be hung by the hangman. Explain why they were hung and write down the excuses given by the hangman.	Imagine you are a newspaper reporter working in the town. Write the story you would hand into your paper at the end of the second day of the hangman's visit.
Will they understand it?	
What do you imagine to be the symbolic relationship between the growth of the gallows and the hangman's progress? How effective is this image?	As the hangman executes more of the town's folk, the gallows gets bigger. Why has the poet described the way the gallows grows? Does the image of a huge gallows affect the way you imagine the hangman?
Is the activity manageable?	
Get into groups of four or five and discuss the problem of racial prejudice and discrimination in the world today using the poem as a starting point. Someone in the group should make notes of your discussion.	When you have both finished writing discuss these questions with your neighbour: 1) Is the poet trying to teach us a lesson with this poem? 2) If you think so, what could it be?

Dead Birds

Have you ever seen, heard, touched, or in any way been involved with a dead bird? Perhaps you have heard a friend (or a complete stranger) speak of one? Describe to the rest of the class the circumstances surrounding your discovery of it, its appearance, and your demeanour, feelings and attitudes (including your attitude to death in general). Use a clear voice and speak in complete sentences. Make sure each one begins and ends with a full stop and a capital letter. Take care in distinguising between *facts* and *opinions*, and remember to use some of the vivid words you have met in this book.

When your teacher tells you, read the following poem.

A DEAD BIRD

Bollards —

This is the landscape of pylons:

lamp-posts parade concretely, oily tarmacadam sweats profusely.

Here, in the land of petroleum fumes and litter baskets, lies a bird once exotic, now squashed.
Its fire-plumed strut is done,
the full-throated warble,
echoing once of the enchanting free,
is silent. The gutter glories.
I ache, and am otherness.

FOR INTERPRETATION

1. What are 'pylons'? When do you sweat profusely?
2. In your own words give the meaning of the phrase 'fire-plumed strut'. See if you can walk around the classroom in this manner.
3. Write a letter to the poet (or phone him if you have his number) saying what you think about the alliteration in this poem.
   (*Alliteration* is the sound that words make when they sound like one another.)

FOR LANGUAGE STUDY: PUZZLE IT OUT

1. Put apostrophes in various places in this sentence:
   The drivers cars whose fenders strike birds wings mustntve, mustntve they?
2. *One* of the words below is *not* a vivid word. Can you spot it?
   (You could work with someone near you on this.)

   vivisection   migratory   sparrow   exterminate

   Now: use the three vivid words in a sentence of your own. (Avoid the use of 'gertcha'.)

FOR WRITING

1. Use the evidence in the poem to write two newspaper accounts of the discovery of a dead bird.
   (a) as it might have appeared in the Stop Press columns of an evening paper and employing not more than three words (e.g., Dead Bird Found);
   (b) as it might have appeared in a 'sensational' newspaper, with banner headlines, interviews with angry local residents, "sob stories" etc.
2. Why is the decline in bird-fatalities *not* explained away by the increase in population since 1938? Present your opinion in the form of a factual essay, avoiding any vivid words you have met in this book.

FOR MORE WRITING

3. A creed is a statement of beliefs — often religious beliefs. Spend some time jotting down notes on the conduct of birds of all ages. Decide which aspects of their behaviour you approve of and disapprove of. Then, imagining you are a bird (a group could imagine they were a *flock* of birds, or a *skein* of geese) write your own personal statement, beginning, "I believe . . . " (Each belief should be a complete sentence.)

4. A friend of yours is ill in hospital, and must remain there for some time. You are sending him three parcels of books to read. Write the letter in which you tell him what the books will be, and why you have chosen them. Do *not* mention dead birds, as to do so may upset him (or her).

FOR VISUAL AWARENESS

This is a painting by Albrecht Durer called 'Dead Bird'.

1. Can you think of another title for this painting?
2. Durer painted this picture using *colours*. Can you work out what *colours* he used?
3. The painting hangs in the Graphische Sammlung Museum in Vienna. Ask your teacher if you can visit this museum. (You should check first that the painting is not out on temporary loan to another museum.)

ACTING OUT

Improvise a scene in which a roadsweeper discovers that a bird which he thought was dead turns out to be merely stunned (or, if you like, in which a bird which he thought was merely stunned turns out to be dead).

You may, if you wish, take the part of the bird or of the roadsweeper's broom — in which case you should use fewer vivid words than is normally necessary.

FOR TOPIC WORK

Collect and record information on *one* of the following topics. You can, if you wish, make a special book on the subject you choose. Mounted and exhibited, your work could be of great interest to others.

A. The Right Attitude to Dead Birds. (Find out about this form local bird-finders, from their assistants, or from trainee bird-finders who have recently left school.)

B. Opportunities for Finding Out about Dead Birds in Your Area. (Study the local pattern of distribution — has Britain's membership of the EEC made an appreciable difference? Compare night findings with day findings. Interview those engaged in the training of bird-removers; you may, with your teacher's permission, harrass and abuse people indifferent to birds' welfare.)

175

There is no simple solution to the problems of addressing pupils in print; and there is certainly no single way of doing it. Many children, especially at the lower end of secondary school, are unaccustomed to making use of print for the purpose of guiding their own work. This means that careful thought has to be given in the preparation of teacher-made materials to the way activities are described so that confusion and uncertainty is reduced to a minimum. One way of thinking through these difficulties is for the teacher to imagine that s/he is talking in print to one of the more unconfident pupils in the class. This may help to keep the style simple and informal, and to produce clear ways into the activities, with useful advice and helpful reminders.

4. DOES IT LOOK GOOD?

If teachers are to be encouraged to produce original material they must have the facilities to present them in an attractive way. The problems which arise when pupils are trying to decipher tatty, colourless, illegible worksheets are at least as harmful as those presented by poor coursebooks. The business of reprographics is considered in detail in *Laying Out and Running Off* (English Centre). It's not just a question of typing and of duplicating equipment and costings; it's also a matter of lay-out, lettering and illustration, for which some items of specialized equipment are required (they can be bought from a good art design shop):
  — a drawing board (with true right angles), T-square and set square;
  — long scissors, scalpel (for detailed cutting out), metal ruler;
  — Rotring 0.35 (or similar) pen (for drawing lines and boxes);
  — Rotring (or similar) plastic stencils and Letraset (for lettering);
  — good quality cartridge paper, cow gum and spatulas, liquid tippex, masking tape, transparent ruler (preferably with lines down the middle to register distances).

Some elementary expertise is needed in using this lay-up equipment — and not everyone is equally gifted in the art of designing attractive materials. Clearly it's useful if one or two members of the department can turn themselves into advisers for the others. If the school has a media resources officer (as all ILEA secondary schools do) s/he should be able to provide valuable advice in this area — though many MROs prefer to be involved at an earlier stage than this in the preparation of materials. Some general points on presentation:
Format
The basic choice is between single sheets, or A4 or A5 booklets. Single sheets may be useful for isolated ideas and extracts, materials devised with a particular class in mind (e.g. in relation to a visit) and

so on. However, the life span of single sheets is not long; more importantly, their regular use may communicate a sense of the fragmentation of work in English. A5 or A4 booklets have a longer lifespan (especially if their covers are printed on thicker paper or card); children also have more respect for a booklet and doodle on them less readily. More importantly, they communicate a more coherent sense of the work in hand, and offer scope to a class for negotiation with the teacher over the choice of activity during any particular lesson. A4 booklets are easier to lay out and duplicate than A5: there are no problems of pagination or folding and they allow for most of the material to be typed or written straight onto a stencil or banda. However, their size and the way they are stapled gives them a shorter life than A5.

Consistency of lay-out
It helps to build on pupils' powers of prediction by having a consistent approach to the sequence of, for example, information and instruction. If each sheet or page is organized differently it is harder for pupils to know where to look for the bits that tell them what to do, or what use to make of the bits that offer new ideas and information. Subheadings are extremely useful here: they make it easier for children to return to the page and find their way around the material.

Space and illustration
Unless paper costs are a real worry, it's worth bearing in mind that pages look and read best when they are not overloaded with print. Short paragraphs, wide spacing and generous margins make the print seem more accessible and easy to tackle. Illustrations also help to break up the text and give a more friendly feel to the material; they can often give substance to an idea more succinctly than words.

5. CAN WE REPRODUCE IT EASILY?
In many schools (including most ILEA schools) reprographic equipment is provided as a central resource to be used by all departments and looked after by a media resources officer (in ILEA and elsewhere) and/or a technician paid for out of the school's capitation (as in ILEA's 'alternative use of resources' scheme (AUR)). The MRO or technician is responsible for the proper functioning of the machines and for buying paper and other necessary items, gives advice and help on design and production, and, in some cases, operates the machines as well. There are obvious advantages in having the full central system. It saves teachers' time and energy and the school's money: it increases the use made of teacher-designed materials and improves their quality; and the machinery is less likely to break down if reprographic work is entirely (or mainly) in the hands of one person. Even in a large school it makes it possible for requests for reprographic work to be met with-

in a short period by use of a simple booking procedure. (For suggestions on getting secretarial help with typing — which completes the picture — see 'Time, Space and Money'.)

If your school doesn't operate the full central system it's worth arguing for along with other departments who make heavy use of teacher-designed materials. Get the facts and figures from a local school which does have such a system and spell out the advantages. If you fail you will obviously need to take into account not only the cost of buying necessary machines for the department (possibly sharing them with other departments) but also the wear and tear on members of the department if they have to operate the machines themselves. A local teachers' centre may have facilities and expertise to cope with a limited amount of reprographic work; the printing department of a local FE college may be willing to take on some sophisticated reprographics as projects for students.

A centrally organized reprographic system needs the following equipment as a minimum:
  — spirit duplicator (banda);
  — stencil cutter;
  — ink duplicator;
  — photocopier
    (the new generation machines can produce good quality copy quickly and painlessly; the more sophisticated of these machines can do double-sided copies on plain paper, including A3 size paper for folded A4 booklets);
  — a collating machine;
  — an electric stapler.

Organizing the Department's Resources

When materials are in stock what system does the department use to store them, to make them available for maximum use and to get them back with minimum loss?

In this section there are descriptions of some common methods of organizing resources. Which method a particular department adopts will partly depend on such things as the size of the department, the geography of the school and the nature of the department's storage areas (and whether or not these can be improved); it will depend partly on how the responsibility for managing the system is allocated. But the method will also be related to the department's views on the teaching of the subject and to the expectations the department has (either consciously or unconsciously) of the way individual teachers should proceed on the business. It is important to establish:

- that there *is* a method;
- that all teachers know what it is;
- that it is a method which suits the department and its way of working;
- that it is carried out with some efficiency.

FOUR METHODS

METHOD 1: THE KLONDYKE RUSH

Under this arrangement the doors of the stock-cupboard are thrown open to all-comers in September. Teachers grab what they can and keep the stuff under lock and key in their own cupboards for the rest of the year. The teachers who get there first take not only their personal sure-fire winners but also anything which looks new and interesting which they might conceivably use during the year. Once the September rush is over, the stock-organizer has virtually nothing to do except check returns at the end of the year.

This method assumes an entirely individual way of working for teachers in the department. It does not encourage sharing and interchange of ideas; it encourages conservatism in the use of material. Since books lie idle in teachers' own cupboards for long periods of time it makes uneconomic use of the resources the department has. It is also unfair on those who miss the rush and find only a depleted set of *The Wind in the Willows* remaining after the others have taken their pick.

METHOD 2: IN-OUT/IN-OUT

Under this arrangement all the stock (perhaps with the exception of exam texts) is put on a temporary loan basis. All the stock is available to be taken out and returned immediately after use. One short story anthology can theoretically be used by 6 or 7 different teachers with different classes during the day.

This system does maximize the use of resources, and at least everything is there for people to see and to choose from. But it presupposes a central stock-room to which all teachers have easy access. It won't work if a number of teachers have to flog up two flights of stairs (and then find the person with the key) before they can take things out or put things back. It also means that pupils can't easily take books home for further reading or whatever; and, because teachers may not be quite sure if the books will be there for 3B's next lesson, it can lead to discontinuity in teaching. Another disadvantage is the wear and tear on the books going in and out of classrooms and stockrooms; here the maximum usage principle increases the likelihood of losses. (This method also tends to lead to the Staffroom Windowsill Syndrome.)

METHOD 3: DUAL LOAN

A system of two types of loaning stock is established: termly or half-termly loan and temporary loan through a booking-out process. At the end of each half-term or term, teachers inform the person in charge of stock which books they wish to use with their classes the next half-term or full-term. The person responsible then tries to meet the requests and hands over the sets of books to the individual teacher who guarantees to return them at the end of the designated period. If two teachers require the same set, then it is possible for an arrangement to be made to share; if the demand for a particular set of books consistently outreaches supply, that is a pointer to buy more copies. Then there are the 'constant usage' books that are booked out only for a double or single period and returned to the shelves immediately after use; poetry anthologies, spelling aids, etc., may come into this category.

This method is a compromise between Klondyke and In-Out/In-Out. It means that all teachers can have a shot at using all the department's materials, provided that they plan in advance; the amount of to-ing and fro-ing is also reduced. But it requires efficiency on the part of the system organizer to make it work, and a willingness from all teachers to meet deadlines for handing over materials to others.

Annotated lists of the department's stock (i.e. not just the titles but a couple of sentences about the books) will of course help teachers to select from what is available, especially if the department and the stock is large. It may also help to set aside a reference collection of books held in quantity (as well as a collection of books which are specifically teacher-resource material) so that people can see what is available without rooting through the whole stockroom.

BEYOND DUAL LOAN

Properly administered, the dual loan method can ensure that teachers have access at the right time to the materials they want to use with a particular class. But it is based on the idea that teachers make their own individual decisions about what materials to use with a class and about how the various bits of a department's resources (anthologies, class readers, non-book and teacher-produced material and so on) can be combined together to make a year's work with a class. There are those who would see this complete freedom of choice as crucial to successful English teaching — and, certainly, classes taught by confident and inventive teachers may consistently benefit from their teachers' freedom to choose and combine materials in whatever way seems appropriate.

But to make this freedom of choice work for you requires time, imagination and full knowledge of what is available. It means being able to construct, say, a unit of work on 'Animals' for a 2nd year by picking *this* story from an anthology to start with, by using *these* ideas from these four different source-books as the basis for small-group assignments, by linking *these* three poems together to raise particular issues and to illustrate three different ways of writing poems on animals . . . and so on. Inexperienced teachers, non-specialists with commitments elsewhere, and teachers who simply don't know the stock-cupboard, may be hard-pressed to use this freedom of choice — let alone to remember to put in the appropriate bookings for a number of different sets of material.

Complete and unsupported freedom of choice may not be much use to these teachers. It may also evaporate the energy and the expertise of other teachers in the department if they are obliged to construct a new curriculum for every class they take — while, at the same time, reducing the in-service possibilities that arise when teachers undertake similar work on the same set of materials.

METHOD 4: THE ORANGE-BOX

For these reasons many departments have found a collectively planned approach to the use of materials helpful to *all* teachers. That is, instead of leaving materials in 'free state' for individual teachers to make their choice from, the department decides to concentrate the majority of its resources into pre-arranged units.

The Orange-Box method is an example of this kind of collective planning of the use of materials.

Firstly a decision is made about 4-6 week units of work for each year and how they are intended to match the department's plans' for each year. Say 10 units: 6 topics ('Neighbourhoods', 'Playing with Words', etc) and 4 units based on agreed class readers for the year. Secondly decisions are made about what kinds of material need to be available on the topic or novel: e.g., a variety of source material, anthologies, slides and tapes, a booklet of activities addressed to the pupils, individual worksheets.

The next step is for all materials currently held (either centrally or by individual teachers) which are appropriate to the unit and the intended way of working to be put into the unit box (large library storage boxes or orange boxes, with plastic wallets or envelope folders for loose-leaf material). Additions come in two ways: a brainstorming department session, and the materials-orderer working systematically through publishers' catalogues to spot materials which might be useful. Once there is a reasonable amount and range of stuff in the boxes a member of department (or a specially formed squad) takes responsibility for knocking it into shape, throwing out the duff stuff, and writing an A4 sheet listing and annotating what's in it (including items like films which aren't in the physical box). Then two teachers agree to work through the unit with their classes, discuss it together, add further materials they have found, write (or rewrite) the pupils' booklet and/or worksheets and draw up an outline map of how the materials can be used.

At the end of this process the boxes will still be in a rough-and-ready state. There now needs to be a department review of how the units mesh together and to what extent they actually encourage the kinds of work the department agrees needs to be done in each year. After ironing these problems out, the process of adding materials and developing and sophisticating approaches can go on in earnest.

Naturally this doesn't mean that all materials go into a box. You still need a filing cabinet for one-off lessons; teachers can still hoard their emergency stuff; sets of plays and anthologies can be kept outside the system for flexible use.

The advantages of this system are:
— it makes available to everyone possible uses of the department's materials;
— good material (including audio-visual material) will get systematically used, rather than under-used or wrongly used;
— it provides an opportunity for shared development and reviewing of sequences of work.

LOSS OF LIBERTY?

The Orange-Box method goes beyond mere storage to the development of common departmental practices; it links with the use the department makes of teacher-produced materials and with syllabus-building from the ground floor up (as suggested in the earlier section on syllabus design). The advantages of the Orange-Box method in terms of developing shared approaches to teaching through the use of materials would seem to outweigh the possible loss of individual liberties. Furthermore, although there is an investment of time required to set up the system, there are also practical advantages for the resources-organizer:
— the materials-gathering effort can be focussed on a narrow range ('we need more stuff for these units') rather than spread over the whole range of possibilities;
— the stuff is all there in one box rather than lying in a number of places, so that the inevitable mess is at least contained and losses are easy to spot by reference to a contents list taped to the box;
— the administration of the booking system is simplified if

people are only required to say which units they will be using next term.

SPECIAL STORAGE PROBLEMS

AUDIO-VISUAL SOFTWARE

Most departments use audio-cassette tapes, rather than reel-to-reel, for both recording children's work and classroom playback. If you are sure you want to keep a particular cassette recording, knock out the square studs at the back to prevent accidental erasure. The problem with retaining both audio and video cassettes is the wastage of blank tape when you've got only 15 minutes of stuff worth keeping on a 60 minute tape. Dubbing onto another tape is time-consuming and loses quality; it's best to have a supply of 30 minute tapes to use to the limit. It's also worth getting into the routine of immediate labelling of cassettes you want to keep; it's surprising how quickly you can forget what it was you wanted to keep.

Slides are best kept in plastic wallets hanging in a filing cabinet for immediate visibility; some wallets have a useful additional pouch for storing accompanying notes. Numbering the slides with little stickers in the top right hand corner of the slide-holder (as it is received by the projector) saves a lot of palaver when you come to set them up.

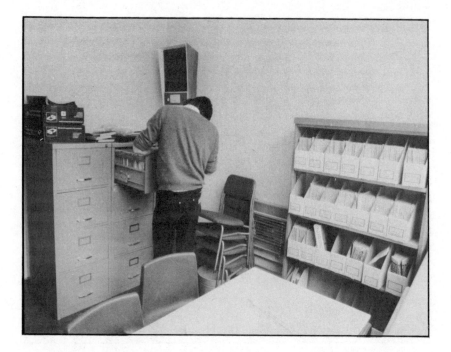

LOOSE-LEAF MATERIALS

Loose-leaf sheets can be something of a problem to store so that they are easily available for use. Labelled manilla envelope folders (of different colours for different categories) in a filing cabinet is the most effective way of storing sheets which are not related to a particular unit of work (sheets on technicalities and so on). Alternatively, plastic wallets kept in labelled upright library boxes are a handy way of storing such materials. Some departments which make heavy use of individual worksheets have developed their own indexing systems (using a list of 'features' and potential uses) to catalogue them. (An example of one department's indexing system is included as an appendix to this section.) Careful planning is needed to devise an effective but simple system like this; maintaining it also takes a lot of time and effort. Other departments may not need such a system — perhaps because they don't make sufficient use of loose-leaf material to warrant the effort. It's a good idea, in any case, to put a copy of each loose-leaf sheet into a master file to be kept in the stockcupboard for easy consultation — and to keep the original artwork somewhere safe.

KEEPING TRACK OF MATERIALS

Recording and keeping track of department materials shouldn't be an onerous business — but it frequently is. What the English department does about it will partly depend on what school policies are on matters such as issuing books to pupils to take home and stock-checking procedures. English departments, because of the attractiveness of at least some of their materials, are likely to suffer more than other departments in terms of stock loss (the question of losses from class libraries is a special case). The point at which stock loss becomes insupportable will vary from department to department; but since *any* expenditure from capitation on replacements of stock loss is wasteful, clearly even the most generously financed department needs to establish procedures which minimize loss — let's say keeping it at an average of under 10% per year. A number of well-worn procedures are worth considering — and, if agreed to, worth sticking to.

STOCK CONTROL PROCEDURES

1. Stamping etc. When new books come in they should be identified as belonging to the department. Many schools use printed labels stuck on the inside front cover; a large departmental rubber-stamp, made up locally, is quicker to apply and more effective. It's also useful to number the books at this stage and to log the full details (including ISBN, publisher and price) on a small filing card for easy checking and replacement. This is tiresome work which some pupils are said to enjoy.

2. Checking returns. It may be worth taping a small card with the title and quantity of a set of books onto the shelf area where it sits. This helps when checking the number of books that have come back, reduces the likelihood of books being piled just anywhere, and enables you to tell at a glance what's in and what's out. Some departments use special forms for teachers to record their takings and returnings; others swear by a large sheet on the back of the cupboard door. Where some variant of the Orange Box method is used, a list of the box's contents taped to the side provides a quick way of checking whether it's intact. This checking can be done by pupils in the class that's just finishing with the box.

3. The Depot. The Staffroom Windowsill Syndrome cannot be eradicated whatever the system. Returning books to the stockcupboard between last period and a staff meeting has a low place on the priority list. Accept the syndrome: establish a large cardboard box in the staffroom, squarely marked 'English Dept. Depot', for people to fling things in.

4. The classic nuisance. The issuing of books for pupils to take home is the locus classicus of stock loss. Pinter-like scenes featuring argument as to whether missing copies of *Ten Great Detective Stories* have or have not been returned are played out in the nation's classrooms daily. Many systems have been developed to overcome the problem. The oldest remains the least unsuccessful: entering the number of the book next to the pupil's name in a markbook and crossing it off when it comes back. If it doesn't come back keep making a nuisance of yourself; avoid the use of comments about the collapse of civilization as we know it when the amount involved is less than £1.50. If it still doesn't come back you might try a note to the form teacher. Some schools operate a deposit system against the return of books across the board; others have a yearly amnesty for prodigal books.

All this is a nuisance; the nuisance may be light when weighed in the balance against the use which most pupils make of books when they are able to take them home.

5. **Equipment control.** Audio-visual equipment like cassette recorders and projectors may be kept in a central school pool and distributed from there. If the department does have its own equipment it is essential that it is properly logged, that the equipment number

and school name is scratched or burned onto the item, and that
rigorous control of its whereabouts is maintained. It helps if the
item is kept in its packing case so that leads and other bits and pieces
stay with it. A regular check of equipment is necessary not only to
see that it still exists but also to ensure that it still works and is safe
to use.

6. **Annual stock-checks.** Some schools insist on frequent and formal
stock-checks when everyone is supposed to spend hours preparing a
report which accounts for missing pencil sharpeners. Others leave
departments to devise appropriate stock-check procedures of their
own. Once a year is quite enough for a full stock-check when everything is returned to the stockroom and lined up in rows. (Don't
count *101 Dalmatians*; they're all still there.) A few suggestions for
this business:

- if the ISBN and price of books have been listed on a card-
  index system when they come in new, then the number
  missing can be recorded on the same card and the re-order
  made from the information on it;
- assign a group of pupils to conduct a sweep of the school,
  including all the nooks and crannies they know about, and
  bring back anything that looks like an English book;
- remember that, after you've finished, nobody in the department wants an updated definitive stock-list which includes
  Three Men in a Boat and BBC *Stop, Look and Listen* pamphlets circa 1958; they would prefer a briefly annotated list
  of relevant stuff categorized according to the department's
  scheme of use.

Class Libraries

**What arrangements are to be made within the department for the
selection, supply and organization of books for independent reading?**

Many English departments would see the provision of books for
independent reading (as well as the time within English lessons to
read them) as a matter of the highest priority, bearing in mind what
we know, on the one hand, about the importance of fluent, confident reading in school and outside it, and what we know, on the other
hand, about the relative decline in the popularity of reading for
pleasure among pupils during the secondary years. Providing access
within English lessons to books in sufficient range and quantity is
only a part of a policy to encourage independent reading: other
issues for a department to consider include making time available
for reading to take place, the need for the promotion of reading and
books, and the role of the school library and the school bookshop.

But this section considers only the resource implications of an English department's commitment to keeping children in contact with reading for pleasure as part of its own programme.

Organizing the supply of books for use in independent reading lessons in English is a particularly time-consuming business; it is a responsibility which two people in a department might share or revolve once the team as a whole has committed itself to taking the business seriously. The responsibility involved the following tasks, some of which may be devolved to willing pupils.

FINANCING THE INITIAL STOCK

The number of books to be made available will be determined largely by how much the department can commit to this kind of spending. A head of department should be able to make a special claim for money from the school capitation (and perhaps PTA funds) to finance stock for independent reading, since the advantages of encouraging it will be felt throughout the school. But even paperback books for children are expensive items, averaging (in 1982) nearly £1.00 each. Assuming that the department is starting to build up a supply of books for class libraries more or less from scratch, it may be necessary to phase the buying over a number of years.

Our estimate is that 2.5 books per pupil (i.e. 75 books for a full class of 30) is the bare minimum for a class library; 4 books per pupil is a more adequate figure to aim at to ensure that a reasonable choice is made available to pupils in a mixed class with a full range of reading interests and abilities. The number of books which need to be bought will also be affected by decisions on how the use of class libraries is to be arranged (see below); a figure of 3 books per pupil may be thought adequate, for example, if there is going to be sharing or a regular exchange of books between classes.

SELECTING THE BOOKS

Obviously there needs to be discussion within the department about the kinds of books which are going to be included in class libraries. It's worth drawing up a rough table showing how the balance between different kinds of fiction books (different, that is, in terms of length, difficulty, genre/type, setting, main characters and preoccupations) should be built for a particular set of books.

Although paperback fiction is the normal mainstay of class library stock, the department may also consider it worthwhile including at least some of these kinds of material:
  — general interest information books;
  — collections of poetry;

- autobiographical and other material produced by community publishers;
- books in languages other than English which are represented in the school;
- writing by children in the school informally published in booklet form;
- material which is only available in hardback;
- light reading/ephemera of the kind which is available in general bookshops.

Some of this kind of material might be kept in separate boxes and shared between classes so that it is not spread too thinly. It's also worth considering having more than one copy of selected fiction titles available in each box so that pupils in the same class can read the same book together and subsequently do some follow-up work on the book. (These books for group reading might be selected to relate thematically to class readers.)

SOURCES OF INFORMATION

In order to add to their own knowledge of books worth buying (i.e. because they are decent, challenging and likely to be popular) teachers responsible for choosing the books might consult:
- the school librarian, the local children's librarian and the LEA library service;
- the school's remedial department;
- a local bookshop with a good children's section (if there is one: see the list produced by the Booksellers Association (154 Buckingham Palace Rd., London SW1W 9TZ));
- neighbouring schools known to have a commitment to the provision of class libraries;
- lists of books produced or distributed by organizations like the Centre for Children's Books at the National Book League (Book House, 45 East Hill, London SW18 2QZ), the School Library Association (Victoria House, 29-31 George Street, Oxford OX1 2AY), the Youth Libraries Group of the Library Association (7 Ridgmount St., London WC1E 7AE), the Federation of Worker Writers and Community Publishers (c/o Centerprise, 136 Kingsland High Street, London E8 2MS), and by LEA advisory services;
- back issues of journals which review children's books (see below; the Centre for Children's Books is one place to consult these);
- the annotated catalogues produced by publishers of children's books (see below) and by educational publishers who publish texts as part of their English lists.

Full lists of sources of information about children's books are given in *Finding Out About Children's Books* (part of the Open University Inset pack 'Children, Language and Literature', OU Press) and *Children's Books: An Information Guide* (Centre for Children's Books, see above).

This initial scouting around to establish a basic class library collection takes a lot of effort and time; but doing it thoroughly is the only way of ensuring that there will be books in class libraries which children in the school will want to read. It's a good idea to requisition this basic stock (or whatever part of it can be afforded in any one year) as a bulk order (with full LEA discount) so that the books arrive more or less together and a definite start to class library use can be made at the beginning of a year. The basic collection can be augmented by dispersing sets of books no longer required as class readers and by asking pupils to bring in (or perhaps sell to the department) useful unwanted books from home.

AUDIO-TAPE READINGS

Having readings of stories available on audio-tape can prove extremely helpful — particularly (though not exclusively) to pupils who find reading difficult; these enable readers to follow what are perhaps demanding texts while they are read at reasonable speed. Some departments (or school librarians) have taken the trouble of producing their own tapes, requesting publishers' permission to do so and using 6th form, staff and parent readers. A number of series on BBC Schools Radio regularly include extended readings of complete stories and substantial extracts which can be recorded and re-used within the copyright period. Some books in series produced by educational publishers (like Longman's 'Knockouts' and 'Imprint' series, Heinemann's 'Graded Reader' series and ILEA Learning Materials Service's primary series 'Share-a-Story') have accompanying cassette readings.

In addition, there are a number of commercial firms who produce audio-tape series (mainly on cassette). Most of these series are aimed at the domestic rather than the educational market; the majority feature largely either books for young children (fairy tales, Beatrix Potter, *Paddington Bear* and so on) or classic novels for adult readers. The texts are normally not provided with the tapes and the readings of adult books are often abridged (with no note of exactly how). Nevertheless, the following series are worth investigating for appropriate material — the easiest way to do so is through a public library which has a good audio section.

Argo: The Decca Record So., Decca House, Albert Embankment, London SE1 7SW.
Caedmon: Teakfield Ltd., 1 Westmead, Farnborough, Hants.
Chivers Audio Books: 93-100 Locksbrook Rd., Bath.

Colophone Cassettes: Audio-Visual Library Services, 10-12 Powdrake Rd., Grangemough, Stirlingshire FK3 9UT.
Listen for Pleasure: Music for Pleasure Ltd., 80 Blyth Rd., Hayes, Middx.
Pinnacle Storytellers: Pinnacle Electronics Ltd., Electron House, Cray Ave., St. Mary Cray, Orpington, Kent BR5 3QJ.
Talking Tapes: The Talking Tape Co., 186 Fulham Rd., London SW10.
Times Cassettes: Ivan Berg Associates, 35A Broadhurst Gardens, London NW6
Tellastory: Bartlett Bliss Productions Ltd., 39 Warwick Gardens, London W14 8PH.
Weston Woods: 14 Friday St., Henley-on-Thames RG9 1PZ.

Obviously a headphone set is needed with the cassette player if children are going to make use of tape readings in a full classroom. The use of a 'group listening unit' (simply a junction box connected to the player which feeds two, four or six sets of headphones) can make the reading available to more than one pupil.

MAKING THE BOOKS AVAILABLE

Most teachers prefer to have their own sets of books which they can then use with classes at will, perhaps swopping sets halfway through the year. Some reduction in the number of books required is possible if books are made into sets suitable for use by 1st and 2nd year classes together, by 3rd year classes alone, and by 4th - 6th year classes together. This three-part division bears some relationship to changes in patterns of reading interest through the secondary years — though other arrangements are of course possible. Where the school's geography and timetable makes it feasible, it may be thought advisable for teachers to share the same set of books for independent reading across classes in the same year. There might be one mobile class library cupboard kept in the stockroom for use by all 1st year classes, for instance, and booked in advance by different teachers. Alternatively, some departments have chosen to equip one of their major teaching rooms as a 'reading room' in which all available books are on display and which all 1st and 2nd year classes visit in turn; the disadvantage of this set-up is its formality and the fact that it to some extent duplicates the school library.

STORAGE

Where teachers have their own set of books these can be supplied to them in special cardboard 'library boxes', in wooden boxes, in shallow trays designed to slide into and out of cupboards, on lockable shelves or on library trolleys. It is worth giving some thought to the storage of books, especially if the classrooms English teachers use are not normally locked between lessons and if sets of books need to be moved from classroom to classroom fairly regularly. Equipment catalogues feature a variety of book storage equipment available from library suppliers and are worth investigating; but the

storage items may be either unsuitable or too expensive. One ILEA
English department gave a 'contract' for the design and construction
of book-boxes to a 5th year woodwork group and duly received a
consignment of shallow, partitioned wooden boxes with lockable
lids, painted in a variety of colours to identify boxes for particular
years.

KEEPING TRACK

Any teacher who has been responsible for organizing class libraries
is aware that the loss of books is a real problem. They disappear.
Opinions differ on what constitutes an acceptable rate of loss. A
small survey of ILEA schools shows figures for book-box loss
ranging from 5% to 35% a year, with an average of around 15%. The
figure seems to be higher where the children are older and where
they are encouraged to take books home regularly; the books which
disappear tend to be the most popular ones. While some degree of
philosophical acceptance of book loss is reasonable, clearly any rate
of loss is high when money is tight — and if the stock is decimated
the whole idea of reading for pleasure can fizzle out for want of
material. The following suggestions may help to minimize losses:

— make a stock-check list for each box, putting one copy into
the box in transparent plastic folder and keeping another
copy in a central file;
— stock-checking is made a great deal easier if all books are
clearly numbered (on the back cover or inside front cover)
with a permanent marker; numbers can then be checked off
against numbers on a list;
— label the books with a large-size school or department
rubber-stamp or sticker;
— cover the books with transparent adhesive plastic; although
this takes time, it protects the numbering and stamping and
makes the books less attractive as personal possessions and
more identifiable as school property — as well as extending
the life of a paperback book by a factor of at least five;
— insist that all teachers try to adhere to a simple procedure
for recording when books are taken out (one at a time!) and
returned; if the books are numbered a sheet of squared
paper will do for each class, with the number being entered
when the book goes out and crossed off when it's returned;
some teachers may prefer a small card-index system which
can double as a quick record of reading;
— ask each teacher to ask a pupil to do a stock-check on the
class bookbox at regular intervals (half-termly, termly or
half-yearly) and return the results to H.Q.; thereafter,
institute an amnesty for books unaccounted for; where books

are accounted for but still stay at home enlist the aid of the form teacher with a pleading pro-forma note; suggest that miscreants don't take any more books home until the missing one re-appears.

ADDING NEW BOOKS

A simple system of recording ins and outs also has a useful function in the procedure for re-ordering books and adding new stock. By checking through class lists it is possible to assess which books are worth replacing or worth buying extra copies of, and which kinds of books are most popular with particular years. A simple questionnaire which asks a sample of pupils to make suggestions for books and kinds of books which might be added can also provide valuable information. (Some teachers might want to involve their classes even more directly in the buying of new books by taking them to a bookshop with some local purchase money in hand.)

The regular injection of new books is clearly essential to maintain the interest of readers — although a certain amount can be done by organizing the exchange of current stock between book-boxes. Referring to publishers' announcements is one way of deciding which new books to buy; publishers of children's books are generally willing to mail these announcements to schools. These are the main net paperback children's books imprints:

Armada/Lions: Fontana Paperbacks, 14 St. James's Place, London SW1A 1PS. 493-7070.
Beaver: Hamlyn Publishing Group, Astronaut House, Hounslow Rd., Feltham, Middx. 741-4441.
Carousel: Transworld Publishers, Century House, 61-63 Uxbridge Rd., Ealing, London W5. 579-2652.
Dragon: Granada Publishing, PO Box 9, 29 Frogmore, St. Albans, Herts. 0727-72727.
Fanfares: Faber & Faber, 3 Queen's Square, London WC1N 3AU. 278-6881.
Grasshopper: Abelard-Schuman, Furnival House, 14-18 High Holborn, London WC1V 6BX. 242-5832.
Hippo: Scholastic Publications, 161 Fulham Rd., London SW3 6SW. 581-0241.
Knight: Hodder & Stoughton Children's Books, 47 Bedford Square, London WC1. 636-9851.
Magnet: Methuen & Co., 11 New Fetter Lane, London EC4P 4EE. 583-9855.
Piccolo: Pan Books, Cavaye Place, London SW10 9PG. 373-6070.
Puffin: Penguin Books, Harmondsworth, Middx. UB7 0DA. 759-5722.
Sparrow: Hutchinson Educational, 3 Fitzroy Square, London W1P 6JD. 387-2888.
Target: Wyndham Publishers, 44 Hill St., London W1X 8LB. 493-6777.

It's also worth looking at the English catalogues of educational publishers (see the list earlier in this section) to find new additions to their non-net fiction lists and to 'remedial' and 'reluctant reader' series.

TED - M

In addition — or perhaps as an alternative — a good children's department in a local bookshop (if there is one) normally buys in copies of most new paperback books. A regular trip (say, once a month) to buy new books from the shelf can save a good deal of time — and is a particularly good idea if the bookshop is able to offer some form of discount to a regular school purchaser. Bookshops don't usually carry non-net fiction produced by educational publishers.

REVIEWING JOURNALS

It is also a good idea to refer to journals which review children's books so as to make an informed judgement of what's new that's worth buying. There are a number of journals, of which the ones listed below are perhaps the most appropriate. It is normal for the school library to have a subscription to journals like these.

Books for Keeps:
6 issues a year, £3.90 p.a.; published by The School Bookshop Association (1 Effingham Rd., Lee, London SE12 8NZ). Reviews net books in hardback and paperback for children of all ages.
Children's Book Bulletin:
3 issues a year, £1.80 p.a.; published by the Children's Rights Workshop (4 Aldebert Terrace, London SW8 1BH). Coverage of books for children of all ages which are non-sexist and reflect the values and ways of life of ethnic groups and working class people; includes selected non-net books of interest to teachers in a variety of subjects.
Recent Children's Fiction:
2 issues a year, £1.00 p.a.; published by the Avon and Gloucestershire Teachers' Children's Books Group (c/o Iain Ball, Senior Adviser for English, Avon House North, St. James' Barton, Bristol BS99 7EB). Covers a selection of net books in hardback and paperback for all ages.
The School Librarian:
4 issues a year, £10.00 p.a. (includes membership of SLA); published by the School Library Association (Victoria House, 29-31 George St., Oxford OX1 2AY). Covers net hardback books and original paperbacks for all ages.
The English Magazine:
3 issues a year, £3.00 p.a.; published by the ILEA English Centre (Sutherland St., London SW1W 0PX). Reviews a selection of net and non-net fiction in paperback and cheaper hardback for secondary age children.

Consumable Stock

What kinds of consumable stock do teachers in the department want

to be able to use?

The range of consumable stock which the English department has available for pupils to use can make a real difference to classroom work and to the way children see the business of writing. The commitment to encouraging interest, care and a sense of satisfaction in a variety of kinds of writing, some of which is to be shown to readers other than the teacher, doesn't sit comfortably with the demand that children write everything in the same anonymous 10x8 exercise book. So it's worth the department discussing what different formats for writing it could provide for teachers and children to choose from. These could include:

— manilla folders with laces;
— simple hardback ring-binder folders;
— plain and lined paper of different sizes;
— sheets of coloured paper for making into stapled booklets of different sizes;
— 'cuttings' books as ready-made display booklets;
— A4 size exercise books and rough books as well as the standard 10x8;
— small 'memo' books for use as personal dictionaries;
— sugar paper and card for wall displays;
— simple clipboards (with elastic bands or bulldog clips);
— banda masters and carbons for instant classroom duplication of pupils' work.

It's also worth ensuring that every teacher has got a decent supply of all the stationery bits and pieces which get called for in English lessons: scissors, staplers, hole-punchers, stencil lettering plates, felt pens, adhesive labels, adhesive cellophane, glue and sellotape, rulers and drawing aids, liquid tippex (if permitted), a gross of spare pens . . . If items like these are stationed in a handy box in a classroom cupboard mundane requests to the teacher are likely to be reduced by at least 25%. Consider, too, the possibility of designing special labels and contents sheets which pupils can use for folders and books; the effect of having items like these available is quite out of proportion to the effort they take to make.

Ordering (whether done centrally or departmentally) and distributing consumable stock is a pleasant task for someone in the department, involving a few happy hours with the LEA equipment catalogue and at a local stationery shop. Keeping copies of LEA requisition forms (and of re-ordering numbers when items are bought locally) saves you having to go through the whole business again next year (including deciding among 8 different tensile strengths of bands (rubber) listed in the catalogue).

APPENDIX

THE ILEA REQUISITION SYSTEM

It is sensible to use the requisition system (rather than 'local purchase') where possible — both for its convenience and for the discount (14% on books). It requires a number of different forms, obtainable from the school office, which are sent eventually to different depots (Tottenham Hale for AV equipment, Southfields for stationery, books and office equipment).

The forms go to the school secretary who deducts the sum from the department capitation and then forwards them to School Equipment Division (DE13) who deduct the sum from the whole school capitation. If there is a query the forms may be referred to DE16; otherwise they go to the appropriate depot who then deliver to the school. If you feel there has been an unusual delay in delivery, check with school secretary that the order went off and then phone the appropriate depot, quoting premises code and order number and date of order.

For books, use the form which gives space for ISBN (10 figures, initial 0 plus publisher's 3 figure prefix plus series and book identifier plus checking digit) and for the title; having the title helps to check arrival of books. The price is also required, but this is re-checked at the depot so what you think you've spent and what you've actually spent may not exactly tally. The incoming books will be accompanied by a pink delivery note which also indicates books you haven't been sent because they are out-of-print or out-of-stock.

For all other orders refer to the GLC Supplies Catalogue (a large brown folder for which periodical updatings are sent) copies of which are jealously guarded in the office. If the item has a stock number it means it's stored at the depot and the only communication you will get back is the green delivery note which comes with the goods. If the item is marked 'D' in the catalogue it means it's not held at the depot and has to be ordered from an outside contractor; you should get a blue or green advice note at about the same time as the firm are sent the top copy in the form of an official order.

NET/NON-NET BOOKS

The most noticeable difference between net and non-net books is that net books are for sale in local bookshops and have prices printed on them. Non-net books are mainly educational textbooks which, because of the minimal discount offered to retailers by their publishers (i.e. 17½% as opposed to 25 - 50%) are not stocked in bookshops. Although bookshops can obtain them for you the mark-up they have to put on them to make a reasonable profit means that it is cheaper to order them from the publisher (via the LEA central purchasing system for further discount).

EXAMPLES OF CHECKLISTS ON TEACHING MATERIALS

1.   A checklist of questions to consider when buying a poetry anthology.

Do you want an anthology which:
- has the poems arranged in themes?
- contains a reasonable number of 'classics' from the past?
- contains a reasonable number of experimental forms?
- shows an awareness of dialect and the speaking voice?
- is attractively and relevantly illustrated with photographs or drawings?
- has a sufficient quantity of poems to enable grouping for specific purposes (e.g. theme, style, form, etc.)?
- specifies a poetry course (with teachers' notes)?

2. A checklist of questions on novels for whole class reading.

Do you want a book which:
  — features characters whose sex or cultural background or social background reflects the make-up of the class?
  — deals with issues of personal concern to pupils?
  — is set in another country or in another time?
  — might help pupils to develop a greater awareness of social and moral concerns?
  — reflects adult genres (like horror, romance, mystery, humour, etc.)?
  — presents opportunities in terms of themes or units of work (e.g. friendship, autobiography, etc.)?
  — is a short read and can easily be read by pupils on their own?
  — presents opportunities for linking to further private reading?

COPYRIGHT

The laws of copyright are complex but what teachers need to know is straightforward.

1. Copyright lasts for 50 years from the death of a writer. Copyright on the typography of books published since 1957 lasts for 25 years, irrespective of whether the text is copyright. Copyright also covers illustrations in books.
2. Single copies of copyright material may be made by individuals for private study provided that not more than a 'reasonable proportion' is copied (usually up to 10% of the whole work).
3. Multiple copies should not be made without the prior permission of the publisher. (Negotiations have been taking place towards a system under which LEAs would buy limited rights for their schools to make multiple copies under certain conditions. Agreement has not yet been reached.)

LOOSE LEAF MATERIALS: AN INDEXING SYSTEM

This example of an organization and retrieval system was devised by an ILEA school. The system can also handle tapes, slides and videotapes. Books, pamphlets and packs of materials do not lend themselves to this system of numbering and are stored on shelves or in labelled pamphlet boxes.

ACCESSIONING
Material going in is recorded on a 'Feature Slip', a pro-forma on which a series of categories are printed. The item is given an accession number. Then:
  — three index cards are made up from the information on the Feature Slip to go into (1) thematic index, (2) an author/title index, and (3) an audio-visual index;
  — the item of material has its number typed on or is labelled and stored;
  — the Feature Slip is put in a ring-binder folder;
  — two copies of typed/duplicated material are placed in (1) a single copy folder and (2) a year/course folder;
  — stencils are numbered and stored in stencil holding boxes.

RETRIEVAL
Reference to any individual item can be found in either any one of the three card indexes or either of the single copy folders.

The Depart- ment & the School

The Department & the School

The School in Mind

The 'thinking school' is a recent addition to the list of catchphrases thrown into the arena of educational debate. It is used to describe schools in which all members of staff work together to seek solutions to those problems which they define as being of the highest priority. So far this book has been about the organization of one department within a school, but the existence of separate departments in a school tends to disguise the potential links between them and the role that they collectively play in shaping the whole curriculum which pupils experience in the course of their school life.

This chapter focusses on the various issues which the English department has to take on board if it is to contribute effectively to the life of the whole school. This process has been catalysed in recent years by the dissemination of ideas about language across the curriculum which has made English departments in particular reflect on what they have to offer and learn from other subjects. This initiative has been closely followed by other whole school developments such as multicultural education and equal opportunities education; both of which have filtered into schools from social policy-making at a local authority level to meet up with an existing set of concerns about race and sex with which classroom teachers have been involved for the last decade. Hopefully, the English department will take a positive, if not a leading role in dissolving the barriers which have divided teachers and inhibited collective discussions about what the school has to offer its pupils, their parents and the local community. This role will engage the department in different levels of activity: from the formulation of 'high priorities' for the whole school curriculum to rethinking everyday matters like the school bookshop, parents evenings and school publications.

Language Across the Curriculum

The language across the curriculum movement grew out of English teachers' attempts in the late 1960's to observe and analyse what actually happens in classrooms in the many interactions between pupil and pupil and teacher and pupil. The idea first emerged as something you could get hold of in *Language, the Learner and the School* (Barnes, Rosen and Britton for the London Association for the Teaching of English, Penguin 1969). The blurb on the back cover pointed readers in the right direction: 'What can we learn about learning by looking at language in classrooms?'. In other words the emphasis was to be on learning rather than language. The decision of LATE to publish its 'manifesto' was in a sense political: it wanted to influence other departments in the secondary school and to re-vitalise the way they talked to one another about children's learning.

The flavour of the document was pleasantly fresh and many LATE and NATE members were inspired to broach the issue in schools. There are now, in various publications, first-hand accounts of the pitfalls, problems, short-cuts and break-throughs which met these early attempts to hold discussions with other colleagues about actual classroom practice rather than about school administration. Moreover most schools which really managed to get immersed in the issue discovered that they were discussing not only learning and language, but also relationships in school and assumptions about schooling. In other schools, however, the complexity of the issue was resolved by sticking to superficial aspects of language — aspects which tended to signify 'control' rather than the development of learning. This latter approach tended to generate vocabulary lists and papers on the presentation of written work.

BULLOCK'S FIVE PAGES

The publication of the Bullock Report in 1975 amplified these developments. In fact the five pages on LAC in Bullock was probably responsible for more action in secondary schools than the rest of the 500 pages put together. Several LEAs circulated schools asking for their 'Language Policy' — a strategy which implied that LAC was something which could be committed to paper for once and for all. But even this approach to LAC seemed to get some fruitful working party discussions under way in schools. There had been a great deal of curriculum development (in separate subjects and in integrated courses) over the previous ten years and teachers were obviously prepared to begin sharing their problems and difficulties.

THE COMMITTEE ON LANGUAGE ACROSS THE CURRICULUM

Are you daunted by the prospect of working out a single Language Policy which takes into account all shades of opinion? We offer below one school's imaginative solution to this problem. This school's Language Policy Working Group (including the heads of RE, Technical Studies, Social Studies and English) presented the report of its discussions in a form which satisfied everyone, with only the instruction: DELETE AS APPROPRIATE.

The Language Policy Working Group was able to decide almost immediately that its area of discussion should be called 'language *alongside/up/interfacing with* the curriculum'. This kind of agreement marked our subsequent discussions; we can say that, despite the difficulties of the subject, the *atmosphere/tea* was rarely strained — although it was, of course, sometimes stirred. We must say that the director of studies' summaries of theoretical work in the field gave us valuable opportunities to examine our own *preconceptions/ fingernails* though some did feel that we tended to reach our conclusions in the subsequent discussions too *prematurely/late to miss the traffic.*

The issue of writing in all subjects proved stimulating. The head of Technical Studies was able to show us some written work produced by pupils in his *practical/peripheral/half-sized* classes. We were in full agreement that, while the pieces may have lacked a little in *subtlety/semi-colons/sense* , they generally had the quality of *neatness/a towel rail* and showed that each sentence had been turned *into proper English/on a lathe* before being committed to paper. It was, however, suggested that here we were seeing the work of *an exceptional teacher/a silly sod* — though this does not mean that we all cannot find ways of encouraging pupils to write well in *the transactional mode/fountain pen* . Some thought, however, was given to the problem of the amount of extra time that would be involved for subject teachers in helping children to write better. Some staff felt that they needed all their available time to make *progress/suet puddings/silk purses out of sows' ears* in their subject lessons and could spare little from their efforts to safeguard their *musical instruments/scale posts/sanity* to assist the head of English in building *pupils' confidence/her own empire.*

Reading is crucial to our *exam results/spiritual salvation/safety regulations.* We agree that our pupils do not do enough close reading of *factual texts/the Bible/the fire notices* . This is to be *regretted/expected/dealt with by form tutors* . But although we live in a predominantly *visual/atheist/centrally-heated* society, this does not mean that teachers should join the rush from *print/god/the classroom when the firebell goes* . Obviously improvement in this matter will be slow: to think otherwise would be to expect *a miracle/ a prolonged TV strike/a firedrill every morning* .

Nevertheless we can look forward to some immediate action on two points.

The Head, in attending the *first/worst* meeting of the group, pointed out that many pupils seemed to be having difficulties in reading their hymn books in assembly. We felt that this was largely because they held them *in disdain/upside down* even though they were *sacred/ free* . There was a suggestion that the hymns be rewritten in *a simpler form/a variety of local dialects* ; at this point the head of *English/RE* offered to *undertake the task/resign immediately* .

We can also announce that having finally agreed to do our first readability analysis on *the Bible/'Metalwork Without Fuss'* , the work is proceeding apace; an interim report indicates that *Genesis/the chapter on rivets* is rather short on *conjunctions/injunctions/jokes* .

Finally, the Head has asked us to include her congratulations to the Working Group on its proposals which, like us, she agrees should be immediately put into *practice/the bin* .

WHY BOTHER?

As the early stages of the LAC movement showed, issues of language and learning can be difficult to get hold of, and finding the right tactics within the school organisation can be difficult too. But if the focus and the tactics are right, LAC can be a powerful vehicle for self-service in-service on the premises. It can provide a way into discussions with the colleagues about the nature and process of learning and this potential gain for both teachers and pupils outweighs the possible dangers of frustration or misdirection. The climate of open and mutual interest generated by such discussions can provide a fruitful soil for other kinds of change within the school. So LAC is worth persevering with in schools where it's still going — and worth re-starting in schools where it got going once and then stalled.

This is a sample list of some of the particular issues which working groups of teachers might consider. A focus on any one of them can very easily broaden to a consideration of general concerns and, at the same time, produce practical suggestions for changes in the way classroom work is organized:

    — supporting and monitoring small group talk;

- how girls and boys participate in classroom discussions;
- extending the range of writing tasks;
- the function and design of worksheets;
- the readability and use of texts in subject lessons;
- encouraging independent reading of fiction and information books;
- pupils who are seen to be unsuccessful in school;
- ESL pupils in subject classrooms;
- subject content and children's interests.

WHO'S INVOLVED?

Members of the English department have often been the people who have been asked to make the first steps. While the English department is probably best able to offer useful information on the language side, there are reasons why teachers in the English department might be content to be active contributors rather than initiators:
- for English teachers to take on the organising role can sometimes lead to diversionary flak ('It's alright for you — you don't have to do glaciers'; 'I can't hear myself teach for the noise in English lessons');
- if the outcomes of discussions are to result in real changes then it will be helpful for someone with a senior position in the school to take responsibility for convening the meetings, guiding the process and channelling recommendations through the school's normal decision-making routes;
- the most effective pattern for sustaining work in this area seems to be a working party with representatives from all departments and all ranges of experience and attitude — a group of people who make ideas their own rather than rely on 'experts'.

The last point does not mean that LAC activities should be confined to a working party. On the contrary such a group is likely to be at its most successful if it manages to encourage small teams of teachers either within or across departments to work together in the kind of ways listed below.

WHAT STRATEGIES?

This is a list of some of the strategies that schools have evolved for starting an exploration of the issues of language and learning in school.

1.   The whole staff meeting with a visiting speaker
Occasionally this has been known to work successfully, although, more often than not, events of this kind can mark the end rather than the beginning of the enterprise. Unless the visiting speaker

knows the school quite well, or is very well briefed, there is a distinct danger of an inappropriate lecture resulting in boredom or resentment. Outside speakers can be most useful when a working group has been working together for a while and really knows why it wants to make use of an outsider. Teachers from other schools can be an exception here and useful at any stage if they are in a position to give a detailed account of their own school's experience.

2. Shared reading

There are now a number of books and articles on language and learning in secondary schools, and a carefully selected extract or article may provoke a lively discussion. On the other hand, print may not be the best thing to start with — and a meeting which depends on people having done the reading beforehand might be sticky. But provided the text is stimulating and fairly short, and provided that the reading of it is made active in some way, a text can make a good 'collecting point' for a group already on its way.

3. The questionnaire

An interesting replication of the Bullock Report itself, this strategy does have the advantage of getting people to think about their own practice especially if it is completed collectively by a whole department. It can also be quite useful as a starting point for a written document. The questionnaire needs to be very carefully thought out if it's to work at all, but even then there is a danger that answers are filled in perfunctorily, which could mean an inauspicious start to a potentially rewarding process of enquiry.

4. Case studies

One relatively safe and interesting way of beginning is to collect all the pieces of writing done in a week by two children — one who appears to be a successful learner and one who appears to be unsuccessful. A meeting of all the teachers involved (preferably with photocopies of the writing) can be a useful way of emphasising that language across the curriculum is about children learning and teachers

sharing. In this way writing, which is the medium that most teachers trade in, gets presented in a way that focusses on the nature and function of different kinds of writing and on the contexts in which they are produced.

5. Taping and video-taping lessons

This can be difficult to arrange but it has the advantage of offering a group shared evidence of pupil or teacher talk: many teacher groups have found that a little bit of such evidence has taken them a considerable distance. It is usually most effective when the teachers involved state beforehand what they particularly want to know more about, or what aspects of current classroom practice are of pressing concern. Without such a framework, there is the danger of the loss of focus when you look at classroom reality.

6. Sharing classrooms

Teachers sitting in on one another's lessons and making detailed observation notes is undoubtedly the simplest method of sharing classroom practice. However, even if discussion is confined to teacher and observer, it can be tricky — especially for the observer, who has to consider which observations are constructive and which might be undermining. (For this reason it's preferable for the observation of lessons to be mutual.) This kind of classroom observation is perhaps most suitable for evaluating a particular item of material or as a way of checking on a subject syllabus in operation.

7. Children's views

Interviewing children about aspects of the curriculum can be very illuminating. A more precise extension of this strategy is to interview a group of pupils after a lesson which has been observed or recorded and then set these views alongside the declared intentions of the teacher. This particular technique (called 'triangulation') has been fully described in the Ford Teaching Project.

8. Shared lesson planning

Getting teachers of different subjects (especially where there is some overlap, as between English and Social Studies) to sit down together and plan a lesson or lesson sequence can be a very useful way of focussing discussion on how to support children's learning. The potential of the activity is obviously maximized if the lessons can then be observed or recorded in some way so that the teachers who planned the lesson can reflect on how it went.

9. Trial lessons

Here teachers agree to take on the role of learners in parts of a lesson presented by a colleague. Although this tactic doesn't always come off, most teachers generally find this kind of experience enjoyable and stimulating in itself. The gain is greatest if the teachers can then get some evidence of how pupils went about doing the same bit of work.

WHAT'S THE OUTCOME?

It is a mistake to think of the outcome of LAC work as a single and final document. There are plenty of those locked away in filing cabinets all over the country. Language across the curriculum is a process. If that process is a fruitful one there may well be implications for school policy and careful thought will need to be given to how recommendations can be implemented and monitored.

Obviously it is not possible to implement policies which relate to classroom practice by crude edict; it can only be done by teachers sharing their concerns and ideas at an informal level. Small voluntary seminars are the most likely outcome for work at this level. However, joint exploration of this kind can be supported by organisational changes, such as timetabling two teachers for one class, or arranging regular early closures so that departments can work on their own language and learning projects. One school, for example, felt that independent reading was such a critical issue that the staff agreed to include on the timetable one period per day specifically for independent reading. Another school decided to introduce integrated studies into the lower school on the grounds that it was the most constructive way to incorporate into the school's life those classroom practices which their LAC discussions had identified as positive. Decisions of this kind need to be agreed by all staff, as well as having the backing of senior staff to ensure that they are efficiently carried out and appropriately resourced.

This is not to deny any place to documents in LAC activity; if it goes well there will be room for all kinds of accounts, reports and bulletins, the role of which is to describe to other staff the work in progress. There may also be a time when writing something more substantial seems like a good idea — perhaps primarily to inform new staff of the background and the status of developments.

English in Integrated Studies

The idea of integrating subjects in the secondary school curriculum gathered force in the mid 1960's; by the time the debate about language across the curriculum got under way in the early 1970's a number of schools had already organised courses with titles like 'World Studies', 'Local Studies' and so on, in which subjects like History, Social Studies, Geography, R.E. and Drama were combined with English to form new courses intended to present a model of learning substantially different from that offered by those subjects taught separately. In some cases the design of these courses reflected a commitment to multicultural schooling.

The original thinking behind integration drew on changing ideas about the nature of knowledge and the way children learn. This was often reflected in timetable arrangements under which large groups of children were taught by teachers in teams for whole morning or afternoon sessions; it was reflected also in the insistence on mixed ability grouping; it also led to intensive use of library facilities and resource areas. At the same time, it was realised that integration provides opportunities for putting into practice ideas about the importance of language in the learning process: the importance of talk, the need for a variety of patterns in the use of writing and reading, and, at least to some extent, the idea of pupils becoming independent learners. A further justification was that the transfer from primary schools is less of a shock for children because integrated studies means that they meet fewer new 'subjects' and are taught by fewer teachers.

ADVANTAGES FOR ENGLISH

In addition to these general advantages, some English teachers saw a benefit to the teaching of their own subject in that the content of an integrated studies course can provide a solid anchoring for reading, writing and talk — an anchoring which is more difficult to provide when English is taught separately. Integrated studies courses can offer a proper information base for speculation, research and imaginative work; there is no need to devise 'special' English work on reading for information, note-making, summary and so on when these activities can occur quite naturally in integrated studies work in response to information texts, films or sets of statistics.

A SURVEY OF COURSES

Not unnaturally, actual practice in courses which have continued to operate since the early 70's may not fully represent the intentions behind the development of integrated studies. For many teachers who arrive at a school where integrated studies is part of their timetable, the course is simply 'there' — and the fact that they have not been involved in the initial discussions can lead to difficulties.

A recent survey (1981) of 24 ILEA schools who have English as part of an integrated scheme reveals some common patterns of organization and suggests some possible sources of difficulty for teachers new to an integrated scheme.

(a) Almost all the schools had courses which catered for the first year and a few for the second year. It was very unusual for a course to go beyond the first two years. The reasons for this seem to be the strength of the primary to secondary transfer motive, and the feeling that subject specialization is needed beyond the second year in preparation for public examinations.

(b) The early ideas about team teaching seem to have been largely abandoned in favour of a single teacher teaching the whole course to a class (invariably a mixed ability class). The reason for this change would appear to be that it proved too difficult in many schools to timetable a team together and to keep up communication within the team about the programme and pupils. The idea of the single teacher may seem attractive because it involves only one person in the job of overseeing the variety of language use and the progress of individuals within a teaching group; it does raise, however, the problem of what kind of language/English teaching a group may get from a teacher who is without training in the discipline.

(c) On average, integrated studies teams meet once a week to discuss and plan their courses. Integrated studies teachers seem to need meetings to agree on the key classroom activities for the forthcoming week. This suggests a high level of co-operation, but it might also indicate a need to negotiate what those key activities should be and to ensure that teachers without training in the range of disciplines from which the course draws are in-serviced by specialist colleagues.

(d) Another reason for meeting so often is that nearly all the schools indicated that their most prominent resource in the classroom was the worksheet. It took precedence over books, commercially-produced packs, audio-visual materials, and library materials. Teachers generally do not feel that ready-made packs or topic books contain the right kind of information at the right level for a course which has often been specially tailored to the needs of the school. Worksheets need to be reviewed or new ones designed as modifications are made to the course.

(e) It seems usual for integrated studies to use about 25% of a first or second year timetable, and for its capitation to be separate from the main subjects involved. Surprisingly, however, the responsibility allowance for the teacher in charge of an integrated studies team in the schools surveyed was rarely more than scale 2. This may mean that the teacher in charge is not in a position to direct the team towards an understanding of the processes which should inform the course — especially language processes.

AREAS OF CONCERN

The best integrated courses succeed because there is a high level of commitment from all the subject departments involved — and in particular an acknowledgement that the course may not satisfy the demands of a subject taught separately. However, an English department needs to consider which aspects of the subject demand space in an integrated studies course, and how this can best be achieved. Many English teachers would single out literature and personal writing as essential components; others might place more emphasis on directed writing and the ability to synthesize information.

The survey of policy and practice referred to above revealed a number of areas of specific concern for English teachers. It seems that in some integrated studies courses:

— very little poetry is read or written;
— scant attention is given to personal reading;
— surprisingly, there is not a great emphasis in pupils talking and working together in groups;
— the range of classroom activities is often narrow and 'worksheet bound';
— literature (in the form of shared texts) is selected to link with the factual content of the course rather than for its experiential qualities;
— creative or personal writing tends to occur within the constraints of a factual framework (for example 'Imagine you are a soldier in India at the time of the Mutiny. Write a letter home about your experiences'), and while this 'imaginative reconstruction' can allow pupils to take on and use new information, imaginative writing in which the writer has a real choice of subject tends to be left out;

— even when 'imaginative reconstruction' tasks are sensibly
framed there is confusion amongst children about whether
they should write a 'good story' or whether they have to
make sure they get all the facts in; teachers are equally
uncertain about responding to such writing, and tend to
mark or assess according to their specialisms.

SUGGESTIONS FOR DEVELOPMENT

The fact that problems of this kind are apparent in some existing
integrated schemes should not be taken as indicating that the principle of integration is itself suspect. Serious problems have also been
noted in evaluations of separate subject teaching from the same
point of view. The following suggestions may be helpful to English
departments already involved in an integrated scheme needing improvement or to departments interested in taking part in a new scheme.

AIMS AND OBJECTIVES

An example of a list of aims for an integrated studies course is given
in the appendix to this section; an agreement on a list of this sort
is the way to ensure that the common ground between the contributing disciplines is established as the basis for the course. But
although 'language development' is often seen as one of the major
aims of an integrated studies course, a great deal of detailed planning needs to be done in order to translate this generalized commitment into specific classroom practice. Discussion of such matters
as handwriting, spelling and punctuation is important — but even
more vital is the need for discussion of varied patterns of work
involving pupils' active use of reading, writing and talk. That kind
of discussion should infuse the thinking behind the preparation of
materials and the design of classroom activities.

COURSE CONTENT

The content of an integrated studies course tends to be the focus of
discussion about it. The content of the course is obviously not
irrelevant: English teachers might want to argue, for example, for
the inclusion of a unit on language and language use or for some
work on storytelling. But questions about the choice of content
(whether organized by theme, chronology or on a geographical
basis) may be less important than questions about how children are
to gain access to the content of the course. A distinction needs to
be made between 'the grand scheme' which dictates the forward
movement of the course and the actual experience children have
of it in the classroom. Most children don't have a vision of the
whole syllabus; they 'do things' in lessons. What children can and
should actually *do* in lessons may be the most valuable focus of

discussion in planning or re-planning an integrated studies course.

LITERATURE

Literature (sharing narratives, poetry and reading for pleasure) and responses to it in talk and writing needs to be given a special role in the course — not necessarily serving in a direct fashion the factual topics covered. While the value of literature in this context can be seen as 'bringing things home', this role doesn't have to be construed literally (i.e. 'We're doing Eskimos and here's a story about them'). Literature can offer a form of experience which illuminates the topic without having an obvious relationship to it. Literature (like language) can also offer a topic for study in its own right (in the form, perhaps, of a unit on 'myths and legends' or 'songs, rhymes and poems'), where the emphasis is on examining a common human activity in a variety of contexts. Equally, the experience of literature can stand on its own — just as something to read and enjoy without any relationship with other work on the course.

WRITING

The same kind of argument can be made for the place of personal and imaginative writing in an integrated scheme. Provided that the task is carefully and generously formulated, 'imaginative reconstruction' can provide a powerful way of taking on new information, but time needs also to be allowed for writing which uses new information in another setting, or which offers pupils a chance to examine and articulate their own experience and views in relation to ideas raised in the course. And, as with literature, writing can also stand on its own as something to enjoy and share.

IMPLICATIONS FOR THE TEAM

Taken together, these suggestions for how an English department might define its contribution to the development of integrated studies work raise implications for the organization of the course and the team's work:

- the course needs sufficient time in the week to allow space for the full range of pupil activities and to ensure that some of them are not crowded out by the course content; in this light, 25% of the timetable seems to be a minimum;
- it is preferable for the course outline to be stable, so that teachers are not in constant pursuit of new materials for new units and so that the emphasis can be put instead on re-tuning the classroom use of materials;
- teachers in the integrated studies team who are without training in English will benefit from in-service help from English colleagues, particularly with reference to approaches to literature and to setting and responding to writing;

English teachers themselves will of course have much to gain in other respects from working with teachers of other subjects.

APPENDIX

THE AIMS OF AN INTEGRATED SCHEME: AN EXAMPLE

INTELLECTUAL SKILLS

1. The ability to find information from a variety of sources in a variety of ways.
2. The ability to communicate findings through an appropriate medium.
3. The ability to interpret pictures, charts, maps, graphs, statistics and print.
4. The ability to relate new information to existing concepts, i.e., the ability to bring together disparate kinds of information and carry them forward as one.
5. The beginnings of an ability to formulate and test hypothesis and generalisations.

SOCIAL SKILLS

1. The ability to participate and work co-operatively within small groups.
2. To value the co-operation and respect the independence of others.
3. A willingness to consider participating constructively in the activities associated with these groups.
4. The ability to exercise empathy — to imagine what it might be like to be someone else.
5. Developing an awareness of the structures and hierarchies within society — that they affect individuals and that they are susceptible to change.

PHYSICAL SKILLS

1. The ability to manipulate equipment.
2. The ability to manipulate equipment to find and communicate information, e.g., CTR and Decimal Classification.
3. The ability to communicate information verbally and to listen.

QUALITIES
Interests, Attitudes, Values

1. The fostering of curiosity through the encouragement of questions.
2. The fostering of a wariness of over-commitment to one framework of explanation and the possible distortion of facts and the omission of evidence.
3. The fostering of a willingness to explore personal attitudes and values and to relate these to other peoples.
4. The encouragement of an openness to the possibility of change in attitudes and values.
5. The encouragement of developing interests in human affairs.

(derived from Place, Time and Society, Schools Council, published by Collins/ ESL Bristol, 1976)

English and the Arts

There was a time, not so long ago, when it would have seemed quite normal to read about the importance of the creative arts in the curriculum and to find accounts in the educational press about schools that had developed exciting programmes and projects involving the English, drama, art and music departments. At that time many teachers believed — and hopefully many still do — that writing a poem or a story was essentially the same kind of activity as making a picture, a tune or a play. It just so happened that writing had a different market value which meant that English tended to be identified as an academic subject, while art, drama and music were regarded as optional extras, marginal to the real business of schooling. This view has steadily gained ground in recent years. The HMI report *Aspects of Secondary Education* (1981) reflected the view in its signal failure to mention the role of music, art or drama in the curriculum. Falling rolls and cutbacks, together with an increasing emphasis on 'the common core' and on work with vocational orientation, have produced a crisis for the arts in schools. The scope of the arts curriculum has shrunk — not in all schools but in many. Those accounts in the *TES* of how a whole first year spent a half-term working on an arts-based inter-disciplinary exploration of the Peasants' Revolt now begin to seem positively abnormal.

FORMS OF CO-OPERATION

However, we are in no doubt that English teaching has key features which identify it as part of the creative arts: fiction, poetry, plays, films and television, in common with art, music and drama offer pupils alternative ways of experiencing the world, of developing the full variety of thinking and creative action and of exploring personal and social values. So we believe that, in spite of the unfavourable climate, the English department should consider making it a major priority to establish links with other creative arts departments in the school. This doesn't necessarily mean complicated liaison work or year-long joint projects; difficulties related to curriculum co-ordination may inhibit this kind of reciprocal arrangement. A department might think instead of modest links and points of contact which could go some way towards extending and strengthening the work which is done in the separate subject areas.

Contact might begin with the English department offering its syllabus to other creative arts departments as a way of beginning discussions on possible points of collaboration. These could include:
  — English teachers using music and art work produced by children as triggers for talk and writing in English lessons;

- working jointly around a 1st year shared reader (like *The Iron Man*) which has clear possibilities for illustration or for musical interpretation. Words and pictures/music could be brought together in a simple display or performance within the year group;
- giving children's own poems and stories a strong presentational emphasis by encouraging them to experiment with different forms of visual illustration and with musical settings. These experiments could easily lead to more ambitious work in which writing/illustration/music/enactment are combined in a live or video presentation;
- agreeing on a small-scale unit of media study looking at, for example, the relationship of image and text in posters or advertising. This kind of project could develop into a more deliberate and extensive co-operation between departments on a form of media study which is both critical and active (See the section on English and Media Studies in 'The Syllabus'.);
- deciding to invest subject lesson time, and perhaps after-school time, in developing a full dramatic production (for performance to school or external audiences) which takes a shared theme (like the local area or transport) and treats it through different creative media.

The Library

The library is a valuable resource for the school as a whole but is often either underused or used with little sense of purpose. For English departments in particular it ought to be seen not so much as a *support* for curriculum but as *part* of the curriculum. The school librarian should be a key figure in helping to develop what we call 'the reading habit', for it is the librarian who can ensure that the library is established as an attractive environment, that the books on the shelves are of the right type and range, and that children are enabled through the library to develop their use of books and socialise their response to what they read.

One important reason why the librarian may not be able to ensure that the library plays an effective role is that s/he is often isolated in the school and receives little support from other staff. This can happen whether s/he is a qualified full-time librarian or a teacher with responsibility for the library. So a simple first step for the English department to take is to invite the librarian to all relevant meetings — and to make sure that the question of library use is put on the agenda. That first step will at least mean that the librarian can start to share the spirit of the department's approach to reading and can begin to suggest opportunities for planned library use within English work which may not be apparent to members of the department. Discussion with the librarian might be focussed more specifically on the issues of access, book choice and library activities outlined below.

WHO USES IT AND WHEN

Decisions about *when* the library can be used may well depend on the English department's ideas about *what* it is going to be used for. These ideas may point, for example, towards a booking system in which each class has a regular lesson timetabled for the library or towards an arrangement by which a whole block of time (perhaps a sequence of 5 or 6 lessons) is booked for a class whose teacher has a specific work unit in mind. Whatever formal arrangements are made, it is important also to retain the facility for individual pupils to gain access during English lesson time if a particular need occurs. If a pupil wants to read a special book or to find a book to get information for work in progress, to be told to wait for next week's library visit is liable to lead to frustration.

GETTING HOLD OF A BOOK

English teachers and librarians agree that it is a good thing for children to choose books themselves on the basis of an understanding of the range of books available. Sometimes we make it quite difficult for them to do this. A library period can easily turn into a scramble to find books — and if books are difficult to get at and if types of books are difficult to identify this can be a frustrating business which leaves little time for actually reading a book.

Members of an English department may be able to suggest to a librarian some ways of helping children to get what they want. These might include:
- creating a special section of popular paperback books (and buying more than one copy of these);
- ordering a selection of magazines and periodicals which children (as opposed to staff) like to read;
- using large, clear signs or posters to help children find particular sections;
- if the Dewey system is in use for non-fiction books, using

a large wide chart to display the main subjects with an abbreviated form of the classification numbers (i.e. not more than one decimal point). This enables pupils to use the system simultaneously rather than queue at a small catalogue drawer; shorter numbers can also be printed larger on book spines and are easier to remember;

— the spines of fiction books presented alphabetically by author are like a blank wall to most children. Other ways of organising fiction could be considered, such as collecting titles together by theme or genre (crime, science fiction, love stories, short stories, etc.) even though these arrangements might be inexact;

— making sure that any theme or genre section has a good mix of books to suit the range of reading abilities (rather than having a separate 'easy books' section which may be avoided out of embarrassment);

— throwing out all books which are inappropriate, dull, damaged, or simply never used, so as to create more space for special displays and for showing books flat rather than by spines only;

— displaying book reviews (including those written by pupils) or distributing a simple newsletter to help children decide which titles they might like to try out;

— the librarian developing special reading programmes for voracious readers, poor readers or those who are particularly difficult to please;

— if possible having carpets and a few armchairs arranged so that small groups can chat and look at books together in corners of the room;

— having readings on cassette available (either of complete stories or of extracts from novels) to give readers access to more difficult texts and as a way of encouraging further reading of the book from which the recording is made (see the section on class libraries in 'Teaching Materials' for further suggestions on this).

ACTIVITIES IN THE LIBRARY

It may be useful for the English department and the librarian to help children to consider the library as having two different functions. The first is that of a place where they can find books to read for pleasure and for personal information; the second is that of a place where there are books and materials which contain information or ideas required for work in other parts of their English programme. The teaching of library skills is a pre-requisite for much of this latter work and an approach jointly planned by the department and the librarian is needed here. However, library skills sessions are best built into real activities in the curriculum where the skills are learned by doing something meaningful rather than presented as a series of isolated exercises. The suggestions below for different types of activity are based on fiction as well as information books and would all involve the librarian in an active rather than merely clerical role.

(a) Reading for pleasure has been referred to earlier. Without affecting the pleasure element it's possible for children to record and share their responses to books — perhaps as part of a system already in use with class libraries. The range of possibilities here includes oral presentations by groups as well as written reviews by individuals.

(b) Special displays related to a book or a topic under consideration in English lessons can be used both as a starting point for the work and as a collecting point for material which the children produce themselves. The displays might include posters, photographs and other artwork as well as books.

(c) English teachers and the librarian could jointly devise a special unit of work with a particular year in which use of library resources is a substantial element. This would involve going beyond the standard 'project' regime towards a scheme in which the use of a selection of books is focussed and supported by guide-sheets.

The School Bookshop

The idea of having a bookshop on the school premises is an example of one of the happier marriages between education and the market-place. Publishers have seized upon the opportunities for promoting their products when there are captive clients and volunteer salespeople; English teachers, on the other hand, sense the positive possibilities of extending the reading curriculum by encouraging the idea of children owning books. More ambitiously, they may see the possibility, particularly in areas where there is no local bookshop, of providing a service to parents and to the wider community.

However, there are many practical difficulties involved in setting up and maintaining a bookshop, and since members of the English department are more liable than others to be involved in the project it is important that these mainly organizational difficulties are faced before a decision to have one is made.

QUESTIONS OF ORGANIZATION

Where will the bookshop be?
A carefully chosen permanent, central and secure site is needed —

one which allows the bookshop to become established as a definite place in the school. A reasonably spacious area is required not only for storage and display but also for children to move around, stand or sit while they browse.

What kind of furniture?
It is an advantage to have permanent display shelving and/or display cabinets which allow books to be presented attractively and avoid the need for the display to be re-set every time the bookshop is open. A number of suppliers sell special lockable display units for use in bookshop areas which aren't themselves lockable. It would be nice but not essential, to have an area which can be carpeted and which has room for a few easy-chairs. Depending on the size of the school, you will need to make storage and display provision for between 300 - 1000 books.

What books to buy?
This is the tricky question — and one on which it is useful to get detailed advice from neighbouring schools which have a successful bookshop. If you buy too much of the wrong kind of book you are liable to financial disaster. It's worth bearing in mind that the bookshop isn't the school library and isn't a reading programme which you might put together for a year group. It should be closer to a real bookshop, where *Dr. Who* sits happily with *Middlemarch*. This means keeping an eye on books which will be popular because they are spin-offs from TV or films, as well as joke and puzzle books, books on popular non-fiction topics and a range of good contemporary fiction for older readers. In other words, there has to be a realistic recognition of what the customers want — without, of course, promoting books which aren't acceptable in a school. Getting the proportions of different kinds of books right is difficult. A survey in the school of what pupils like to read in their spare time would be helpful at the pre-ordering stage. How many books you start with will depend on how much capital the school can invest in the stock. (See the section on ordering books for class libraries in 'Teaching Materials' for sources of information on children's books.)

Where do the books come from?
Booksellers offer a variety of deals, so it is worth investigating at least two or three possible suppliers. These might range from an independent local bookshop to a large bookshop chain or distribution firm like 'Books for Students' (Catteshall Lane, Godalming, Surrey). The source you choose should be one which can supply the range of books you want, delivers orders quickly, gives at least 10% discount, uses a simple accounting system and is prepared to offer sale-or-return, sale-or-exchange or at least extended credit facilities.

Who does the work?
Running the bookshop and handling finance and stock records is a

lot of work, and the person who takes charge ought to have either a responsibility allowance or a couple of periods of extra non-teaching time to do it in. In some schools, office staff assist with the admin. The work of staffing the shop when it's open can be minimised by involving other staff or parents and a group of pupils who have learnt the routines and rules of the shop counter but who are directly responsible to the manager.

Where does the money come from?

Most of the considerations above need to be thought through, contacts with suppliers made, and stock requirements investigated, *before* approaching the head and other colleagues about the idea of a bookshop, because knowing all the details and costs is valuable when arguing for initial capital to get the thing going. Some schools have been given a special grant from school capitation, others have approached the PTA or have raised money from sponsored activities.

HOW TO BE A SUCCESS

The school bookshops which have succeeded have done so for easily identifiable reasons.

1. The bookshop has not been regarded merely as an extra-curricular activity which is the special hobby of one member of staff. Instead, it has been seen as a definite part in a whole school reading policy in which staff and parents are prepared to actively encourage children to buy books.
2. This commitment has been backed up by publicity in the form of letters home, posters, competitions, gimmicks, occasional visits by children's authors and book-token rewards for contributing to school life or for special achievements.
3. The running of the shop has been efficient and imaginative. This means that the stock is large and varied enough (and refreshed often enough) to satisfy needs; that it opens regularly at routine times (normally 2 or 3 times a week); that special orders can be taken from pupils with the guarantee that the books will be available quickly; and that the environment, especially the way books are displayed, is welcoming.

Talking to teachers who are running successful bookshops would be an excellent way for a department interested in setting up a bookshop to begin its own investigations. Valuable detailed advice can also be obtained from the School Bookshop Association (1 Effingham Rd, London SE12 8NZ; 852-4953), particularly on the technical aspects of the business (including accounting, display furniture, book suppliers, licensing, stock insurance, etc.) and on promotional schemes which can stimulate interest in the bookshop. (The Association's handbook, *How to Set Up and Run A School Bookshop* is useful in this respect, as is *Running A School Bookshop*, Peter Kennerley, (Ward Lock Educational, 1978)).

Outings and Visits

English teachers arrange outings and visits for pupils of all ages on the principle that the stimulus of direct experience is a valuable complement to experience in the classroom.English teachers know why they take children out — but as most trips involve some disruption of the school's routine it's a good idea to ensure that other staff do too, since the purpose of an 'English' trip down the river may not be as evident as that of a 'Geography' trip down the river.

WHERE TO NEXT?

Outings and visits organized by an English department will serve a wide variety of purposes. They may include, for example:
- looking at material connected with literary texts (the manuscripts and artefacts in the Dickens' House Museum, for instance, or the locations in Leon Garfield's *Smith*);
- seeing what goes on in a workplace like a newspaper office or a photography workshop, as an element in the study of

a topic;
- becoming familiar with the local library or with a bookshop in the neighbourhood;
- collecting material (interviews, surveys, impressions, etc.) in the local area for use in a guide to facilities in the area;
- seeing what goes on backstage in a theatre prior to attending a performance;
- having an opportunity to see a special showing of a film version of a play or novel in the comfort of a cinema;
- spending time in a grand house, a park, a cemetery, a market . . . , perhaps simply to gather and share impressions of it, perhaps to use the experience for writing back in class;
- having an intensive period of work on writing, drama or reading at a residential centre;
- putting on a drama performance at a local primary school or community centre;
- (or more ambitiously) temporarily exchanging pupils with some in a school in another area of the country, as part of a larger programme of exchanges of letters, stories, tapes and other material.

Visits of all these kinds — and others not mentioned — allow English teachers to let the world into the classroom by letting children out of it. (And, of course, the same thing can happen the other way about — when visitors come into the school.) It's easy to find places to go and excellent reasons for going to them. *What Every English Teacher Needs to Know about Resources and London* (English Centre) has a list of over a hundred places to visit with school parties in and around London; each place has a teacher's comment on how a visit went. It's a good idea to have a system of simple departmental reports, so that when people go somewhere new with a group they make a note on a filing card after they get back of useful details and comments.

PLANNING THE VISIT

Finding good places to go is easier than making the arrangements. Outings are like good dinners: they invariably take longer to prepare than they do to enjoy (and there's usually some bit of tough admin. that should have been marinating since last week). The planning diagram and examples of permissions letters which follow should adapt to most schools' requirements.

Not all the planning is pure admin. One maxim is worth noting: the classroom preparation necessary for a successful visit is better done before the visit rather than after it. Once you've made the five vital phone-calls and bought the tickets there's a natural tendency to think that the children will know what to do when they get there.

They may: but they are likely to get a lot more out of the trip if they've done some preliminary talking, reading and planning of their own.

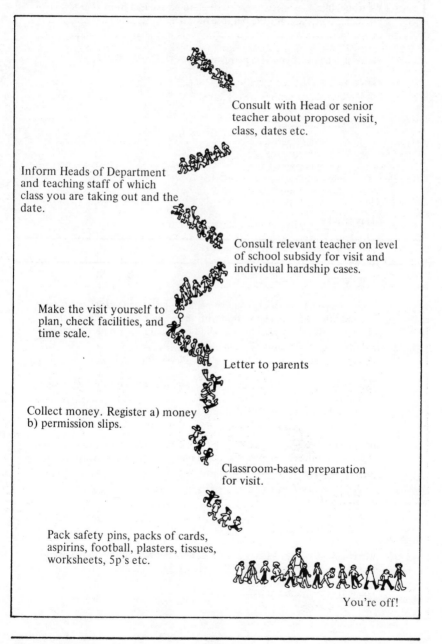

Consult with Head or senior teacher about proposed visit, class, dates etc.

Inform Heads of Department and teaching staff of which class you are taking out and the date.

Consult relevant teacher on level of school subsidy for visit and individual hardship cases.

Make the visit yourself to plan, check facilities, and time scale.

Letter to parents

Collect money. Register a) money b) permission slips.

Classroom-based preparation for visit.

Pack safety pins, packs of cards, aspirins, football, plasters, tissues, worksheets, 5p's etc.

You're off!

TED - O

PERMISSIONS

We would like .... to be excused from your lesson
on .... for the purpose of ....
....

Please sign below if you give permission.

Period 1......................
2......................
3......................
4......................
5......................
6......................
7......................
8......................

Tutor..........................
Many thanks.   Signed ....

Dear Parent,

As you know, we encourage pupils to join a wide variety of theatre,
film and other visits in connection with their English lessons during the
school year. On this occasion your child is invited to join a party which is
going to ....
on.................................... The party will be accompanied by........................

The group will travel by............... and the total cost of the outing to
each pupil will be...................................
They will be leaving the school at........................ and returning to school
by..

If you would like your child to join this party, would you please allow him
or her to return the completed slip and money to the accompanying teacher
by ....

Yours sincerely,

- -

My child.. has my permission to join the party going
to.. on ....

(signed)..

Commonsense suggests that you
- ask parents to give their written permission if their children are going to be out of school for a substantial period of time (or, to play safe, for all visits) and inform them as necessary of times of departure and return;
- know the pupils that you are taking out;
- establish firm guidelines for behaviour during the trip;
- know the nature of the place you are going to (where the toilets are, where you can eat sandwiches if it rains . . .);
- make sure the pupils know what to do if they get separated from the group and check periodically that nobody is missing;
- bring with you a few necessaries for minor emergencies;
- do not dismiss children before the official end of school time;
- check that everyone can get home safely if you arrive back at school at night.

The teacher in charge of a group of pupils is deemed to be 'in loco parentis' even when a visit takes place out of school hours. This means, according to the well-known legal judgement, that the teacher must 'take such reasonable care of his pupils as a careful father (*sic*) would take of his children having regard to all circumstances', and is legally responsible to the LEA, the head of the school and the parents. As precise regulations vary between LEAs and from school to school it is vital that you know the regulations which apply in your case and that you have a written copy of such regulations.

It is particularly important for you to know your insurance position; for instance, the ILEA's insurance is usually effective for supervised class visits but special insurance cover may be needed for unusual visits (for example, when a teacher's own car is used for transport). For more detailed information and advice, particularly on these aspects of school visits, see the Schools Council publication *Out and About* (Evans/Methuen, 1976).

Primary/Secondary Liaison

Ideally, there should be considerable contact between an English department and the primary schools which provide the secondary school with its intake. In reality, there is probably very little contact — and there are considerable practical difficulties which account for this. Contact may, in fact, be limited to the provision by the primary school to the secondary school of assessment records on pupils transferring. The question of assessment, including information at this transfer stage, is considered elsewhere. But, apart from this, what other contacts are possible?

If there were all the time in the world, there might be discussions between all primary and secondary teachers in a particular area about work done on language and literature, and attempts made to ensure that there is at least a minimum of continuity. However, teachers have not got the time or opportunity to hold a large number of meetings, even where the willingness exists. This difficulty is compounded for a secondary school which has as many as 20 feeder primaries.

SMALL-SCALE INITIATIVES

The best way forward for an English department might be simply to contact the two or three neighbouring primary schools which provide a large part of the school's intake and convene a meeting at which key areas of interest can be identified. This could provide the best opportunity for an exchange of documentation and for talk around it. Once one important area is defined (comprehension, for example), a further meeting could take place at which theory and practice is examined more closely, preferably with some examples of materials present. A series of such meetings spread over two or three years,

perhaps one per term, would cover quite a lot of ground and would provide a fairly comprehensive range of insights into similarities and differences of approach. A bonus on this scheme would be to arrange for occasional exchange of classroom visits. Those departments which have been able to establish a pattern of meetings like this have reported not only that the meetings are interesting in themselves but also that they have had a significant effect on the subsequent planning of the 1st year programme.

Two other schemes seem to have worked in places where they've been tried. One is for secondary pupils to write stories, perform plays and so on for an audience of primary children; the second is to run a 'headstart' programme during the summer holidays for pupils about to enter the secondary school. The latter scheme has had considerable success in some areas of London, particularly with children who have difficulties with reading and writing.

Relations with Parents

English teaching is a major focus of parents' concern for their children's progress in school. They know power over language is vital in itself and they are also likely to see performance in English lessons as a litmus to judge their children's general development. English teaching exists in a rather more public arena than most other school subjects, and while by no means all parents have strong views on the way it should be taught, some do — and others may quietly worry. The great majority of parents appreciate any information they can get from teachers about the basis and the method of English practice in the school — and appreciate too specific suggestions on what they might do to encourage and help their own children.

An English department ought to try to meet parents' concern and desire for information. That doesn't mean a department turning itself over to intensive PR for the sake of it, but simply that it should acknowledge the right of parents to know and the need to avoid misunderstanding — and recognize that children have a lot to gain from their parents' active, well-informed interest. The benefit is mutual, not least because it can be easy to encourage some parents to turn an active interest in their own children's work into an active commitment within the school in schemes for special reading help, in drama productions, in the school bookshop and so on.

PARENTS EVENINGS

Policies on parents evenings are decided by the school as a whole. Where the procedure is simply that parents of children in a particular year see individual teachers about their children's work, the English department could consider getting together beforehand to discuss whether there is an issue (like encouraging reading at home, or exam coursework or the assessment of writing) which might be raised with all parents in the course of discussion. A simple information sheet on such an issue might be helpful for parents to take away. Many departments have also found it useful on these occasions to have children's written work available to show to parents so that specific examples of strengths and weaknesses can be pointed out.

Parents evenings of the traditional kind do not allow much space for teachers and parents to discuss the business of English teaching in any great detail. To overcome this problem, a number of English departments have developed the idea of a special evening (or day-time) event on English teaching for parents. Often this is done as part of a programme of information for parents of 1st year pupils, but there is no reason why it cannot be opened up to all parents. These are some suggestions for an evening such as this:
  — putting on a display of pupils' work and teaching materials, organized so as to illustrate the range of resources used and the ways in which pupils' work emerges from their use;
  — providing examples of pupils at work (preferably on drama or talk) — on videotape, or, more dramatically, a small group having a bit of a typical English lesson 'live';

- running through slides of activities in English lessons with a spoken commentary;
- giving parents a condensed English lesson in which they can experience for themselves practices with which they are not familiar;
- giving parents photocopies of children's writing to consider and discuss.

Activities like these are ways of giving parents an insight into what goes on in English lessons. However, there is still a place for a short talk by a member of the department (or possibly by somebody from outside the school with particular expertise) on an issue like development in reading, for example. A talk like this obviously needs to be short and untechnical, and organized so as to allow parents to raise questions. If appropriate, the talk might involve the parents themselves in some practical work and offer some suggestions for how parents might support their children at home. Using people in the department as leaders of discussion in groups and subsequently as members of a panel to take questions is an alternative to a single speaker addressing the whole audience.

HOMEWORK

Some parents tend to equate the quantity of homework set by a school with the school's commitment to academic standards; others may welcome vast quantities of homework as a form of social control extending the discipline of schools into the home. The desire to meet such expectations often leads schools into setting worthless tasks in order to maintain the required quota of hours. The English department may want to pursue a different policy from the rest of the school; for example, setting independent reading as a regular assignment, or setting homework only when it arises naturally out of on-going classwork. It may be worth the English department formalising its homework policy so as to identify for both parents and pupils the variety and the purpose of homework tasks. These may include:
- a reading scheme in which pupils are expected to keep a record of books read (whether chosen by themselves or supplied by the teacher);
- a long-term writing project (e.g., an extended story in chapters, an autobiography, a journal of personal writing, an information project) which pupils are expected to organize themselves over a period of time;
- short-term writing tasks (finishing off classroom work; choices for writing from a specially devised 'In your own time' homework booklet);

— finding out information relevant to classroom work from relatives, friends, local sources and so on.

These kinds of homework tasks, and the justifications for them, could be explained to parents by means of a short leaflet, sent home or stuck into the last pages of the exercise book/folder. This leaflet might also explain the department's procedure on marking children's written work, as this is a question on which there can also be some misunderstanding. Alternatively the information needed here could be part of a longer publication for parents intended to describe the aims and practices of the department in a short and accessible form (see the section on 'The Syllabus').

COMPLAINTS ABOUT BOOKS

The problem of parents complaining about books and other classroom materials does not rear its head too often but when it does it can create unpleasant conflicts. The worst effect of such conflicts, especially if they escalate to involve governors and the local press, is that they tend to activate teachers' self-censorship mechanisms in order to avoid a repeat of the unpleasant ordeal. Most complaints relate to bad language or 'immoral behaviour' in books which are read with the whole class; some are to do with the treatment of social issues in English lessons.

Teachers should be able to justify their choice of shared texts and explaining the value of children taking on a range of important personal and social issues should not prove too problematic. Heads of school usually like to take charge of (or at least oversee) negotiations with parents who have complaints of this kind; they have a right to expect that teachers have arguments to marshal, even if complainants (some of whom may have particular religious or political convictions) are not necessarily to be persuaded by them. We should, of course, warn ourselves against the habit of thinking that the complainant is always wrong; the point is that there should be rational dialogue.

The problem may have a special dimension if the complainant is speaking for a pressure group and seems to be prepared to mobilize other people. Cases have arisen, for example, in which members of the National Front or the National Viewers and Listeners Association have been involved. Belonging to an organization does not itself affect the right of parents to complain. But, it can affect the intensity with which the cause is pursued and the mounting pressure can sway the judgement of the head, who may well waver in giving support to the department rather than risk an unseemly public debate. On the other hand, locating an organizational context for the complaint may avert panic.

Clearly there is no way that a department can hope to guarantee itself against all possibility of complaint, whatever its source; and it would be unhealthy for a department to try to do so. But it's worth bearing in mind that *well-informed pupils* (i.e. pupils with whom teachers have discussed why certain books and other materials are studied) are invariably the best line of pre-emptive defence for practices to which the department is committed. In special cases where, for example, the department considers an X certificate film appropriate for use in the classroom, it would be wise to write to all parents of children in that class informing them of the reasons for the choice of film (pointing out the date of the certificate if relevant) and asking them to reply if they would prefer their child not to see the film.

PUBLICATIONS AND PERFORMANCES

An active department is constantly on the lookout for outlets for children's work, whether writing, drama or in other forms. That's good for children — to have a sense that what they do can be seen and appreciated by people other than teachers. And it's good for parents (among others) as well — to get a chance to see what English in the school is actually about and to see the range and quality of work which children are capable of. When work from English lessons is displayed, published or performed it becomes real and tangible to both parties and gives recognition and a sense of occasion to the effort of learning.

The advantages of making English work visible are so great that there is no danger of over-doing it. The likely constraints on the activity are to do with time and energy, since it can take a lot of both to turn a good idea into something worthwhile. But many departments have found that, by drawing up a rough calendar for the year, by sharing the work-load and by balancing formal and informal presentation, they can manage to have something on the go most of the time. While any of the following possibilities may be undertaken with an audience of parents in mind, they may of course also be intended as ways of engaging the interest and attention of other pupils in school or of people in the local community generally; in some cases, indeed, they may have parents in mind only as a friendly secondary audience:
- class magazines (designed and possibly printed by pupils on a spirit or ink duplicator);
- school magazines (an amalgam of pupils' writing and school news usually associated with close staff involvement and commercial printing);
- anthologies (collections of poems or stories or autobiograph-

ies);
- class newspapers (as a wall display or as a series of mock-ups made by groups);
- school newspapers (presenting articles which reflect pupils' own interests and sold cheaply to other pupils and parents);
- displays of work in the school foyer or waiting area;
- displays of work in a local community centre or library (or even in a shopping precinct);
- space in a local newspaper (some schools have successfully negotiated for an occasional section or whole page);
- arts festivals (a two or three day period in which there are constant day-time and evening performances, readings and exhibitions);
- school plays (an evening of playlets, an old-time variety show, a multi-media event with video and film . . . as well as the standard single play).

Bibliography

Bibliography

The following list of books may be useful to a department which wishes to start or extend a department library. The selection is personal and is not exhaustive.

Language and English Teaching

LANGUAGE AND LEARNING Britton Penguin 1970 0140214569
LANGUAGE PERSPECTIVES ed. Wade Heinemann 1982 0435109103
A LANGUAGE FOR LIFE (The Bullock Report) DES HMSO 1975 0112703267
LANGUAGE AND SOCIAL MAN Halliday Longman 1974 0582314763
LANGUAGE IN EDUCATION ed. Cashdan and Grugeon OU/Routledge and Kegan Paul 1972 071007431X
THE FOUNDATIONS OF LANGUAGE Wilkinson Oxford 1975 0199110166
LANGUAGE STUDY, THE TEACHER AND THE LEARNER Doughty and Thornton Edward Arnold 1976 0713117559
THE POLITICS OF LITERACY ed. Hoyles Writers and Readers 1977 0904613461
THE WORLD IN A CLASSROOM Searle Writers and Readers 1977 0904613461
ACCENT, DIALECT AND THE SCHOOL Trudgill Edward Arnold 1976 0713119837
GROWTH THROUGH ENGLISH Dixon Oxford 1975 (second edition) 0199110921
CLASSROOM ENCOUNTERS: LANGUAGE AND ENGLISH TEACHING ed. Torbe and Protherough Ward Lock 1976 070623619X
FINDING A LANGUAGE Medway Writers and Readers 1981 0906495415
YES, THEY CAN! Weber OU 1980 0335002447
EVERY ENGLISH TEACHER Adams and Pierce Oxford 1974 0199190577
ENGLISH: THE WOOD AND THE TREES Sharpe Pergamon 1980 080245528
TEACHING ENGLISH ACROSS THE ABILITY RANGE Mills et al. Ward Lock 1977 0706236432
ENGLISH 16-19: THE ROLE OF ENGLISH AND COMMUNICATION Dixon Macmillan 1979 0333270061

Talk

FROM COMMUNICATION TO CURRICULUM Barnes Penguin 1976 0140803823
UNDERSTANDING CHILDREN TALKING Martin et al. Penguin 1976 0140803483
TALK: A PRACTICAL GUIDE TO ORAL WORK IN THE SECONDARY SCHOOL Self Ward Lock 1976 0706234332
LEARNING THROUGH TALKING 11-16 Schools Council Project Evans/Methuen 1980 0423507109

Writing

THE DEVELOPMENT OF WRITING ABILITIES 11-18 Britton et al. Macmillan 1975 0333178629
UNDERSTANDING CHILDREN WRITING Burgess et al. Penguin 1973 0140807004
WISHES, LIES AND DREAMS Koch Vintage 1970 0394710827
ERRORS AND EXPECTATIONS Shaughnessy Oxford 1978 0195025075
TEACHING WRITING Thornton Edward Arnold 1980 0713162821
TEACHING SPELLING Torbe Ward Lock 1978 070623856

Reading and Books

THE FOUNDATIONS OF LITERACY Holdaway Ashton Scholastic 1979 0868960144
READING: FROM PROCESS TO PRACTICE ed. Chapman and Czerniewska
OU/Routledge Kegan Paul 1978 0710000642
READING Smith Cambridge 1978 0521293553
READING, HOW TO Kohl Penguin 1974 0140803440
THE READING CURRICULUM ed. Melnik and Merrick OU/University of London
Press 1972 0340167815
READING: TESTS AND ASSESSMENT TECHNIQUES Pumfrey UKRA/Hodder and
Stoughton 1976 0340165545
PRINT AND PREJUDICE Goodman Zimet UKRA/Hodder and Stoughton 1976
0340210265
READING DEVELOPMENT AND EXTENSION Walker Ward Lock 1974 0706233646
CHILDREN AND THEIR BOOKS Whitehead et al. Macmillan 1977 0333223225
RELUCTANT TO READ ed. Foster Ward Lock 1978 0706236424
THE SIGNAL APPROACH TO CHILDREN'S BOOKS ed. Chambers Kestrel 0722656416
LITERATURE AND LEARNING ed. Grugeon and Walden OU/Ward Lock 1979 070623769?
RACISM AND SEXISM IN CHILDREN'S BOOKS ed. Stinton Writers and Readers 1979
0906495191
TEENAGE READING ed. Kennerley Ward Lock 1979 0706238893
THE COOL WEB ed. Meek et al. Bodley Head 1977 0370301447

Drama

GAMES AND SIMULATIONS IN ACTION Davison and Gordon Woburn Press 1978
0713040025
DRAMA GUIDELINES O'Neill et al. Heinemann 1977 0435185659
A PRACTICAL GUIDE TO DRAMA IN THE SECONDARY SCHOOL Self Ward Lock
1975 0706234405
TOWARDS A THEORY OF DRAMA IN EDUCATION Bolton Longman 1981
0582361389
DRAMA STRUCTURES O'Neill and Lambert Hutchinson 1982 0091478111
DRAMA AND THE WHOLE CURRICULUM ed. Nixon Hutchinson 1982
0091492513

Film and Media Studies

MASS MEDIA AND THE SECONDARY SCHOOL Murdock and Phelps Macmillan 1973
0333148452
FILM IN ENGLISH TEACHING ed. Knight Hutchinson 1972 0091135117
TEACHING ABOUT TELEVISION Masterman Macmillan 1981 0333266773

English As a Second Language

SECOND LANGUAGE LEARNING AND TEACHING Wilkins Edward Arnold 1974
0713157593
THE COMMUNICATIVE APPROACH TO LANGUAGE TEACHING ed. Brumfit and
Johnson Oxford 1979 019437078X
UNDERSTANDING SECOND AND FOREIGN LANGUAGE LEARNING ed. Richards
Newbury House 1978

Assessment and Examinations

ASSESSING CHILDREN'S LANGUAGE Stibbs Ward Lock 1979 0706238532

Language Across the Curriculum

LANGUAGE, THE LEARNER AND THE SCHOOL Barnes et al. Penguin 1971
0140800948
LANGUAGE ACROSS THE CURRICULUM ed. Marland Heinemann 1977 0435806319
WRITING AND LEARNING ACROSS THE CURRICULUM 11-16 Martin et al. Ward
Lock 1976 0706234987
LANGUAGE POLICIES IN ACTION ed. Torbe Ward Lock 1980 0706239784
LANGUAGE ACROSS THE CURRICULUM: GUIDELINES FOR SCHOOLS NATE
Ward Lock 1976 070623619X
THE EFFECTIVE USE OF READING Lunzer and Gardner Heinemann 1979
0435104985
A GUIDE TO CLASSROOM OBSERVATION Walker and Adelman Methuen 1975
0416812104
THE LANGUAGE OF TEACHING Edwards and Furlong Heinemann 1978 0435802941
BECOMING OUR OWN EXPERTS ed. Eyres and Richmond 1982 0950791008 (English
Centre, Sutherland Street, London SW1)
THE WEST INDIAN LANGUAGE ISSUE IN BRITISH SCHOOLS Edwards Routledge
and Kegan Paul 1979 0710001938
THE CLIMATE FOR LEARNING Medway and Torbe Ward Lock 1980 0706241037
READABILITY IN THE CLASSROOM Harrison Cambridge 1980 0521296218
THE RESOURCES OF CLASSROOM LANGUAGE Richmond Edward Arnold
1982 0713162341